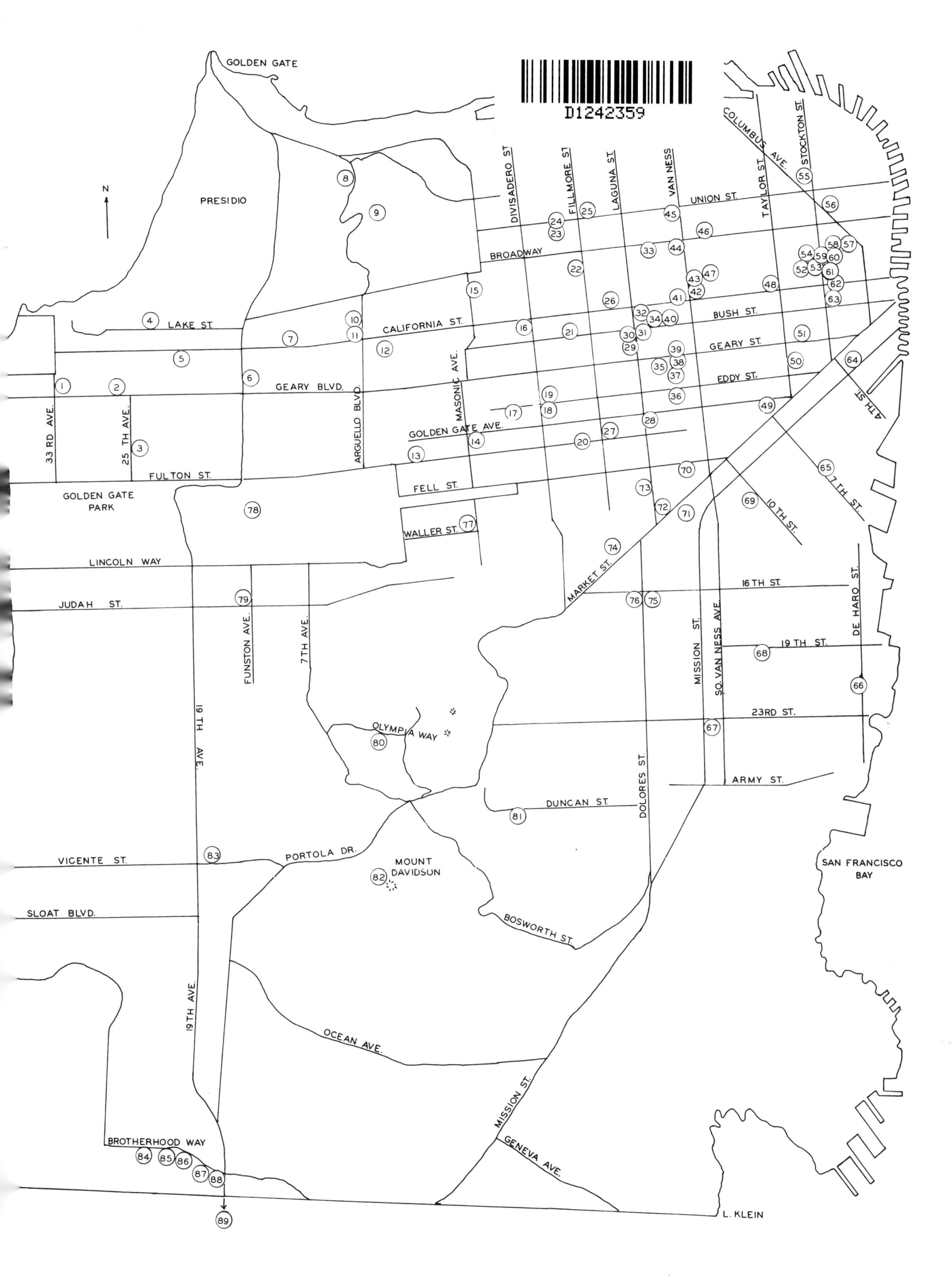
D1242359
GOLDEN GATE
PRESIDIO
N
LAKE ST.
CALIFORNIA ST.
GEARY BLVD.
33 RD AVE.
25 TH AVE.
ARGUELLO BLVD.
MASONIC AVE.
GOLDEN GATE AVE.
FULTON ST.
GOLDEN GATE PARK
FELL ST.
WALLER ST.
LINCOLN WAY
JUDAH ST.
FUNSTON AVE.
7TH AVE.
19 TH AVE.
OLYMPIA WAY
VICENTE ST.
PORTOLA DR.
MOUNT DAVIDSON
SLOAT BLVD.
BOSWORTH ST.
OCEAN AVE.
19TH AVE.
BROTHERHOOD WAY
MISSION ST.
GENEVA AVE.
L. KLEIN
DIVISADERO ST
FILLMORE ST
LAGUNA ST.
VAN NESS
UNION ST.
BROADWAY
TAYLOR ST.
STOCKTON ST.
COLUMBUS AVE.
BUSH ST.
GEARY ST.
EDDY ST.
4TH ST
7TH ST.
10 TH ST.
MARKET ST.
16 TH ST.
DE HARO ST.
19 TH ST.
MISSION ST.
SO. VAN NESS AVE.
23RD ST.
DOLORES ST.
ARMY ST.
DUNCAN ST.
SAN FRANCISCO BAY

Sacred Places
of
San Francisco

Sacred Places
of
San Francisco

Narrative by Ruth Hendricks Willard and Carol Green Wilson
Photographs by Roy Flamm
Architectural comment by Joseph Armstrong Baird, Jr.
Sponsored by San Francisco Alumnae Panhellenic

Published by Presidio Press, 31 Pamaron Way, Novato, CA 94947

Library of Congress Cataloging in Publication Data

Willard, Ruth Hendricks..
Sacred places of San Francisco

Bibliography: p.
Includes index.
1. San Francisco (Calif.)--Church history. 2. San Francisco (Calif.)--Religion. 3. San Francisco (Calif.)--Churches. 4. San Francisco (Calif.)--Temples.
I. Wilson, Carol Green, 1892- . II. Flamm, Roy.
III. Baird, Joseph Armstrong. IV. San Francisco Alumnae Panhellenic. V. Title.
BR560.S3F42 1984 726'.09794'61 85-9337
ISBN 0-89141-192-5

frontispiece:

The simple vertical Victorian Gothic thrust of Old St. Hilary's, built of wood in 1888, forms a prelude to the soaring shapes of twentieth century skyscrapers.

Printed in the United States of America

Dedicated to
Carol Green Wilson
1892-1981
whose keen biographer's insight
brought this story to life

Contents

Photographer's Note

Most photographs were made using a 4 × 5 inch Sinar camera equipped with a 65mm Super Angulon, a 75mm Goerz Rectagon, and a 190mm Wide Field Ektar. Film was Kodak Plus X. For the interiors, film was exposed at an E. I. (exposure index) of 12 and 25, a reduction equal to 4 stops or so of the film's "normal" E. I. exposures of 30 to 120 seconds at f. stops 16, 22, and 32.

The negatives were processed in highly diluted developers of the FX series originated by Geoffrey Crawley, editor of the *British Journal of Photography*, to control the contrast encountered. These contrast ratios in the building interiors were up to 2,000 to 4,000 to 1. No illumination of any kind was introduced by the photographer. Only lighting, both artificial and natural, indigenous to the buildings was utilized.

Exterior photographs were exposed and processed more normally except for the use of Pinacryptol Yellow.

Because the photography lasted about a year it was done in all kinds of weather and light conditions.

A serious effort was made to produce straightforward photographs with as little of the photographer's interpretation as possible. Camera positions were between 5 and 5½ feet off the surface holding the tripod, about average eye height. Oblique angles, unusual viewpoints, and "trick" or overly dramatic approaches were not used.

This photography would have been almost impossible without the cooperation and enthusiasm of Ruth Willard. She made the work more pleasant and enjoyable than any project this photographer has undertaken in many years of photography.

Roy Flamm
Windsor, California
May 3, 1985

Foreword

The churches of San Francisco are both numerous and of widely varied style. Indeed, in pursuit of architectural data for this book, I was astonished to see how many they are for a city of San Francisco's size. Some are in the heart of the inner city, but many are appropriately in the several residential areas of the outer city. Most of the older congregations have moved several times from one location to another; all in the path of the earthquake and fire of 1906 have either scars to prove their survival or new structures to replace fire-devastated shells that were not rebuildable. Inevitably, because the extent of the fire was so wide (destroying almost everything from the eastern, northern, and southern waterfronts to Van Ness Avenue on the west), a majority of the churches of San Francisco are post-1906. After the dignified concepts seen in Father Serra's chain of churches, of which one link was Mission Dolores, the venerable trio of Old St. Mary's, St. Francis on Vallejo Street, and St. Patrick's on Mission Street indicate the supplanting of Hispanic-Mexican late Baroque and Neoclassical traditions by American Gothic Revival, and the change from the modest colonial character of late eighteenth and early nineteenth century Yerba Buena to the vigor of Victorian San Francisco. Several other veteran churches are in a form of Richardson Romanesque or of later nineteenth century Gothic. The massive strength of the Richardsonian mode, usually in stone or brick, and the aspirant verticality of the Gothic left a marked trail upon these more venerable buildings. Buttresses, pointed arches, and traceried rose windows for the Gothic, and majestic low rounded arches and richly textured surfaces for the Richardsonian are commonplace. Indeed, the legacy of the Romanesque and Gothic, in more historically accurate transcriptions from the medieval period, continued with particular power down into the twentieth century. Use of variant forms of rounded and pointed arches, of corbel tables (decorative reductions of what were once structural support systems along the upper parts of buildings), and of a galaxy of stained glass windows have descended like a benediction upon generations of San Francisco's churches. Old Hispanic-Mexican traditions from the mission era have touched several of the larger edifices of the early twentieth century, notably in tiled exterior roofs and painted interior wooden roofs. The assertive power of the Baroque, with its rich panoply of parts that lead irresistibly to a single focus, has not been overlooked—nor has the simple beauty of the Classical past, seen usually in Baroque contexts.

The exoticism of the Near and Far East are only minimally apparent in San Francisco, despite one of the world's largest concentrations of Chinese population here. Most of Chinatown's "Oriental" architecture revolves around a decorative use of uptilted roof forms, occasional carvings of columns and other parts, and reliance on bright color and lively Oriental-language signs. The Old Vedanta Temple is almost unique in its use of Moorish and Hindu orientalisms, as those styles were more usually reserved for movie palaces in the twentieth century. The most widespread exotic aspect of style in San Francisco is that of the various Eastern Christian churches, whether Russian, Serbian, Greek, Armenian, or whatever else, in origin. The traditional "five spot," or five-domed church, of Constantinople and its later developments in Russia, Greece, Armenia, and what is now Yugoslavia, has numerous descendants in a city that Herb Caen has called Bagdad by the Bay, but which might more accurately be styled Constantinople by the Bay, from both its location on a large body of water (rather than Baghdad's river) and its vividly cosmopolitan and sophisticated style. Some of these churches are so modest in material and detail as to virtually lose all architectural precedent; others are proudly evocative of the great periods of Orthodox design and are brilliantly colored and gilded. Most share a heritage of specialized design in their interiors, with an iconostasis, or altar screen, replacing the usual altar and apse or pulpit as focus of the church's service.

Not surprisingly, the vernacular simplicity of wood, masonry, and metal seen so widely in Northern California's nineteenth-century commercial architecture from San Francisco to the Mother Lode is notably absent from the city's churches. It was used in certain early shrines, but most of these were destroyed in San Francisco's numerous fires before the development of more fireproof buildings in the later 1850s and 1860s. These were quickly replaced with structures considered more appropriate for houses of faith, repositories of the community's devotion to architectural glory. The widespread Mannerist inspired Italianate and the later, more magniloquent Second Empire, which might have seemed useful for ecclesiastic buildings, were preferably used in domestic design. Perhaps mercifully, also, the excesses of the end of the Victorian era in capricious invention and distorted forms were little employed for churches. The basic fact is that wooden buildings were doomed to fire damage; for symbolic and practical reasons, masonry was deemed best for the majority of religious structures.

Fortunately, a few charming, simple wooden or wood and stucco churches dot the city's convoluted landscape. The quiet serenity of the Swedenborgian Church and the equally calming interior of the St. Mary the Virgin Episcopal Church are agreeable reminders of a country tradition of modest design applied to the metropolis. In both, suggestions of plain Gothic are evident; both, additionally, represent a fine use of a court or garden to turn the noise of the city into the quiet of a rural setting. These miniparks serve as delightful breathing spaces in the hurly-burly of the town and augment urban green areas. Their streetside plantings continue a more recent enthusiasm for street greenery, noticeably lacking in nineteenth-century western cities.

In modern design, and in the contemporary, the churches of San Francisco have generally had little real interest. There are a few, like St. Mary's Cathedral or the Pine United Methodist Church, that have wholeheartedly embraced the language of engineering and purely functional forms. There are others, like the Unitarian Church on Franklin Street, that have admirably combined old and new. Furthermore, some simplified Japanese ideas (notably from Shinto sources) have been quite successfully combined with contemporary materials. By and large, the feeling has been strong that churches, like their faiths, represent traditional forms—witness Grace Cathedral with its splendid Gothic concepts and stained glass windows in concrete dress. It is difficult to strip all of the allusiveness of past architectural forms from the sects they house. Though most churches built since 1906 have steel frames with concrete and stucco exteriors (for obvious safety reasons), they do wrap themselves in the colors and clothes of a more remote past.

A word is in order concerning the choice of the particular examples and what constitutes *Sacred Places*. As to the latter, in general, architecturally defined structures were selected, not hallowed sites—although the Cross on Mount Davidson and the large bronze Buddha in Golden Gate Park are clear exceptions. As to the former, any individual or group of individuals would inevitably choose a slightly different ensemble of buildings to represent the ecclesiastic architectural traditions and achievements of a city. It was imperative to not repeat many variants of the same basic design and to avoid numerous works of the same faith. Thus, there are both monumental and modest churches of San Francisco that will not be found in this book. The final group represents a thoughtful evaluation of a difficult problem, where aesthetics, quality of workmanship, and size were not inevitably the criteria. This choice was somewhat affected, also, by the photogeniality of the subjects. Some notable ensembles do not photograph well in their particular environments or in terms of fine interior features. Some are obscured by those scarifications of the modern city, utility poles and wires. If these could be eliminated, along with the cacophonous multiplicity of poorly designed signs and lettering omnipresent in urban America, it would do more than anything to make our "Cities Beautiful."

In the last analysis, any book is the result of many points of view: in this case of the San Francisco Alumnae Panhellenic, of the several writers who have administered to the interpretation of a complex mass of historical and architectural data (of which some aspects can never be verified due to incomplete historical records or conflicts in them), and of the staff of Presidio Press—all working with the photographs taken by Roy Flamm. I personally saw as much of each building as was feasible, and my impressions were many and mixed. Sometimes the honest simplicity of a modest building was more impressive than the lavish grandeur of a larger one. Sometimes the quietly worshiping parishioners, or even sleeping vagrants, seemed more holy than all the images.

It is a fact that the twentieth century has not been distinguished by a renaissance of ecclesiastic art. Of stained glass, there has been the notable example of Charles Connick, and other studios, where glorious approximations of Chartres have been created. For modern glass, there is the local and effective example of Mark Adams, who has worked his magic with tapestry also. The stunning elegance and craftsmanly perfection of a Samuel Yellin in wrought iron is not commonly seen outside the great modern cathedrals of New York and Washington; but San Francisco's Dirk van Erp, in more modest fashion, provided some handsome examples of metal work for our churches. In the realm of imagery of saint or other holy figure, achievements are less successful; there are few Ghibertis or Fra Angelicos among us. Jacques Schnier points a way in his admirable sculptures of abstract form; it may well be that the future will offer some equally "lucid" examples of more realist type—mirroring the move to variant forms of realism in painting. Though church furniture is often not as much studied as architecture in San Francisco churches, it is an important part of the ensemble; the almost always anonymous craftsmen are unjustly forgotten.

If there is a single lesson in the study of San Francisco's churches, or the churches of any American city, it is that, as in the playing of a great symphony orchestra, a better conductor elicits a better performance. Architectural ensembles sometimes lack that kind of inspired overall direction. Some modern churchly artistic goals are confused with the expenditure of funds for grandiloquent and costly effects. No deity has ever been more suitably worshiped than in a handsome grove of trees—like the glorious redwoods of Northern California. If we might make our churches exemplars of fitting materials, executed with architectural creativity and craftsmanly distinction—buildings in which there is a happy marriage of all the arts like several of those in San Francisco's past and present—there would be continuing success in ecclesiastic design. Sacred places are best interpreted as places where the mind, heart, and spirit work harmoniously together; always when this happens, the results will be memorable.

Joseph Armstrong Baird, Jr.

Preface

In the late 1960s and early 1970s, Americans generally, and San Franciscans especially, awakened to the richness of their cultural background and the significant way in which architecture makes that heritage visible. In an effort to preserve important buildings and sites, registries were established at the local, state, and national level. In San Francisco, five of the first six structures given landmark status were churches.

Several members of the San Francisco Alumnae Panhellenic, on returning from travels abroad, observed that the sacred places of their city—the temples, churches, and synagogues of many faiths—rival those of Europe and Asia in beauty and diversity. Casting about for a new public service project, the group agreed that a photographic study of these awe-inspiring structures would serve to make San Franciscans, as well as visitors, aware of the city's wealth of ecclesiastical architecture while at the same time contributing to Panhellenic's ongoing program of academic scholarships.

Members first surveyed every religious group listed in the San Francisco telephone book, evaluating each for architectural interest. Researchers then interviewed clergymen, church historians, and pioneer members to learn each congregation's religious philosophy and distinctive ceremonies, the reason for its establishment in San Francisco, information about the founders and other outstanding leaders, the nature of the membership, programs of interest, and facts about the architect. Church leaders of all faiths gave freely of their time and knowledge, made their congregational histories and other publications available, and gave permission for photography. The initial selection of sacred places was based on the research reports prepared from those interviews.

Members of Panhellenic attended services of the various faiths and congregations selected. In order to place the various groups in historical perspective, researchers examined possible sources of information in the libraries of the California Historical Society, the Mechanics' Institute, the University of California, San Francisco State University, and the University of San Francisco; the History and Archives rooms at the San Francisco Public Library; and the architects' file at the Foundation for San Francisco's Architectural Heritage. Others scrutinized early city directories, historic telephone books, unpublished masters' theses, and microfilmed newspapers and records of the city building and water departments. The writers consulted frequently with religious leaders and historians.

Sacred Places is a cooperative and collaborative work. The book itself is the brainchild of Terys Saville, who conceived and organized the project, directed the initial survey, and continued to inspire the efforts necessary to bring so ambitious an undertaking to completion.

The late Carol Green Wilson, whose historical and biographical works (including *Gump's Treasure Trade* and *Chinatown Quest*) have delighted Californians for half a century, graciously volunteered to write the text. She brought a wealth of knowledge to the project. An active churchwoman, she was among the organizers of the interracial, ecumenical Festival of Faith held at the Cow Palace to commemorate the tenth anniversary of the United Nations in 1955. Mrs. Wilson made time in her busy personal life to visit many of the churches, arrange for the use of several unpublished memoirs and diaries, lay out the book, and write the preliminary text. It is with great affection that *Sacred Places* is dedicated to her memory.

As project director, Ruth Hendricks Willard was responsible for overseeing the work of a staff composed entirely of volunteers. She selected and worked with the photographer, planned and directed the research, and found consultants as needed. Her energy, dedication, and scholarly approach assured successful completion of the book. At the publisher's request, Mrs. Willard wrote the final text. She is a historical consultant to a public television station; her published work includes *The White House: Treasury of our Heritage*.

The index was prepared by Jane Wilson, most recently the International Relations Officer for the American Library Association and previously a member of the California Library Association committee that prepared the second edition of *California Local History: A Bibliography and Union List of Library Holdings*. Miss Wilson also gave expert editorial assistance. Lucy Klein, a statistician with a penchant for cartography, prepared the map.

The foreword, architectural commentary, glossary, and photo captions are contributed by the distinguished professor and arts consultant, Dr. Joseph Armstrong Baird, Jr., whose published work includes *Time's Wondrous Changes: San Francisco Architecture 1776–1915* and *Churches of Mexico*.

The photographs were taken over a one-year period by Roy Flamm, whose work has been published in Europe, Japan, and the United States. Mr. Flamm is a Fellow of the Royal Photographic Society of Great Britain and of the Society of Architectural Illustrators; his work is in the permanent collections of both. His photos of Bernard Maybeck buildings have been circulated throughout the United States and Canada by the Smithsonian Institution.

Special words of appreciation must be extended to Joan Griffin, senior editor of Presidio Press, for her patient and expert guidance during preparation of the final text, and to L. Jay Stewart, who served as consulting editor earlier in the project. Daniel Drapiewski graciously provided legal advice. Editorial costs were met in part by a generous grant from the Crown Zellerbach Foundation.

As far as can be learned, *Sacred Places* represents the first interpretation of the growth and development of any cosmopolitan American city from the perspective of its religious groups. Producing the book has served to increase the cultural awareness of all who have worked on it. It is our hope that its publication will do the same for others.

San Francisco Alumnae Panhellenic
Dorothy A. Praeger, President

Book Committee Members

Margot Buckley
Dorothy Coon
Margaret Loader Davis
Carolyn Anderson Gerrans
Jean Greene
Barbara Heller
Jewel McKenna
Lucia McKenzie
Idabelle Norton
Dorothy A. Praeger
Christine Schaezlein
Ann Sherwood
Carolyn Thomas
Barbara Thompson
Jean Tokarek
Marie Weaver
Ruth Hendricks Willard
Carol Green Wilson
Jane Wilson
Ruth Wright

Terys Saville, Chairman

Researchers: Helen Anderton, Barbara Baker, Katherine Bading, Jane Bressler, Rhea Burr, Rosalind Champeau, Marjorie Cullen, Helen Daly, Medora Deason, Ruth Flowers, Lani Friedel, Barbara Hart, Jeanne Hexberg, Charlotte Higginbotham, Mildred Johnson, Charlotte Jones, Eveline Kenney, Charlotte Kingore, Jodi Conway Linsin, Barbara Lyons, Luita Merrill, Connie Mitchell, Helene Montgomery, Mary Stewart Newman, Cecile Opsahl, Carolyn Pierce, Emily Plake, Lubov Poole, Bonita Rossberg, June Shafer, Mary Sherman, Constance Simpson, Lynn Stewart, Mary Twohy, Rebecca Walker, Marilyn Whittaker.

San Francisco Alumnae Panhellenic is an unincorporated, nonprofit association of alumnae members of National Panhellenic Conference sororities on university campuses in the United States and Canada.

Introduction

Temples and churches add diversity and richness to the cityscape. Small or large, they stand recognizable and apart. No special training in architecture is needed to identify a house of worship; even a small church built closely between neighboring houses is as obviously a religious structure as a cathedral. A passing glance reveals its function. Even those who are not religious can appreciate the presence of these architectural grace notes that enhance the city and please the eye. Given time to linger and reflect, this appreciation deepens.

Alone among the buildings that make up a town or city, churches and temples suggest something beyond the ordinary. Though fashioned of such common materials as masonry and wood, they are dedicated to the pursuit of the non-material—the spiritual. In their architecture and internal appointments they express a particular culture's concept of the sacred (the faith) and how best to relate to that mysterious presence (the ritual). Sacred writings disclose the third element common to all religions, the criteria for living with other human beings (the ethics). If architecture, then, is said to reflect the character of a city, ecclesiastical architecture reveals its spirit.

The religious impulse, like the impulse to talk, is universal. All human beings speak, but everywhere in different ways. Likewise, the feeling of reverence for something beyond the concerns of daily life is found among all people, but the forms that it takes are infinitely varied. Some worship many gods; some, one all-powerful deity; others, a deity that is somehow a trinity. People worship their ancestors or revere an enlightened human being who is not a god. Yet differences aside, all people share an impulse to harbor the sacred and set aside certain places as holy.

Nowhere is the diversity in America's religious life more apparent than in the city of San Francisco, where a village became a metropolis almost overnight as fortune-seekers from all over the globe converged on this western gateway to the mines. These immigrants brought with them a kaleidoscopic array of cultural and spiritual traditions, and they built places to enshrine their beliefs. Many of today's most lavish temples serve descendants of those pioneer congregations.

The sacred places of San Francisco are a present heritage of other times and other places. In their form and symbolism they reflect the incredible diversity of humanity's concepts of the sacred and how best to relate to that mysterious presence. Together they tell the story of San Francisco, revealing not only the rich panorama of her heritage, but also the substantial, though often overlooked, contribution of the religious community. Priests, pastors, and rabbis and their congregations have played an integral role in forging a city out of bedlam, rebuilding a city out of destruction, ministering to the wounds that grew out of the tumult and the shouting of the 1960s and the 1970s. From the very beginning the city of Saint Francis has relied upon its religious community to take the lead in establishing benevolence societies, schools, orphanages, hospitals, and community centers. Every state is accorded statues of two outstanding leaders in the Statuary Hall in Washington, D.C., and it is noteworthy that California's representatives are both clergymen: Father Junipero Serra and the Reverend Thomas Starr King.

Regardless of the diversity of religious approaches to the sacred, there is an underlying universality in their teaching of how and why human beings ought to relate to one another. The same concept—popularly described as the Golden Rule—appears in one form or another in the scriptures of all the major religions.

> Brahmanism: "This is the sum of duty: Do naught unto others which would cause you pain if done to you." Mahabharata 5, 1517
>
> Buddhism: "Hurt not others in ways that you yourself would find hurtful." Udana-Varga 5, 18
>
> Confucianism: "Is there one maxim which ought to be acted upon throughout one's whole life? Surely it is the maxim of lovingkindness: Do not unto others what you would not have them do unto you." Analects 15, 23
>
> Christianity: "All things whatsoever ye would that men should do to you, do ye even so to them; for this is the Law and the Prophets." Matthew 7:12
>
> Islam: "No one of you is a believer until he desires for his brother that which he desires for himself." Sunnah
>
> Judaism: "What is hateful to you, do not to your fellowman. That is the entire law: all the rest is commentary." Talmud, Shabbat 31a
>
> Taoism: "Regard your neighbor's gain as your own gain, and your neighbor's loss as your own loss." T'ai Shang Kan Ying P'ien
>
> Zoroastrianism: "That nature alone is good which refrains from doing unto another whatsoever is not good for itself." Dadistan-i-dinik 94, 5

All of the world's major religions and many lesser-known sects are represented in San Francisco today, each with its own concept of spiritual reality. Roy Flamm interprets these masterful structures with his camera, and, Dr. Joseph Armstrong Baird, Jr., defines their architectural significance. Although most congregations now inhabit their third or fourth structures—Old St. Mary's, St. Francis Lutheran, and St. Mary the Virgin Episcopal being notable exceptions—traditional elements originating in older cultures still exist in San Francisco churches. A brief summary of those ancient traditions serves to increase the visual enjoyment of their local descendants. Most large formal churches and temples, for example, follow one of the two basic plans inherited in part from the Greeks and Romans and further developed by the early Christian communions. The Roman Catholic church is derived from the Roman basilica, a long, rectangular hall or nave with a semicircular apse at one end and colonnaded aisles or porticoes along the sides. A transept extending the full width of the building between the nave and the apse divides the interior space in the form of the Latin cross. Eastern Orthodox churches have a central dome over a squared building that represents the Greek cross with its arms of equal length. These forms have been adapted to serve both Protestant and Jewish congregations as well.

Roman Catholicism, the dominant faith in San Francisco thoughout most of its history, is also the most architecturally evident. Developed when only clerics could read, Catholic church architecture relies upon symbols and designs to instruct people in religion. From this tradition came much religious architecture, painting, and sculpture. The church building itself, with its cruciform shape, brilliantly colored windows, carved images, and flickering light, helps to create a feeling of awe and reverence.

European religion and hence religious architecture was introduced by the Franciscan fathers, who built the missions using Indian laborers and local materials. The early missions were the simplest buildings possible, having thick adobe walls, small, unglassed windows, and red tile roofs. The maximum width of the mission buildings was logically determined by the length of straight timbers available locally for roof beams. But even these simple structures must have seemed impressive to the Indians. Building styles had accompanied the missionaries from Mexico, in turn influenced by Spain. After 1787, the fathers carried an illustrated Spanish translation of the handbook *Ten Books of Architecture* written about the time of Jesus by the Roman engineer-architect Vitruvius. For this reason the Alta California missions were somewhat more adorned with period elements than those built earlier in the Southwest. The present Mission Dolores, dedicated in 1791, furnishes a good example.

In Europe, the basic basilica gradually evolved into the varying forms of churches and cathedrals of the Middle Ages. The nave was often entered from a colonnaded courtyard, or atrium, usually located on the west. Side aisles were not as high as the nave, and light entered principally through the clerestory (upper story) of the nave as well as through other windows along the aisles. Eventually these openings were filled with pieces of colored glass set in lead joints to form designs or pictures. Interior spaces of European churches were divided according to use. The Second Council of Tours in A.D. 567, for example, forbade persons from standing among the clergy during the mass; the sanctuary was, from then on, physically separated from the worshipers.

In Europe a church building came to be regarded as a major expression of religious feeling; the building itself was a great work of art. Design went through several stages of development. The style now called Romanesque evolved during the eleventh and twelfth centuries. Although primarily Western European in origin, Romanesque incorporates elements from other cultures as well. Rounded arches used for windows and doorways are a highly visible characteristic of the style. Transepts, symbolic at first, became structurally necessary when more elaborate crossings and towers were added to the buildings. It was during this time, also, that stonemasons mastered the building of vaulted and ribbed roofs; this made it possible to construct the high interior ceilings of stone for fire protection. Romanesque architecture emerged from a feudal, hierarchic society. The men who built the churches were usually clerics and their associates or assistants. Carvings in stone and wood were teaching devices used to instruct the large peasant class, who could not read, in the lessons of the church. Sermons were rare during most of the Middle Ages, except for an era of preaching and reformation in Italy during the thirteenth and fourteenth centuries. But the mass, with or without music, filled these halls with resonance.

During the Middle Ages in the European Christian world, God was considered a remote and mysterious spirit. The Gothic cathedral, with its high, vaulted ceilings, subdued lighting, mysterious echoes, and sensuous aroma of candles and incense, was the highest expression of this concept. Inside, a person felt dwarfed and awestruck. It was Mary the mother who was especially to be revered as the intercessor with God, and all Gothic cathedrals were dedicated to her.

The Gothic church developed out of the technical advances created by the designers and workmen of the Romanesque period, but the builders of the Gothic church were even more skilled craftsmen. Gothic architecture tried to "make gravity seem an illusion," and the characteristic Gothic line is vertical, always striving upwards. Gothic structures were taller, airier, more imaginative in their design than their predecessors. The Gothic arch was usually tall and pointed in its earlier development, becoming more complex later. Walls were opened with magnificent stained glass windows that became larger as time went on. A triforium, or extra story beneath the clerestory, helped lift the nave windows even higher. Thin ribbed vaults were developed, permitting the construction of ever higher stone ceilings supported by ever thinner supports under a great trussed and gabled wood roof. Flying buttresses added visual and structural reinforcement to the dynamic thrusts of the church's masonry construction.

The Gothic church was built by many people working together under the direction of a generally anonymous designer; the style is sometimes said to be an expression of the religious zeal and deep pride these people took in their creations. Churches and cathedrals were built and paid for by entire towns, though overseen by the local bishops. Costly and complex, many took centuries to complete; some have been finished only recently, and some not yet. The word Gothic was originally a derisive term applied by later generations to this noble style, which was to have such a profound impact even as far away as Northern California.

The Renaissance church of the fifteenth century came to be regarded as the design of a single well-known individual, and thus the importance of the church architect was established. During this period, designing a church became more of an aesthetic effort than the complex solution of structural problems or a mass community effort to praise God. Churches like St. Peter's in Rome seemed to be the dwelling place of a more earthly God. The character of the times had changed. Now the interiors were richly ornamented with fine marbles, woven tapestries, painting, and sculpture befitting a princely personage. The Baroque church of the seventeenth and eighteenth centuries was a richly orchestrated ensemble of all the arts, with a strong sense of the theater; carefully organized parts created a powerful central emphasis in design.

Protestants, the second religious group to arrive in San Francisco, represent a religious tradition that grew out of the thoughts and writings of such men as Martin Luther, Ulrich Zwingli, and John Calvin. One of Luther's major contributions was a translation of the Bible from Latin into German, making it available to people who could not read the classical language. The Word is essential to Protestant worship. The theologian Paul Tillich describes Protestantism as a religion of the ear and not of the eye; he credits it with producing great music and poetry but not great architecture, painting, or sculpture. Protestants differ from Catholics in the predominance of the Word over the sacrament (the sermon over the Eucharist). The architectural expression of these differences is often seen in the proximity of the pastor to the congregation, who are usually seated close to the pulpit, and in the absence of sculpture and paintings used as teaching devices in the Catholic church.

Protestant churches do, however, run the gamut from elaborate to understated. Episcopal churches, derived from the Anglican communion and closer theologically to the church of Rome, tend to be more elegant, depending upon how "high" they are, "high" here meaning close to the Catholic liturgy. Quakers, by contrast, gather in meetinghouses that resemble ordinary residences, somewhat like the early New England churches. Baptist, Congregational, and Christian Science congregations tend to build churches that are straightforward and plain. Architectural environment is relatively unimportant to such groups as the Seventh Day Adventists, the Salvation Army, and Jehovah's Witnesses. (These generalizations, however, share the weakness of all such comments.)

The third major branch of Christianity, Eastern Orthodoxy, was introduced to San Francisco by chaplains from visiting vessels of the Russian Imperial Navy in 1859; the first Orthodox parish was established in 1864. The Eastern Orthodox church developed an architectural style based on the squared, central-domed Byzantine temples of the early church. These buildings were a symbolic representation of the Greek cross, with its arms of equal length. (The occasional round temples are considered to represent a circumscribed Greek cross.) Characteristically, the temple exteriors are plain, while interior walls and sometimes vaults are covered by glass mosaics in gold and brilliant colors. Windows are relatively small, both as a protection from harsh climates and to leave a maximum wall surface free for decoration. The dome, which symbolizes heaven, may be supported by columns, and is often decorated with an image of Christ *Pantocrator* (Ruler over All), especially in Greek churches.

The temple interior reflects the distinctive Eastern view of the sacred ritual. Unlike the Western church, where the mass is celebrated before the worshipers as if on a stage, in an Orthodox church the altar and some of the ritual are hidden behind the *iconostasis*, a kind of rood screen. During the ritual, priests pass through openings called the Royal Doors, affording mysterious glimpses of the altar. The inconostasis is decorated with *icons*, two-dimensional mosaic or painted images of Mary, Jesus, and the saints. Often solid today, the iconostasis started out centuries ago as an open grill.

The Russian version of the Eastern Orthodox temple was originally constructed of wood, and later of masonry. Interiors were richly decorated. The place of worship was frequently located on the second floor because of routine spring floods. The characteristic onion-shaped dome was designed to shed the heavy snowfall more effectively. Complex and sometimes bizarre roof forms were developed to serve as vertical landmarks. Towers were taller on churches built on the flat Russian steppes than on those in the hilly Serbian countryside. Frequently there were three apses and four small domes arranged around the large central dome. Some of these features can be found in Russian Orthodox churches in America, even though they have lost their original practical function. Some American Orthodox congregations have westernized their temples by installing seating for the worshipers, and their services by replacing the cantor with a choir. Instrumental music is not permitted.

The Jewish faith was among the earliest to be established in San Francisco; not one, but two congregations were founded in April 1851. The Jewish people, historically dispersed all over the world, have frequently found themselves in disfavor and thus unable to build freely. Consequently, their synagogues have tended to resemble the religious architecture of their host countries. Architecture is of little importance in Judaism; the Book or Torah is sacred rather than the temple as such. According to Jewish law, a synagogue consists of the Torah and ten men, wherever they can meet.

Changes in the temple focus on the interior and largely reflect the Reform movement of nineteenth-century German Judaism. All Jewish congregations retain the liturgical furniture—the Torah, the ark, and the menorah, as well as the everburning lamp over the ark. In some Conservative and Orthodox congregations, the reader of the Torah faces toward the ark. In Reform Judaism the reader faces the congregations, and women are no longer restricted to a separate part of the temple. There are proscriptions against graven images in Jewish temples, and the teaching function of Christian visual art was never necessary, because Jewish law required that all Jews be able to read the holy books. Nonetheless, many synagogues have fine works of art and support artists with grants.

The indigenous religions of China and Japan do not involve congregational worship, and so the temples often started out as shrines set up in open courtyards or courtyards with porticoes. In Japan the Shinto shrines, like the houses, were built in wood using simple post-and-lintel construction. Shinto was based on love of nature, of the family, and above all, of the ruling family as direct descendants of the gods. Pictorial representation was not permitted: Shinto art was symbolic. Since the third century, Shinto shrines in Japan have been destroyed every twenty years and then replaced by exact duplicates, thus assuring the preservation of ancient building forms and technologies.

Chinese popular religion—a blend of Taoism, Buddhism, Confucianism, reverence for one's ancestors, and other beliefs—was permitted to continue after the 1945 Chinese Revolution, although shrines to some of the household gods were replaced with shrines to public leaders. Temples are regarded as the dwelling of the god to whom they are dedicated, but they include shrines to a number of other gods and sages. In San Francisco such temples usually occupy the top floor of a building, to be closer to heaven, and are frequently sponsored by one of the Chinese benevolent associations. There are no formal services; worshipers visit the temples on an individual basis whenever they feel the need, or have something to pray about. Westerners came to refer to these temples as joss houses, a corruption of the Portuguese *deus* or god.

Buddhism characteristically involves congregational assembly to study the teachings of the faith. Beginning in the third century B.C., *chaitas* (sanctuaries or assembly halls) were cut into the hills of central India from the west to the east coast. Parts of the exteriors (and later, interiors) of these caves were carved to imitate in accurate detail the wooden structures of the period. San Francisco Buddhists continue the tradition of group study. Their temples, often referred to as churches, frequently provide space for such auxiliary programs as language classes, recreation, and social services. Some Buddhist churches have westernized their music by installing organs.

The arts of many Asian countries derive from Indian Buddhism. The most distinctive architectural hallmark of the faith is the stupa—a domed masonry mass of highly symbolic associations. The stupa was originally used to enshrine the relics of a holy person or a great teacher—notably the Buddha or Enlightened One—and later sometimes employed as a depository for sutras (scriptures), which were usually placed in the foundation stone. As Buddhism spread from India through China and Korea to Japan, the upper forms of the stupa were adapted to traditional architecture, producing the pagoda, a towerlike storied structure of stone, brick, or wood having prominent, upturned eaves on every story. Historically, the first floors in larger pagoda shrines were furnished and contained an altar, while the upper stories were plain and unfurnished.

Another characteristic of Eastern liturgical art is the use of sculpture to express the infinite. China, Japan, Southeast Asia, and India have a rich artistic heritage of religious sculpture. In San Francisco, most Asian temples are enclosed within buildings of Western construction, sometimes having an upturned roof and columns with Oriental detailing, but otherwise giving no hint of their distinctive interior appointments.

San Francisco, America's first Eurasian city, is heir to this rich legacy. All of the world's major faiths and many of the lesser known are represented in San Francisco today, and their sacred places enhance and enliven the cityscape. This book was originally conceived as a photographic study of the most magnificent and exotic structures. But it quickly became apparent that such buildings have an importance transcending their aesthetic appeal.

The churches and temples of San Francisco are comparable to the volumes in a fine old library; there are treasured first editions and contemporary works, often side by side. Each tells a story of people coming together to define ancestral beliefs and customs in relation to a uniquely cosmopolitan environment, of congregations sponsoring refugee families, establishing prison and street ministries, providing homestays for foreign students and, during the sixties, young runaways, and developing leadership roles for women. Together they tell a refreshingly different story of a city more often publicized for its excesses than for its spiritual vitality.

It has been our objective to tell that story. The subject is a vast one, and there are few precedents. As far as could be learned, no one has ever examined the social history of a major city in relation to the religious beliefs and practices of so diverse a population. This book is but a beginning. Inevitably, choices had to be made. Not all could be included. We have tried to present the historically and architecturally significant, and a balance of religious, cultural, and ethnic backgrounds.

The book is divided into four time periods, each introducing approximately twenty newly established faiths, sects, denominations, or congregations. The date given is that which seemed most appropriate in each case, whether the first religious services or the official founding. The individual essays vary considerably, due in part to the nature of the material available but also to the particular focus of the congregation as expressed in interviews or in the published materials supplied by them.

To minimize repetition, we have introduced each clergyman by his title and referred to him thereafter by first or last name, according to the custom of his sect. Eastern Orthodox and Roman Catholic priests are introduced as "Father" unless another title has been requested by a specific congregation. Protestant and Buddhist ministers are generally referred to as "The Reverend," Jewish clergymen as "Rabbi," and Vedanta Society spiritual leaders as "Swami." Bishops, archbishops, monsignors, and archimandrites are so designated. Generally speaking, the founding clergyman and several leaders from earlier times are mentioned. A current minister may be included if, for example, he was instrumental in the construction of the present church or temple. The significant contribution of the city's largest minority—the women—is poorly covered, primarily because the early records so seldom mention their participation in religious affairs.

In the fifth century B.C. Herodotus, since known as the Father of History, interpreted the culture of ancient Egypt to his Greek countrymen by describing the monumental temples he had visited while on a visit there. Ever since that time, travelers have followed his example, forming their impressions of other lands and other peoples in part from their ecclesiastical architecture. Many Americans travel the world over, visiting churches, temples, and synagogues, scarcely conscious of what is to be seen beneath the spires and within the walls of their own places of worship.

Here is presented the first study of an American city as revealed in the sacred places built by its people and the stories that those structures tell. Here is a view of the city in relation to its innermost self—the aspirations, beliefs, and contributions of its religious community of all faiths and all races.

Ruth Hendricks Willard

1

Days of Old, Days of Gold

1776–1851

San Franciscans have always had a sense of the past, perhaps because the past is so close to them. Though relatively young in years—scarcely more than two hundred birthdays have been celebrated—the city includes among its functioning sacred places a simple adobe chapel in which the present space-age population receives the same sacraments as those administered to the Neolithic people for whose salvation the building was constructed. More tangibly than any other structure in the city it serves, Mission San Francisco de Asis, popularly known as Mission Dolores, encompasses the panorama of human existence.

The recorded religious history of Alta California predates the birth of the missions, however. The earliest known Christian services on the Pacific Coast were those conducted according to the Anglican *Book of Common Prayer* by Francis Fletcher, the chaplain who accompanied Sir Francis Drake aboard the *Golden Hinde* in 1579. Catholic services began sixteen years later when the Spanish explorer Sebastian Rodriguez Cermeño entered the present Drake's Bay, naming it La Bahia de San Francisco. But it was not until the late eighteenth century that Spanish exploration parties reached the great bay now called by that name.

It was the responsibility of the Franciscan order, under the direction of Father Junipero Serra, to carry the cross to Alta California. Five missions had already been established when Father Francisco Palou, Serra's close friend (and later, his biographer) set out with a group of settlers and soldiers who had come from Mexico with Capt. Juan Bautista de Anza to establish an outpost of the Spanish dominion at the port of Saint Francis. Spanish colonization was controlled by the king, whose interests were paramount in all things. The soldiers established presidios, or outposts, to protect the holding; the settlers were required to settle in little pueblos similar to medieval Spanish towns; and the clergy established missions to Christianize the Indians, teaching them the Spanish language and the rudiments of the white man's way of life.

In March of 1776, de Anza marked the spot for the presidio, and on June 27 the expedition arrived near the Indian village of Petlenum, at the site selected for the mission. Palou, generally recognized as California's first historian, recorded the event: "A camp was formed consisting of fifteen tents erected on the edge of a large lake [Laguna de las Dolores] which empties into the arm of the sea or inlet of the port . . . a great many of the pagans came in, making signs of friendship and expressing their pleasure at our arrival. . . . On the next day after our arrival an arbor was built in which an altar was set up and there I said the first Mass on the day of Saint Peter and Saint Paul." The missionaries with six soldiers and two colonists began building houses, a storehouse, and a chapel while the rest of the company returned to the garrison to start the construction of the presidio. Formal possession of the presidio was taken on September 17, and dedication of the mission on October 9, when the necessary documents had arrived from Mexico.

For the next seventy-five years, California was Roman Catholic country. Beginning in the 1820s Yankee ships could occasionally be seen in the harbor. Spanish administration of the San Francisco colony was lackadaisical at best, and in 1822 California became a Mexican province. The influence of the missions began to wane. The old Pious Fund on which the fathers depended largely for their support gradually dried up because the various governments under the Mexican flag needed funds—and they took them. By 1834 the missions were secularized, the Indians dispersed, and most of the lands transferred to private ownership. During the early 1840s, the Holy See established several new dioceses to serve the Catholics living in western North America—California (1840), Texas (1841), and Oregon (1843). The Right Reverend Francisco Garcia Diego y Moreno, a Franciscan, served as Bishop of Upper and Lower California until his death in 1846.

The pueblo of San Francisco was officially founded on June 25, 1835, with the erection of the first building—a little trading post—at Yerba Buena Cove by the Englishman, William Richardson, who, like several other settlers, had become a Mexican citizen after accepting the Roman Catholic faith. By the mid-1840s the United States and Mexico were at war, and on June 7, 1846, Captain John B. Montgomery sailed into the bay to hoist the American flag over Yerba Buena. Montgomery was a Presbyterian elder, and he conducted divine services aboard ship before coming ashore. It was a portent of things to come. The Americans, a predominantly Protestant people, would bring a fundamentally different view of the world to the territory. The days of the plantation economy, caste society, and graciously hospitable Californio culture were numbered.

Although small, the population already had a cosmopolitan cast. Joseph Downey, an eyewitness, described the flag raising ("Filings from an Old Saw," in *The Golden Era*). Aides from Montgomery's ship, the *Portsmouth*, "by entreaties, menaces, and promises at last gathered some thirty or forty persons of all nations, colors, and languages and penned them in the square formed by the soldier-sailors" for the flag-raising. "This was an eventful moment," says Downey. "Something was about to be done that could not easily be undone."

Three weeks later the chartered ship *Brooklyn* put into port bearing 238 members of the Church of Jesus Christ of Latter Day Saints (Mormons). The new arrivals more than doubled the population. A second religious doctrine was proclaimed in the pueblo of Yerba Buena when their leader, Samuel Brannan, began holding services in the plaza on the last Sunday in July. The group included a hundred children needing schooling; their families found housing in some vacant outbuildings of the secularized mission and employed a Miss Angela Lovett as teacher, thereby establishing the first school to serve the pueblo. The Mormons were soon followed by a modest stream of settlers. While most were white males born in the United States, there were also visible minorities of South Americans, New Zealanders, English, Scots, Irish, Germans, Spanish-speaking Californios, and Indians.

Among the new arrivals were two circuit-riding Methodist preachers—Asa White, who came with his family from Oregon, and William Roberts, who was appointed by the Baltimore General Conference to do missionary work in the West. Together they established the First Methodist Society, California's first Protestant congregation, on April 25, 1847. Roberts was the preacher, and White's house, known as the Shanty with the Blue Cover, the meeting place. That same month, the Reverend Thaddeus Leavenworth, who had come to San Francisco with Stevenson's Regiment, preached the pueblo's first Protestant Episcopal sermon in the adobe hotel on the plaza. Leavenworth apparently found the pueblo's prospects appealing, for he resigned his chaplaincy abroad the *Brutus*, moved ashore, and opened a drug-store. The following August, he was elected *alcalde*, or chief administrative officer, of the village which had by that time been renamed San Francisco.

On February 2, 1848, the Treaty of Guadalupe Hidalgo ended America's war with Mexico; the young nation had achieved its "Manifest Destiny" to extend the benefits of American traditions and beliefs from the Atlantic to the Pacific. The timing could not have been better, for only about a week earlier James Marshall had discovered gold at Sutter's

Mill on the American River. Now the newly discovered wealth would enrich both the fledgling territory and the nation. On the very day the treaty was signed, the brig *Eagle* dropped anchor in the bay, bringing the first Chinese to California.

The rush for gold started slowly, with a kind of man-in-the-street scepticism. Almost no one believed the early rumors of the discovery. The few people in town went on about their business until the day Sam Brannan ran through the streets brandishing a bottle of gold dust and shouting "Gold! Gold! Gold from the American River!" One imagines San Francisco instantly crowded with forty-niners as a result, but in fact both news and people traveled slowly at that time. As late as October of 1848, both the American (interdenominational) and the Baptist home missionary societies routinely dispatched emissaries to the newly acquired frontier area before learning of the discovery of gold; the clergymen heard the news upon arriving at New Orleans.

Californians had the Gold Rush pretty much to themselves that first year. The town of San Francisco was bereft of a working force within days. Both weekly papers stopped publication, *The Californian* observing that "the field is left untended, the house half-built, and everything neglected but the manufacture of shovels and pickaxes." San Franciscans were just beginning to return home when adventurers from the rest of the world began flooding through this western gateway to the mines. Word reached Hawaii in June; by July vessels began disgorging crowds of white and Kanaka treasure-seekers from the Pacific Islands. Oregon got the news in July and began sending delegations in August. Experienced miners from Peru, Chile, and Mexico began to arrive late in 1848. One of the early Chinese arrivals went up into the mountains, found gold, and wrote to friends at home about the new country. Soon throngs of Chinese gold-seekers joined the mass migration to the land that they called *Gam San*, or "Gold Mountain." Already, San Francisco had become a teeming, brawling city, its harbor filled with tall masts and its few boardwalks crowded with men from many lands. When the Reverend Timothy Dwight Hunt followed his flock from Maui to San Francisco, arriving in October, a committee of citizens arranged to hire him as the official city chaplain, to provide nondenominational religious services for the rapidly growing community.

On February 18, 1849, the first Argonauts from the eastern states steamed into the harbor aboard the Pacific Mail's *California*. Sixty-one sailing ships, each with a full cargo of men, left the East Coast during one month late in 1848; the vanguard of these Cape Horn vessels made port in the summer of forty-nine. Overland caravans began to straggle in during August and September. Europeans, too, had heard the news. British, German, and French adventurers, as well as Australians, began arriving in the autumn.

The civic headaches of today hardly compare to the migraine of a town whose population had jumped twentyfold in one year. Sailing ships were abandoned, fully loaded, in the harbor, as seamen and officers jumped ship to head for the Sierra. George Osborne Wilson, arriving abroad the brig *Oriental* on March 3, 1850, wrote in his diary: "We were soon winding our way among thousands of gold seekers through streets and lanes, the mud knee deep and the rain descending in copious torrents. . . . At sunset, found all hands on the beach ready to go aboard our brig with faces a foot longer than when we landed. . . . All came to the conclusion that the prospect was not very flattering." The town suffered acute shortages of food, shelter, goods, services—everything except young, adventurous males from all over the continent and the globe. Never had there been a city of so many, "peopled by men alone."

Though San Francisco is famous as a place where gamblers and other rough-and-readys came to pursue their fortunes, many of the gold-seekers were professional, well-educated men. Not all came to dig for gold; as the months went by, an increasing number of young men, hearing opportunity knocking, came to mine the miners. Almost immediately, the city became a lively center of trade and commerce. Still, there was a topsy-turvy quality to this population—a kind of mixing-bowl democracy noted by early commentators. The Chilean aristocrat Vincente Rosales recalled in his *California Adventure*, "No actor played the role that had fallen to his lot in his own country . . . the lawyer, a mover of freight, the doctor, a porter." Or, as observed by Bayard Taylor, ace reporter dispatched by the *New York Tribune*, "Lawyers, physicians, and ex-professors dug cellars, drove ox teams, sawed wood [illegible] sailors, cooks, or day laborers were at the head of profitable establishments." One of the local surveyors was a former Congregational minister, the Reverend Chester W. Lyman.

In a town of few women, and fewer ladies, men lived in hotels and pleasured themselves with eating, drinking, and gambling. This is all part of the conventional image of early San Francisco—a wild, wide-open city—and to a point it is true. Less generally touted, this same boisterous setting provided the beginnings of the city's religious life. At first, churchmen in the East considered California a threat. The lure of the gold was draining their congregations of young men, the future community leaders. From the pulpit, they exhorted young men to forego the adventure. When that approach proved futile, the clergymen sometimes packed their Bibles and went along, to provide spiritual leadership in a wild and profligate land. Other missionaries were transfered by their denominations from previous assignments around the world. San Francisco was seen as another Puritan City on a Hill—the focal point for transmitting their Protestant beliefs and values to western America and even the pagan Orient.

On arriving in the burgeoning city, the missionaries gathered their flocks and established new congregations. Four, or six, or twenty people—Methodists, Presbyterians, Episcopalians, Baptists, Congregationalists—met in homes, hotels, courtrooms, rented halls, aboard ships abandoned in the harbor, or even under canvas, and made their compacts with the Lord. A Lutheran minister arrived, unsponsored, from Germany to bring the gospel to "this wicked city"; he quickly gathered a congregation.

The Catholic church was struggling to meet the needs of its rapidly increasing immigrant constituency all over America. The only priest assigned to Mission Dolores, a Mexican Indian who spoke only Spanish, divided his time among several missions. In order to meet the spiritual needs of the rapidly growing Catholic population, the administrator of the Diocese of Upper and Lower California recruited priests from outside the area in the spring of 1849, authorizing them to establish an auxiliary chapel within the area of the pueblo itself. This little church, also named St. Francis of Assisi, offered multilingual services from the very beginning.

After several San Francisco laymen wrote East requesting more priests, a new diocese was created, and on December 7, 1850, the Catholic community gathered at St. Francis of Assisi church to welcome the bishop of the newly created Diocese of Monterey, the Right Reverend Joseph Sadoc Alemany, a Dominican born in Spain. Though educated and consecrated in Europe, the new bishop was a naturalized American citizen with a decade of service in Ohio and Tennessee. Erudite, compassionate, and totally committed to his assignment, Bishop (and later Archbishop) Alemany proved the ideal prelate to adapt the rapidly growing, multinational, immigrant church to an individualistic, democratic society.

The ministers were few and the needs staggering in the overcrowded, makeshift city. Clergymen of all faiths were likely to spend their mornings in study and the preparation of sermons; afternoons were often devoted to visiting the sick and the imprisoned, and conducting funerals and weddings (sometimes three or four of each in a week). With their congregations, ministers formed associations and committees to provide such necessary services as schools, orphanages, asylums for the destitute and the insane, and counseling for the sick and the dying.

The *Annals of San Francisco* describes a "novel and interesting ceremony" in Portsmouth Square on August 28, 1850. Mayor John Geary, some other civic officials, and the Reverend Albert Williams presented the Chinese residents with religious tracts, papers, and books printed in Chinese characters. The Chinese, richly dressed in native costume, made a "fine and pleasing appearance," and accepted the mayor's invitation to participate the following day in a civic memorial service honoring President Zachary Taylor.

As observed by Owen C. Coy in *Golden Days*: "It is wonderful to think that these few Christian leaders were able to turn the quiet village of Yerba Buena into San Francisco, and to establish in the midst of the seething stream of recklessness a highway for the worship of God." Financial support for these efforts came from the denominational or national missionary societies, and from the people of San Francisco as well. As the historian Hubert H. Bancroft characterized the typical gambler, "his philanthropy knows no formula; he will contribute to establish a church or a brothel, to support a Sunday school or a swindle." In other words, money was at least available to build churches, though it was broadly distributed elsewhere too.

In September of 1849, Jewish Argonauts came down from the mines to celebrate the High Holy Days with their co-religionists; by the following autumn they were making plans for a synagogue. Liberal theology came to San Francisco in 1850, as little groups gathered in private homes to study the teachings of Emanuel Swedenborg; later that same year a group of New Englanders established the First Unitarian Church. As for the Chinese population, they too brought their religious beliefs and customs with them, establishing at least two temples before the end of 1851. By the time California became a state, San Francisco was a city of from twenty to twenty-five thousand people. At least a dozen Protestant and two Catholic churches had been established, and a synagogue was about to be formed. Those pioneer congregations are among the most influential in the city today.

Mission San Francisco de Asis (Mission Dolores)

320 Dolores Street, near Sixteenth Street
First services June 29, 1776

The simple dignity of this small chapel, the oldest intact building in the city of San Francisco—and still in daily use—befits its position at the crossroads of history. It sits near the site of the village of Petlenum, one of nine or ten Neolithic settlements within what is now San Francisco. It was founded by Franciscan friars under the leadership of Father Francisco Palou. They had the responsibility of bringing to the inhabitants of this remote territory the benefits of both Christian salvation and Spanish civilization, and they undertook their work with great earnestness. In time, the Spanish would be supplanted by the Mexicans and the Mexicans by the Americans, and the American city surrounding the little adobe chapel would fall to an earthquake and a fire; but the mission itself would continue to serve its sacred function.

The first mass was celebrated on June 29, 1776—five days before the American colonies declared themselves a nation—in a small *enramada*, or arbor of leafy branches, constructed on the bank of a lagoon named Nuestra Senõra de los Dolores because it was discovered on the feast day of the seven sorrows of Mary. By coincidence, the fathers had given a similarly doleful name to the creek that emptied from the lagoon into the bay—Los Llorones, or "The Weepers"—because of the "kind of weeping greeting" the first exploration party had received from a young Indian at that spot a year earlier.

The first of several small chapels was put into service and the mission registers opened in late July; however, formal dedication was postponed until October 9, when the necessary documents had arrived from Mexico. Palou noted that he "blessed the site, set up the Holy Cross, and made a procession in honor of our Father San Francisco, using an image of that Saint which was carried on a platform and afterwards placed on the altar." The people of the presidio, the supply vessel *San Carlos*, and the mission "gave the salvos in all services." No Indians were present because in the month of August they had been driven away by their enemies from the southeast (the present San Mateo County), who set fire to their villages, wounding and killing the inhabitants.

The distinction of becoming the first entry in the mission register belongs to Francisco José de los Dolores Soto, newborn son of a couple in the Anza party and the first white child born within the confines of the present San Francisco; he was baptized on August 10, 1776. The Indians began returning to Petlenum the following March, and in June 1777, the first three neophytes were baptized. Palou relates with satisfaction that on the occasion of Father Junipero Serra's final visit to the mission in 1784, the registers listed the names of 394 neophytes.

Other early baptisms of historic interest include that of la Doña Concepción Arguello, on February 26, 1791, whose romance with a Russian naval officer was to become one of San Francisco's tragic stories; and the June 16, 1823, baptism of Guillermo Antonio (born William Anthony) Richardson, who renounced his English citizenship and religious affiliation in order to marry Maria Antonio Martinez, daughter of the commandant of the Presidio.

On April 25, 1782, Palou laid the cornerstone of the present chapel (a few blocks away from the original location). Within the stone he placed "the image of Our Holy Father Saint Francis, some relics in the form of bones of Saint Pius and other holy martyrs, five medals of various saints, and a goodly portion of silver coin." In 1875 Palou returned to Mexico while Father Pedro Cambon, his successor, began work on the present building. Construction proceeded slowly; six years were to pass before the formal dedication on August 2, 1791.

With the exception of the chapel at the Presidio, Mission Dolores (as it was called almost from the beginning) was the only religious institution serving the settlement until the arrival of Sam Brannan's Mormon colony in 1846. The number of Indians living at the mission fluctuated from year to year, reaching its pinnacle of 1,252 in 1820 and declining to 200 by 1834, when the mission was secularized, the Indians dispersed, and lands transferred to private ownership. The burden of sustaining the California missions during this period of financial deprivation fell upon the Franciscan friar Francisco Garcia Diego y Moreno, who was consecrated as Bishop of Upper and Lower California in 1840. From the time of his death in 1846 until the arrival of Bishop Joseph Sadoc Alemany in 1850, the vast diocese was administered by Father José Gonzales Rubio. In the late 1840s, as the English-speaking population of the pueblo continued to grow, Rubio recruited additional priests and authorized the establishment of an auxiliary chapel within the pueblo itself—the church now known as St. Francis of Assisi.

Bear and bull fights, so popular with the early settlers, constituted the main activity at the mission during these years, although the cemetery continued to be used for religious burials. In 1857 the old mission—several miles from the center of town, largely ignored and in disrepair—was officially restored to the Roman Catholic Church under the leadership of Archbishop Joseph Sadoc Alemany. When the town began to grow out toward the mission area, a large Gothic Revival parish church was built next door. Several other religious groups also built churches nearby.

Father John Patrick Tobin, assigned to Mission Dolores parish in 1902 by Archbishop Riordan, began a program of rehabilitation which probably resulted in the little adobe chapel's surviving the earthquake and fire of 1906. Both the new church and the parish school were demolished. Tobin organized crews to care for the stricken and conducted outdoor religious services in Mission Park until a temporary church was put up. He then oversaw the construction of the Ultra Baroque church that hovers over the humble mission today.

The venerable mission was further restored in the 1920s, when the architect Willis Polk created what he considered to be his masterpiece by inserting steel reinforcing to strengthen the structure without altering its appearance. By that time the sturdy structure had withstood the disaster of 1906 plus one hundred fifty years of wear that included several lesser quakes. In 1955 Mission Dolores was designated a Minor Basilica by Pope Pius XII—the fourth such designation in the United States and the first west of the Mississippi River. As the mission and the nation celebrated their bicentennial in 1976, a permanent exhibiton of historic artifacts was established in a former classroom.

A walk through the peaceful little garden cemetery (along with the National Cemetery in the Presidio the only burial grounds remaining within the city limits) is a lively yet poignant historical adventure. Among the earliest names carved into the headstones—of Irish, Chilean, French, Spanish, Italian, Yugoslavian, English, Scottish, Portuguese and German derivation—are many now bestowed upon the streets of San Francisco. The city's tempestuous past is recalled by the headstone of James P. Casey, who was executed by the Committee of Vigilance for the murder of journalist James King of William. A Lourdes grotto keeps the memory of those whose early wooden gravemarkers have disintegrated. The five thousand unmarked Indian burials are commemorated by a statue of Kateri Tekakwitha, a Mohawk-Iroquois maiden who represents all Indians by virtue of her 1932 nomination for sainthood.

The mission is a characteristic small elongated rectangle, 114 feet long by 22 feet wide, the width being limited by the length of straight timbers available to support the roof. The adobe walls are four feet thick. The architectural details combine modified late Baroque and Neoclassical styles. The arched entrance is flanked by thick engaged columns with stereotyped Tuscan capitals below a wooden balcony. Six similar half-columns above the balcony extend upward to the broad eaves of the roof. A stepped ornamental band linking these upper half columns is reminiscent of the curvetting cornices of eighteenth-century Mexico, while the overhanging eaves protect the mud walls from erosion by the rain.

The bells of Mission Dolores came from Mexico, a gift of the viceroy. Inside, the struts and ridge-joints are bound with the only material available—rawhide thongs; the door and window frame joints are secured by manzanita pegs. The local Indians, who did the actual work, had no building tradition of their own and hence few building skills. The ceiling timbers and sanctuary arch were originally painted by Indian neophytes using vegetable and mineral pigments. Restored today, the chevrons are done in green, tan, red, white, and gray. The retable, a screen behind the altar, was brought overland (in sections) from Mexico. It is handcarved and painted, and in its rich late Baroque rhythms is the most elaborate such eighteenth-century screen found in the California missions. There are thirteen carved statues of saints on the retable. Indians made the Pascal candle; the original

The holy and unholy dead lie quietly together in the old Mission Dolores cemetery.

confessional doors line the wall to the left of the entrance. Midway on the left side is the baptistry. To this day all parish baptisms are performed here. As the year 1984 drew to a close, the sacrament of baptism had been administered to a total of 28,826 persons, from Neolithic men and women to space-age infants, in this chapel. Mission Dolores is the simple ancestor of San Francisco churches and temples.

San Francisco Registered Landmark #1
California Registered Landmark #327
National Register of Historic Places, March 16, 1972

Mission Dolores' simple Baroque emphasis, in plain adaptations of columnar forms, contrasts with the rich period vocabulary of the new church nearby, with much the same basic pattern of focus.

Chapel of Our Lady

Moraga Avenue, at Mesa Street, Presidio of San Francisco
Founded September 17, 1776

What is now the Presidio of the United States Army in San Francisco was once a small military outpost of the Spanish domain, established on three thousand *varas* of land selected by Captain Juan Bautista de Anza early in 1776. Cross and crown were inseparably linked in Spanish culture: it was the function of this northernmost garrison to protect the surrounding missions (ultimately including San Jose, Santa Clara, San Francisco de Asis, San Rafael, and San Francisco Solano) and to forestall any incursions into New Spain by such foreign powers as Britain or Russia. The missionaries, in turn, were held responsible for both the spiritual sustenance and the physical development of each new settlement.

Anza was soon recalled to Mexico, and it fell to Lieutenant José Joaquin Moraga to supervise construction of the new post. On July 26, 1776, the soldiers and settlers began building barracks of tules, setting the first one aside for a chapel, and on July 28, Father Francisco Palou celebrated the first mass. The Presidio was formally dedicated on September 17, 1776—the day of the Stigmata of Saint Francis. Palou, assisted by several other friars, offered mass in a tiny temporary chapel hastily constructed for the occasion by carpenters from the supply ship *San Carlos*. A bronze tablet in the garden of the present Chapel of Our Lady commemorates that event.

Those early soldiers were served by a series of small adobe chapels, all of them crumbled and long since gone. The chapel became ecumenical when the United States Army took possession of the Presidio in 1847. In 1873 a small frame house of worship rose on the same site. With its turreted spire surmounted by a cross rising some thirty feet above the ground, the chapel resembled a miniature New England village church. In 1883 Archbishop Alemany appealed to the Jesuits to supply spiritual guidance to the soldiers at the Presidio. They did so for twenty-four years, from 1883 until 1907. Father Francis Ignatius Prelato, a man beloved by the entire military community, served for seventeen of those years, during which time the little church was called the Chapel of Saint Sebastian, for the Roman soldier-martyr. Catholic, Protestant, and Jewish services were conducted in the chapel until 1932, when the new Ecumenical Post Chapel was completed. At that time, the old chapel became known as the Chapel of Our Lady and was reserved for Roman Catholic services.

In 1952 Monsignor Patrick J. Ryan, then Sixth Army Chaplain (later, Chief of Chaplains), oversaw the reconstruction of the building in accordance with the sensitive plans submitted by the architect Hewlitt Wells. The modernized building, done in redwood with clear and colored glass, retains the old belfry and some of the original trusses. Inside, a large wooden cross hangs above the variegated marble altar table. Wood carvings depict the stations of the cross and Mary and Joseph. Dorff Studios of San Francisco did the decorative elements of the shrine. Handwrought iron is used for the large chandelier and flower stand, which reflect the Hispanic-Mexican origins of the Presidio. Brilliantly colored windows on the west add sunset glow to afternoon weddings, as brides enter under crossed swords. Blue and gold illumination provides a spectacular setting for evening ceremonies. The entire wall behind the altar table is of clear glass, bringing the chapel and the worshipers into oneness with nature.

California Registered Landmark #79
(Presidio of San Francisco)

Reminiscent of a late medieval Gothic arch and England's tie beams are the details in the Chapel of Our Lady.

Church of Jesus Christ of Latter Day Saints

1900 Pacific Avenue, at Gough Street
First Services July 31, 1846

Only three weeks after Captain Montgomery posted the American flag over Yerba Buena, the religious character of the little village was abruptly transformed by the arrival of the schooner *Brooklyn*. Under the leadership of Elder Samuel Brannan, 238 members of the Church of Jesus Christ of Latter Day Saints—a hundred of them children—had made the long voyage by way of Cape Horn and Hawaii in search of a place where they could establish an agricultural colony and follow the dictates of their distinctive faith without interference. The shipload of newcomers more than doubled the local population, thereby transforming the nominally Catholic village to a mostly Mormon settlement overnight.

They were members of one of the most striking religious movements to originate in the United States—the church founded in 1830 by Joseph Smith after a series of divine revelations which led to his producing the *Book of Mormon*, the *Doctrine and Covenants*, and the *Pearl of Great Price*. It is a basic tenet of Mormonism that the living God continues to make divine revelations to his followers, or Saints, even in these latter days; these books and also later revelations are considered to have validity equal to that of the Bible. Some of the Mormon beliefs and customs were so offensive to other Christian denominations that they were forced to move from place to place to escape persecution. After the murder of Joseph Smith in Illinois in 1844, Brigham Young led the group westward in search of a new Zion, preferably outside the United States. On the same day the exodus began from Nauvoo, Illinois—February 4, 1846—Elder Samuel Brannan and the Saints who had remained in the New York area embarked for California. Both groups entertained hopes of establishing the new headquarters for their faith.

Curiosity was widespread as the *Brooklyn* put into port. Stories of the group's adventures in Illinois and Missouri had preceded them, wrote eyewitness Joseph Downey ("Filings from an Old Saw" in *The Golden Era*), and "a vague idea seemed to predominate in the minds of all that they were a sort of wild, desperate people, and that trouble would soon arise from their arrival." Montgomery, however, after conferring with Brannan and several other elders, invited the entire contingent to attend divine worship aboard the *Portsmouth* the following day. At the appointed hour, wrote Downey, "every eye was fixed on the ladder, anxious to get a peep, especially at the women," but when the last one had been seated, "a dilapidated specimen of a Quarter-Gunner growled out, in no very sweet tones, 'D-mnation, why they are just like other women!' And so they were; sect, creed, or religion had not changed the human form divine, and they sat as meek and smiling as though they had no religion at all."

Brannan lost no time in getting started. John Henry Brown's *Reminiscences and Incidents of the "Early Days" of San Francisco* describes the first sermon delivered in the English language in Yerba Buena: "preached by Samuel Brannan on the last Sunday of July, 1846, as good a sermon as anyone could wish to hear," and the first wedding, performed by Brannan "according to the Mormon faith in a room generally used by the

Mexicans as a calaboose or prison." Everyone was invited; refreshments were ample; and the wedding was pronounced a "grand success."

The new arrivals set up their tents along the shores of Yerba Buena Cove. Brannan had brought along a printing press, and in January 1847 he began publication of the *California Star*, San Francisco's first (and California's second) newspaper. After it was learned that the Mormon headquarters would remain in Salt Lake City, many of the San Francisco contingent moved either to Utah or to southern California. Brannan, meanwhile, had gone on to more secular pursuits, becoming San Francisco's first millionaire, donating land for the city's first schoolhouse, and probably instigating the Gold Rush, since few people really believed the story of the discovery until he personally verified it. He was also influential in forming the Committees of Vigilance that brought order to the boisterous city during the 1850s.

The San Francisco branch of the Mormon church acquired a new president on December 2, 1847, when Addison Pratt returned from a mission to the Society Islands (Tahiti). By 1849, worship services were held in the Public Institute on the plaza (Portsmouth Square). In 1854 Pratt reported that there were missionaries laboring in San Francisco, Union City, Santa Clara, Santa Cruz, and Sacramento. While on church assignment in San Francisco, Elder George Q. Cannon published the *Book of Mormon* in the Hawaiian language in 1855 and began the *Western Standard*, a church magazine, early in 1856.

Through the years, San Francisco continued to be the port through which missionaries passed enroute to and from the Pacific Islands, but little missionary work was done within California until the 1890s, when both the Oakland Branch and the California Mission of the Church of Jesus Christ of Latter Day Saints were activated. In 1894 the church presented an exhibit at the California Mid-Winter Exposition and established a meeting place at 29 Eleventh Street in San Francisco. After the earthquake and fire of 1906, headquarters of the California Mission were moved to Los Angeles. The first stake, or diocese, in present day California was established in Los Angeles in 1923; the San Francisco Stake was organized May 10, 1927. In 1964, the church proudly dedicated the Oakland Temple, one of fifteen such located around the world for the performance of sacred ordinances. By 1983, Mormons were once again the second-largest religious group in California. There are currently three churches belonging to this Christian group within the city.

The Pacific Avenue church is the chapel for the Bay Ward, or parish. The architect Emil B. Fetzer did the original design for this church, and the firm of Markling and Yamasaki executed the final concept. (Although the firm had not been considered church architects before they did this building, they have since designed the Mormon temple in Washington, D.C.) Completed in 1970, the building is modern—made of concrete and brick—but it has sharply pointed Gothic arches and tall slender pseudo-buttresses or pillars repeated along its entire length. These are echoed in the slender tower and the side elevator. This starkly austere church is surrounded by lush plantings of ivy, hedges, and trees to accommodate its contemporaneous appearance to a more traditional residential setting.

Post Chapel

Fisher Loop, Presidio of San Francisco
Founded March 27, 1847

Although the United States established possession in 1846, it was not until the following March that the Presidio of San Francisco was formally occupied by American troops under the command of Major James A. Hardie. For the most part, the Americans simply took over existing buildings. The chapel became a post chapel, caring for both Catholics and Protestants although officially under Episcopalian jurisdiction. A new post chapel was constructed some time before 1873. Like other army chapels of the period, this one showed the strong architectural influence of New England, but in homage to the Spanish Mexican heritage of the Presidio, it was built in the area occupied by the previous chapels, near the site blessed by Father Francisco Palou nearly a century earlier. Elements of that building are incorporated in the present Chapel of Our Lady, which now, once again, serves only Roman Catholics.

Army architects designed the present Mexican Colonial Revival chapel, which was dedicated in 1932. The white textured stucco exterior with red tile roof relates to other buildings on the post. Paired, twisted (Solomonic) columns flank the entrance, which has a tabernacle motif above crowned with a broken spiraled pediment. A Moorish mixtilinear outlined window on the low tower gives added zest. Twelve stained glass windows represent such virtues as Honor, Mercy, Justice, Sacrifice, Faith, Love, Loyalty, Courage, and Obedience. They were designed by Willemina Ogterop, a Netherlands-born resident of Berkeley. Ogterop worked for Cummings Studio in San Francisco for twenty-five years, until she was seventy-two years old. During that time she designed windows for many churches and synagogues, including those at St. Ignatius.

The mural in the long space beyond the chapel's side entryway was done by the State Emergency Relief Administration (S.E.R.A.) division of the Works Progress Administration under the direction of Lucien Labaudt. Victor Arnautoff, the artist of this work, studied in Mexico under Diego Rivera. He said, "When Rivera came to San Francisco, he left me in charge of the wall decoration in the National Palace [in Mexico]. I also worked with him in the Palace of Cortés at Cuernavaca. Under his guidance, I became familiar with the chemical composition of plaster and the principles of mural painting." The Post Chapel fresco measures ten feet high by thirty-five feet long. The left portion shows the early history of the post; the Presidio of the late 1930s appears on the right; in the middle is an image of St. Francis, patron of the city.

Interior altar appointments can be changed to accommodate Christian or Jewish services. A screen of wrought iron behind the altar suggests older Hispanic types. Commemorative plaques from various regiments line the walls of the nave, and regimental standards hang from the beams of the wooden-trussed and timbered ceiling. The dimensions are suggestive of the California mission buildings, long and narrow. The building provides a feeling of reverence similar to that found in many more elaborate places of worship.

California Registered Landmark #79
(Presidio of San Francisco)

Mixing medieval and modern, the Post Chapel's interior has powerful lighting to create a dramatic effect.

First St. John's United Methodist Church

1600 Clay Street, at Larkin Street
Founded April 25, 1847

This historic congregation descends from the oldest Protestant church in California. By the mid-1840s, missionaries who had followed the Lewis and Clark Trail to the Oregon territory were casting thoughtful eyes upon Catholic dominated California. Asa White, an itinerant Methodist preacher, was the first to sail southward, bringing his family and the makings for a rough board shanty with blue cloth for a roof. They set up housekeeping on the shores of Yerba Buena Cove. Early in 1847, they were joined by another Methodist preacher, William Roberts, who had been appointed by the Baltimore General Conference to do mission work in the West.

The arrival of any clergyman in San Francisco was a novelty. Roberts' first act upon arrival was to offer to give a sermon in the hotel dining room. Signs were posted, and the room soon filled. According to the report of the hotel manager, the congregation was "not very fashionable, but deeply attentive, and well pleased with the sermon." Many had not been in a place of worship for ten or fifteen years. An old sailor passed the hat and reported to Roberts, "That was a damn good sermon!" There were "preaching, drinking, card-playing, and billiards all going on at the same time" under one roof, but reportedly the gamblers were somewhat quiet in honor of the occasion.

The population was too small for more than a single congregation. White appears to have deferred to Roberts as the minister chosen by the church. From then on, Roberts preached in the Whites' house, which became known as the Shanty with the Blue Cover. On Sunday, April 25, 1847, Roberts, the Whites, and a congregation of six people officially founded the First Methodist Church of San Francisco. Eventually the membership grew large enough to buy a lot and make plans for a permanent church.

Two years later, the news of gold in California had reached the world, and San Francisco had become a teeming, brawling city, its harbor filled with ships and its streets crowded with men from around the world. In Baltimore, the Conference had appointed the first ordained Methodist minister to carry on the work in California, and the Reverend William Taylor, with his wife and family, sailed into port aboard the *Andalusia* in April 1849. Born in Virginia to hill-dwelling Scots-Irish parents, physically strong, energetic, and compassionate, Taylor was ideally suited to life in the burgeoning city. The very day of his arrival (and nearly every day after that), he visited the City Hospital, attending the sick, writing letters for them, and consoling the dying. Two days later, he preached his first sermon in the Shanty with twenty-three in his audience. As the little church begun by Roberts was not finished, Taylor rowed across the bay to what is now Oakland to cut timbers with which to complete the building. With the help of the congregation, the rough building at Washington and Powell streets was completed and dedicated three weeks later. A much more elaborate church was built in the same location in 1852.

Taylor was, at heart, a street preacher, and on the third of December he startled his congregation with the announcement that at three o'clock that day he planned to preach in the open air, on Portsmouth Square. The plaza was surrounded by gambling halls, and

Sunday was their best business day. No one was sure how they might respond to such an intrusion. Undeterred, Taylor borrowed a bench from the front of a gambling hall, seated his wife and some family friends on it, and proceeded to "sing up a crowd" before delivering a sermon in his powerful voice. The crowd that "gathered to jeer, stayed to listen," as he exhorted the fast-living citizens with "What shall it advantage a man if he gain the whole world and lose his soul?" Over the next seven years, Taylor, who was called the singing crusader, preached more than six hundred sermons standing on boxes, whiskey barrels, ships' decks, and once, on top of a bar. Whenever a ship was docking, Taylor would stand on the pier, singing hymns and preaching the gospel. His audiences frequently numbered a thousand people, and on one occasion, in the plaza, ten thousand were said to be present. Taylor's autobiographical *Seven Years' Street Preaching* gives a typical Sunday schedule in 1852: leading a class at the Powell Street church at 9:00 A.M., followed by preaching on Long Wharf at 10:00, at the Seamen's Bethel at 11:00, at the State Marine Hospital at 2:30, on the Plaza at 4:00, and back at the Bethel at 7:00.

Taylor had quickly assumed the unofficial position of port chaplain. In 1851, he organized the Seamen's Bethel aboard an abandoned ship, the *Panama*, then docked on Davis Street. The Bethel provided religious and social services for sailors in port and living accommodations for shipwrecked and destitute seamen. Subsequently, the ship was moved to the foot of Mission Street, and a church built on the deck. For a time, Taylor and his family also lived on board the ship. In 1857, the church was dismantled and rebuilt on Mission Street between First and Second.

Working with two other Methodist ministers, Isaac Owens and Edward Bannister, Taylor was instrumental in founding California's first chartered college in Santa Clara in 1851. Originally called Wesleyan College, this institution evolved into today's University of the Pacific. Other organizations founded at First Methodist Church included the California Bible Society, 1849; the Methodist Book Concern, 1850; and the *California Christian Advocate*, first published in 1850.

The Reverend Edward Bannister became pastor of First Methodist in 1856, holding the post for two years. His wife noted in a letter to her parents in the East that things had changed after the first flood of wealth from gold had subsided: "Money is not so abundant in California as it was four or five years since. How many there are, who then thought themselves rich, and indeed were, and are now *poor*. Economy is much more practised." In 1895, during the pastorate of the Reverend Thomas Filben, the church hosted a world conference of the Epworth League, the Methodist youth group. With the help of Mayor Adolph Sutro, who ordered banners printed with the Epworth League symbol and hung over Market Street, Filben was able to honor his pledge to find rooms in private homes at the rate of a dollar a day for 12,000 of the 16,700 delegates.

First Methodist continued to use their church on Powell Street until it was destroyed in the earthquake and fire of 1906. Not only the building, but also a fine library and extensive collection of pioneer records were destroyed. Undaunted, the congregation "made do" in a temporary structure, ironically called "The Shanty," for four years.

The congregation reached its peak membership during the period from 1922 to 1947, perhaps because of the double influence of the Great Depression and World War II. "The grave crises of the world sent people to churches seeking not only comfort, but a new understanding of what it meant to be human in such a world," according to the church's history. During this same period, the Methodist Mission Conference established the St. John's Italian Methodist Church, the first Italian Methodist Church west of the Mississippi

River, with the Reverend Ettore DiGiantomasso as pastor. The church offered Americanization classes, counseling, youth groups, and worship services in both Italian and English. In 1967, St. John's and First Methodist agreed to merge, adopting the name First St. John's United Methodist Church. Two years later, recognizing the presence of yet another minority group within the parish, First St. John's also began ministering in Cantonese and providing facilities for a variety of community activities, including a Tai Chi class.

The present church, built in 1911 at a cost of seventy thousand dollars, was designed by John G. Kramer of New York. The stucco building represents typical early twentieth-century church architecture, a form of rural late Mission Revival style. The gabled entrances suggest village English Tudor Gothic in their heavy bracketed wood shapes; the tower is more Mission Revival, with high, rounded openings and balconies. Stained glass windows on two sides, with arched divider bars, give an overall medieval flavor to a twentieth-century building.

The large scale of the parts creates a strong overall effect in First St. John's United Methodist.

Old First Presbyterian Church

1751 Sacramento Street, at Van Ness Avenue
Founded May 20, 1849

As young men set out to seek their fortunes in the California gold fields, church leaders took steps to provide them with religious guidance in the wild new land. Among the first eastern ministers to set out for San Francisco was the Reverend Albert Williams, who resigned his pastorate in Clinton, New Jersey, to accept a joint commission from the American Home boards of Missions and Education. He left New York on February 4, 1849, aboard the streamer *Crescent City* bound for Chagres and the fastest route to California—overland across the Isthmus of Panama and then north to San Francisco by the Pacific Mail steamer *Oregon*. It was a fortuitous choice, for by the time he arrived in San Francisco Williams had gathered the nucleus of his future congregation from among his shipmates. They were a cosmopolitan group, hailing from such diverse points as China and Chile as well as Massachusetts, Michigan, Vermont, and Pennsylvania. Among them were the family of Colonel John White Geary, the newly appointed postmaster, who brought with him the first regular mail from the Atlantic states to be opened in San Francisco. (Geary later had the distinction of being the only person ever to serve as both *alcalde* and mayor of San Francisco, the title being changed during his term of office.) Williams and six charter members informally established the First Presbyterian Church of San Francisco before going ashore on April 1, 1849.

After preaching a few times at the Public Institute building on Portsmouth Square, Williams formally organized the church on May 20, 1849. The little congregation held services in various places—the schoolhouse, the newly built First Baptist Church, a Customs House storeroom, and the Superior Court chambers in the City Hall. Then, on Saturday, August 18, they gathered on the west side of Dupont Street (now Grant Avenue) to erect their first official meeting place—a large tent purchased from a mining company. While certainly unimposing, the tent was neatly furnished with matting, pulpit, and seats for two hundred people, and it served the congregation well until Janury 19, 1851.

On that day, the congregation dedicated a prefabricated church building designed in "early Gothic style" by the New York architect J. Coleman Hart. The new church, which had arrived in November, 1850, on the bark *George Henry*, was erected on Stockton Street between Pacific and Broadway. Thirty-two women, "the largest number ever collected in one place of worship in The City," attended the dedication. Friends in the Scotch Presbyterian Church of New York supplied a bell, a pulpit, lamps, and seats. Six months later, this structure fell victim to one of the city's recurrent fires, and the congregation put up a plain wood hall.

Williams opened a school for twenty-five children in the public schoolhouse on April 23, 1849, but by the following September the pressure of his ministerial duties forced him to abandon that effort. He then took the initiative in extending the Christian ministry to the rapidly growing Chinese population. By mid-1850 he was distributing religious tracts, papers, and books printed in the Chinese language. Two years later he was influential in the establishment of a mission to the Chinese under the pastorate of the Reverend William Speer, a veteran of five years' service in China. First Presbyterian contributed to the founding of the San Francisco chapter of the American Bible Society in 1849, the Protestant Orphanage (now Edgewood Children's Center) in 1851, and the San Francisco chapter of the Young Men's Christian Association in 1853. Calvary and Welsh Presbyterian churches also grew out of First Presbyterian.

The ministers of First Presbyterian actively participated in community affairs. The Reverend William C. Anderson, pastor from 1856 to 1864, was instrumental in founding the College of California in Oakland (one of the institutions that evolved into the University of California). As a delegate to the 1861 Presbyterian General Assembly, Anderson held out for the Union in the War between the States; this conflict led to the split of Presbyterians into northern and southern factions. The Reverend Robert Mackenzie, pastor from 1886 to 1901, was among the founders of the San Francisco Theological Seminary in San Anselmo.

First Presbyterian's fourth home, built in 1857 on Stockton Street between Clay and Washington, was a brick Gothic Revival structure with a ninety-six-foot tower. After twenty-five years in this location, they sold the building to the newly organized Chinese Presbyterian Church (formerly the Chinese Mission), and joined several other pioneer congregations in moving to the Western Addition. Their fifth church, on Van Ness Avenue, survived the earthquake but was one of those dynamited to stop the spreading fire. Bernard Maybeck was commissioned to design a temporary building on Washington Street; in 1911, when the present structure was completed, that church was sold to the Lutheran Church of the Holy Spirit.

Today Old First Presbyterian Church continues its honorable tradition of community service. The church individually sustains a program of weekly concerts of classical music, a senior activity center, and a children's tutorial program, and also supports a number of community programs including the San Francisco Night Ministry and the Larkin Street Youth Center.

The present church was designed by William Charles Hays, Sr., a professor of architecture at the University of California at Berkeley. It is modern North Italian Romanesque and one of the best examples of this style in San Francisco. The interior is a high, beamed hall with an ample balcony over the front and numerous arched stained glass windows that march down the sides to a deep chancel, with its pulpit, seats for dignitaries, and ramped choir. Built of brick of varying tones of tan and gold, the building is dominated by a large rose window with plate tracery, which is in turn divided by a Greek cross with the symbols of the Evangelists and patterned corners with grapes and vine leaves around it in terra cotta. Terra cotta, a fired clay masonry form capable of great variety of shape and color, was used to decorate many churches. Architectural terra cotta was also used in the old Hall of Justice, the Chronicle Building, and many more San Francisco buildings. (Most of this local terra cotta work was executed by the Gladding McBean Company, founded in 1875, and the single remaining maker of large-scale architectural terra cotta in this country. Today the company has several operations, but they also supply the terra cotta necessary to restore old buildings, matching the original workmanship. Samples are sent to them for restoration projects all over the United States.)

Old First suggests an early medieval Italian Romanesque basilica like St. Ambrogio in Milan with its modest upper facade arcade and paneled surface; a modest right side entrance allows the facade undivided attention. The equal-armed Greek cross has within it a design motif that is both Celtic and Buddhist—the knot of eternity. The terra cotta grapes symbolize the fertility of California. Heritage of many rich and diverse cultures, this church unifies them in its stately temple.

A great Celtic cross and plate traceried rose window dominate the facade of Old First Presbyterian.

St. Francis of Assisi Church

610 Vallejo Street, at Columbus Avenue
Founded June 17, 1849

Since its inception the Church of St. Francis of Assisi has reflected the richly international population of San Francisco. As gold-seekers started to arrive from Oregon, Canada, and the Pacific Islands in the summer of 1848, it became evident to Father José Gonzalez Rubio, administrator of the diocese, that Father Prudencio Santillan, the Spanish-speaking priest assigned to Mission Dolores, would be unable to meet the spiritual needs of the rapidly growing population. Rubio sent out appeals for help to bishops throughout the United States. The first to respond was the archbishop of Oregon City, who sent the only priest available, the Very Reverend J. B. A. Brouillet, vicar-general of the diocese of Walla Walla. Arriving in December 1848, Brouillet was soon joined by a French-Canadian priest, Father Antoine Langlois, and they set about establishing an auxiliary to the mission within the newly incorporated city of San Francisco.

Father Langlois became the pastor. At first, services were held in the Vallejo Street home of Major James A. Hardie, commander of the Presidio and a convert to the Catholic faith. A group of the "more zealous" Catholics raised a subscription of five thousand dollars to buy a piece of ground and build a church on the west side of Telegraph Hill, close to the waters of the bay. They covered the walls and ceiling with white cloth, "some ladies adorned its little altar," and the first services were held in the new church on July 19, 1849. As an auxiliary chapel of the mission parish, the church was named St. Francis of Assisi.

Within a year, the Right Reverend Joseph Sadoc Alemany, newly appointed Bishop of California, arrived in San Francisco. On Sunday, December 8, 1850, he offered mass at St. Francis Church, delivering both English and Spanish sermons in the morning and preaching in French in the afternoon. Two days later, a large reception was held at the church to welcome him to the city. Although the Royal Presidio Chapel of Monterey was his official cathedral, Alemany designated St. Francis Church his pro-cathedral and made it the scene of many of his episcopal ceremonies in the years 1851–1853. When in San Francisco, he lived in a small shanty on the church grounds.

The present church building was started in 1857 and dedicated on March 17, 1860. Five years later, Archbishop Alemany put the Dominicans in charge of St. Francis, with Father James Henry Aerden, the founder of St. Dominic's Church, as pastor. In response to the needs of the expanding congregation, Alemany appointed two assistant pastors in 1868—Father John Valenti for the Italians and Father Andrew Garriga for the Spanish. (Garriga was later placed in charge of founding a separate church for the Spanish, Portuguese, and Italian parishioners; first services were held on December 25, 1875, in the new church of Our Lady of Guadalupe.) A mission for the German-speaking was established in 1869 under Father Francis Xavier Weninger.

St. Francis Church has several firsts. It was the first Catholic parish church in San Francisco proper, and it opened the first parochial school in California in 1851. The first ordination of a priest in California was performed there in 1852, and in 1863, the church had a Chinese curate, Father Thomas Chan, brought to America by the archbishop to minister to his countrymen. The first mass in the Chinese language anywhere in the United

States was offered at St. Francis Church in 1969. In 1972, Bishop Mark J. Hurley of Santa Rosa said in his last mass before retiring that St. Francis Church "has proved that men of all races, colors, and creeds can pray together and live together." To serve its present-day congregation, the priests at the church can hear confessions in English, Spanish, Chinese, French, German, Italian, and Tagalog.

The architecture of the church is Gothic Revival. Following the twin-towered concepts of many medieval churches, the ninety-five-foot towers have paneled buttresses and at their apex, crocketed finials and simple crenellations. The towers frame a plain gabled roof. The building is now painted a rich cream color with white trim. The entrance has three portals, each with an arched top, and wood-traceried stained glass windows, echoed by similar ones surmounted by hood molds on the tower faces. A delicate small rose-traceried window crowns the front above a tall, traceried window framed by pointed niches with statues.

Old marble panels above the doors have inscriptions in gold leaf. Simple handrails lead up the steps to the recessed wooden doors embellished with fine hand-wrought ironwork on each leaf. Cruciform and arched designs in wood at either side of each entrance exhibit period craftsmanship. The building's east and west sides are divided by pier buttresses and have large arched and traceried windows that light the church. Interior frescoes depict the life of Saint Francis. The church bells, fifty-three inches in diameter, are said to have come from California missions. After 1906, when the church was damaged but not destroyed, steel girders were installed to strengthen the building. St. Francis is considered the mother of Roman Catholic parish churches in San Francisco.

San Francisco Registered Landmark #5
California Point of Historical Interest #SFr 003

An early example in San Francisco of the historically important twin-towered Gothic church of northern Europe is St. Francis on Vallejo Street.

First Baptist Church

21 Octavia Street, at Waller Street
Founded July 8, 1849

Though among the earliest denominations functioning in the New World (Roger Williams established the First Baptist Church of Providence, Rhode Island, in 1639), the Baptist church grew very slowly until about the time of the Revolution, when people began moving westward. To meet the needs of an isolated population, the church encouraged unpaid lay preachers to spread the gospel of Jesus by preaching to their neighbors and those in nearby areas. So successful was this approach that the Baptists became America's first convert faith, and by 1800 they were the country's largest Protestant denomination. (They relinquished this status to the Methodists in 1820, but regained it in the 1920s.)

As the war with Mexico drew to a close, the Baptist Home Mission Society decided to establish a mission in California and selected the Reverend Osgood C. Wheeler, then in his first pastorate at Jersey City, New Jersey, for the difficult assignment. Reluctant at first, Wheeler finally agreed. He and his wife left New York aboard the steamer *Falcon* on December 1, 1848, expecting to carry out their missionary duties in an isolated western outpost called San Francisco.

Three days later, word of the discovery of gold reached Washington. By the time they had crossed the Isthmus of Panama by mule and canoe, waited thirty-four days at Panama City for a steamer, and spent twenty-eight more days aboard the *California* enroute to San Francisco, their destination was irrevocably transformed from a sequestered frontier village to a bustling seaport. Besides the Wheelers, there were three other missionaries from New York aboard the little steamer—two new-school Presbyterians, the Reverends Samuel H. Willey and J. W. Douglass, of whom more later, and an old-school Presbyterian, the Reverend Sylvester Woodbridge, who went on to found the first Presbyterian church in the state at Benicia.

Arriving in San Francisco on February 28, 1849, Wheeler immediately set out to get acquainted with the chaotic community. A layman, C. L. Ross, helped him canvas the city for Baptists, and for children, in order to form a Sunday school. By the end of May, regular services were being held in a private home, and the Sunday school attendance had grown from the lone little boy who showed up the first Sunday to more than forty. On Friday, July 6, six people presented church letters and were recognized as the constituent members of the First Baptist Church of California, which was formally founded the following Sunday. Within the month they had erected their first church on Washington Street near Stockton. This simple frame building, thirty by fifty feet in size, having a ship's sail for a roof and costing six thousand dollars to construct, served not only the Baptists but also the newly formed Presbyterian church for a time. From December 26, 1849, to June 22, 1851, the building was also made available, free of charge, for a free public school operated by John Pelton, a former Massachusetts schoolmaster, and supported by city funds. A plaque in Chinatown commemorates this little building, the first Protestant house of worship in San Francisco.

The first candidate for baptism came on October 21, 1849. Since the little church had no proper baptistry, it was decided to hold the ceremony on the shores of North Beach. The pastor, church members with the candidate, and ministers of the other churches marched toward the bay followed by the mayor and other government officials, representatives of the Navy and the Marines, and a large crowd of observers including even the visiting prime minister of Hawaii.

By 1850, Wheeler had established Baptist churches in San Jose and Sacramento, and the combined membership of the three churches had reached a total of fifty-three. In 1851 while Wheeler was in southern California recuperating from an illness, the church building and the businesses of many of the members were destroyed in one of the city's disastrous fires. Exhausted and discouraged, Wheeler resigned his pastorate. The Reverend Benjamin Byerly, described as a man of "unusual ability and eloquence," became the pastor of First Baptist in 1852. During his ministry membership increased to 131. Plans were made for the erection of a new brick church on Washington Street, and finally, on September 27, 1857, the congregation once more gathered under its own roof.

In the 1860s, under the leadership of the Reverend David B. Cheney, First Baptist became the largest congregation in the state. In 1879 a Sunday school was opened for Chinese children, that same year the first Chinese convert, Dong Gong, was baptized. In 1877 the congregation moved into a new, twin-spired Gothic Revival church on Eddy Street between Jones and Leavenworth; this church was demolished on April 18, 1906. Their new pastor, the Reverend George E. Burlingame, obtained a large tent through friends in Chicago. While waiting for their tent to arrive, First Baptist shared the facilities of the Swedenborgian Church. Money for a new building was collected from Baptists all over the United States; the devout Baptist John D. Rockefeller gave seventy-five thousand dollars. The present site was bought in 1908 and the building was dedicated on September 14, 1910.

During the troubled 1940s the church reached its peak membership of forty-six hundred. Today the congregation, though reduced in size, includes members of thirty nationalities. Social programs include a day-care center, a senior citizen facility, and a Christian day school that serves the multiracial neighborhood's students in grades kindergarten through six.

The building is in a modified Baroque–Classical Revival style popular in the early 1900s; the architect was James E. Stewart. It has a classical modillioned pediment above Ionic pilasters, which alternate with stained glass memorial windows. The grouped windows and pilasters, though like a temple front, serve to create a Baroque centralization; all of the structure rides on a basement of rusticated stone. The interior is semicircular, with dark oak pews ornamented by Ionic details. The inside of the large overhead dome is painted light blue and set with striated marble.

Trinity Episcopal Church

1668 Bush Street, at Gough Street
Founded July 17, 1849

During the height of the Gold Rush, six Episcopalians wrote to New York asking that a rector be sent out to them. The Reverend Flavel Scott Mines, a Virginian who had previously served in the West Indies, was given an unofficial commission. He traveled by way of Panama, arriving in San Francisco on July 4, 1849. Mines conducted the first services of his new church at the American Hotel on Stockton Street, where two hundred people gathered together and raised seven thousand dollars for a church building. A wooden structure that was to house the first Episcopal church on the Pacific Coast was put up on the southwest corner of Jackson and Powell streets.

Mines, however, was not the missionary officially appointed to California; the Reverend Jean Leonhard Ver Mehr was. A near-fatal attack of smallpox had delayed Ver Mehr's departure date, and the ship he took had traveled by way of Cape Horn. He was surprised to find himself without a post when he finally arrived in San Francisco. Fortunately, the two men were able to see the humor in the situation and soon became good friends. Ver Mehr gathered a second congregation and became rector of Grace Chapel, the forerunner of Grace Cathedral.

Trinity's second home, located at Pine Street between Kearny and Montgomery, was of corrugated iron of the type frequently imported in sections and assembled in San Francisco during this period when the city had no regular fire department. "Let San Francisco become another Antioch, mother-city of churches," urged Mines at the dedication of the sixty thousand dollar structure in 1851. San Francisco was, indeed, the mother city of church life in California, but during that year the city became far better known as a center of lawlessness, violence, and "vigilante justice." Outraged by increasing numbers of robberies and murders, and suspecting corruption in the courts, a group of five hundred men, mostly merchants and community leaders, organized a Committee of Vigilance on June 9 to restore order. A majority of Trinity's forty pioneer members participated, with Mines serving as unofficial chaplain for the committee. A year later, Mines' health failed. His sudden death was mourned by the entire city. His successor was the Reverend Christopher B. Wyatt, formerly assistant minister of the Church of the Holy Apostles in New York.

The Right Reverend William Ingraham Kip, the first Episcopal bishop to California, arrived in San Francisco on January 29, 1854. A committee from Trinity was at the dock to welcome the Kips, inviting the new bishop to preach that very day at the "Mother Church of the Pacific." The following Sunday, he was filling the pulpit at Grace Church, more or less vacant since Dr. Ver Mehr had partially retired to Sonoma. Within a short time, Kip assumed the rectorship of Grace Church, moving his *cathedra* from Trinity and proclaiming Grace to be the Cathedral. Most church historians consider this to be the first such designation in America. During Kip's long episcopate, Trinity and other congregations contributed to the founding of St. Luke's Hospital, the Episcopal Old Ladies' Home, and the Maria Kip Orphanage. In addition to his San Francisco church duties, Bishop Kip continued his missionary journeys throughout the state for thirty-seven years. He died in 1893, having served his adopted state for nearly four decades. His last official act in Grace Cathedral was the ordination of his namesake grandson, Canon William Ingraham Kip

III. After his death his official *cathedra* was returned to Trinity Church, where it remains in the chapel.

Unlike many churches, Trinity has endured without any major crises, either financial or philosophical. The congregation has been as steadfast and enduring as the building in which they worship. Three Episcopal bishops have come from the parish. One, Charles Brent, was the first bishop of the Philippines, and there is now a school in Manila named for him. A Gothic Revival structure at the corner of Post and Powell streets served as Trinity's home from 1867 until 1892, when they sold that property and made what was considered a daring move to the suburbs—their present location at the corner of Bush and Gough.

Trinity's building is a simple reduction of basic Romanesque and Gothic elements. The massive church is one of the few built of stone in San Francisco, here from gray sandstone quarried in Colusa. The architect was A. Page Brown, with consultants later on. The church with its short pier buttresses, crenellation, octagonal turrets, crocketed finials, and tall, narrow, pointed windows, suggests a fortified structure on an unruly frontier, like its parent at Durham, England. It has also been compared to the architecture of the eastern Ivy League colleges—Princeton in particular—where Collegiate Gothic is common.

The interior has two small stained glass windows and a lectern supported by a bronze angel designed by Louis Tiffany. The other stained glass windows were made by Fritz Mayer and Company in Munich. The pews, altar, and communion rail in this church were brought from Trinity's third building. The church has a four-manual Skinner organ built in 1924. An echo organ was added to the rear of the church in 1926.

San Francisco Registered Landmark #65

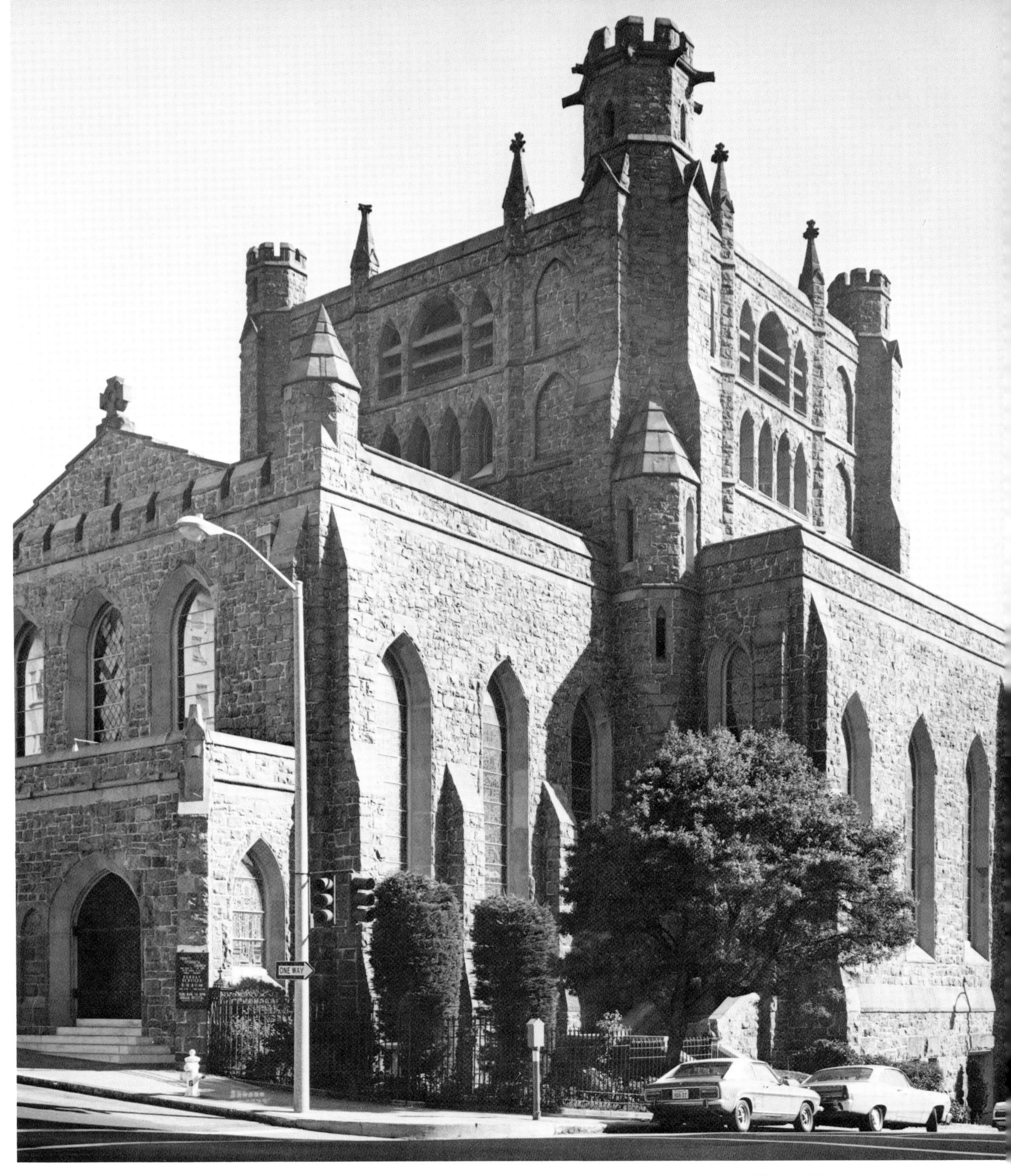

Massively wrought out of stone, Trinity Episcopal looms on San Francisco's skyline like an English-Scottish border cathedral of the late Middle Ages.

First Congregational Church

Post Street at Mason Street
Founded July 29, 1849

First Congregational Church of San Francisco was founded by the man who was San Francisco's first and only city chaplain. The Reverend Timothy Dwight Hunt, a graduate of Yale University, had gone to Hawaii as a missionary. When the Gold Rush began, at least half of Hawaii's English-speaking inhabitants left the islands for San Francisco. After consulting his church leaders Hunt followed his parishioners to San Francisco on the ship *Honolulu*. He was given free passage and arrived in October 1848. The citizens had heard of his coming and were enthusiastic because there were as yet so few Protestant clergymen. He was met by a committee who offered him a position as city chaplain for a salary of twenty-five hundred dollars per year. This was high but appropriate, as everything was inflated due to the great influx of gold. Hunt accepted. His family followed him, and Mrs. Hunt's father shipped a prefabricated house to them around Cape Horn. It had five rooms and the then common calico-lined walls with white cotton ceilings. The house was put up on a steep hill on Vallejo Street.

For seven months, Hunt preached nondenominational sermons on Sundays, performing other pastoral duties during the week. One of his services was particularly successful: The steamer *Falcon* had arrived in the city, bringing Mrs. Bezer Simmons, who agreed to sing at the church services. When the singing began, "men in all sorts of attire, pants in boots and over boots, with red, blue, white, and checkered shirts filled the room" and gathered outside "to a depth of twenty to thirty feet . . . as soon as the lady's voice had been heard. . . . The news spread like wildfire . . . and completely broke up, for the time being, the gambling circles . . . in the famous Parker House." Even the proprietor, Robert Parker, went to the church, it was so rare to hear a woman sing.

With the establishment of several Protestant churches, the need for a city chaplain ceased, and Hunt preached his last sermon in that capacity on July 22, 1849. At three o'clock that same afternoon, the newly organized First Congregational Church held its own first service in the same schoolhouse, and asked Hunt to become minister. A Presbyterian minister, Albert Williams, who took part in the service of induction on July 24, wrote in his autobiography, "It has ever seemed strange to me that Mr. Hunt, a Presbyterian, did not adhere to the formation of a church of his own religious faith."

Actually, Presbyterians and Congregationalists had been worshiping together in newly developing areas for half a century. Under the Plan of Union of 1801, they had agreed that western congregations would vote for a minister from either communion and then affiliate with the church of his membership. (By the early nineteenth century, more Scots-Irish Presbyterians than New England Congregationalists were moving west, with the result that the Plan of Union served to curtail the expansion of Congregationalism—the church brought to America by the Pilgrims and the Puritans.) By reversing the customary procedure and asking the minister to adopt their affiliation, these pioneers may have started the city's tradition of maverick voting patterns.

Places of worship were makeshift and hard to come by. Soon, the schoolhouse was needed for a jail. The church moved from the jail to store space until its own first building—wooden, cloth-lined, and only twenty-five by fifty feet in size, but located outside the path of the great fires that continually swept the city—was ready in February 1850. The continuing influx of New Englanders increased the membership so rapidly that by July 1853, First Congregational dedicated a new red brick church diagonally across Dupont and California streets from the present location of Old St. Mary's Church. The church cost fifty-seven thousand dollars and seated seven hundred people. Two years later the congregation finished the basement, graded Dupont Street outside the church, and built exterior stairways.

In the 1870s, young Japanese students began coming to America seeking a western education. Several attended services at First Congregational Church. With the financial support of the Women's Society, these young men joined with a similar group at the Chinese Methodist Mission to form the Japanese Gospel Society (the first Japanese organization in the United States) in 1877, and later withdrew to form a separate group, the Tyler Gospel Society. The Women's Society continued sponsoring the society until it became a mission of the Presbyterian church in 1885.

In 1870, as the city moved to the south and west, First Congregational purchased the lot at Post and Mason where the church has remained to the present time. The new edifice, dedicated on May 19, 1872, was described by the *San Francisco Bulletin:* "Rivals the best in America . . . walls of red brick with ornaments of artificial stone . . . surmounted by a spire . . . which rises 225 feet from the sidewalk . . . pew capacity is 1,600." On April 15, 1906, the Reverend Dr. George C. Adams, celebrating his tenth anniversary as minister, had before him "the largest congregation of any Protestant church in the city." Three days later the beautiful church was reduced to rubble and ashes.

For the next six years, services were held in the refurbished basement level. By August of 1913, having united with Plymouth (founded in 1862), they determined to build a permanent church edifice. Interim services were held at Temple Emanu-El, and ladies' weekday programs at Central Methodist, by invitation of those two congregations.

The present Congregational church was opened for services on February 28, 1915, the year of the Panama-Pacific Exposition. Both members and visitors flocked to hear the invigorating sermons of the Reverend Dr. Charles F. Aked, who had come from New York's Fifth Avenue Baptist Church in 1910. At this time the church adopted the slogan, "The church with a heart, in the heart of the city," and prepared for an urban ministry. As international conditions worsened on the eve of World War I, industrialist Henry Ford formed the hope that a delegation of ten or twelve social and religious leaders might be able to reason with their European counterparts and effect an end to hostilities. Aked, an internationally known clergyman, was among the leaders selected to participate. This unofficial but hopeful delegation sailed to Europe on a vessel called *Peace Ship;* their mission was, as we know, unsuccessful.

First Congregational's ministry today includes a lunch program for the elderly, a coffee house primarily for young adults, and a counseling service in the evenings for anyone who drops in with a problem. It is characteristically a congregation of single people, many of them elderly, some old-time San Franciscans, and a sprinkling of tourists staying in downtown hotels.

The distinguished structure, finished in 1915, was designed to be compatible with both the New England origins of the denomination and the character of the surrounding business district. The church resembles early American meeting halls in interior arrangement. There is an art glass skylight in the coffered ceiling. The quietly classicist, ramped interior in cream color echoes the exterior. The building itself was designed by the Reid brothers in

Beaux-Arts Roman. On the Post Street facade, four massive Corinthian columns in terra cotta are set in front of a deep reveal with arched windows. Two slightly projecting "wings" at the sides, with pedimented doorways, frame the center. The whole is dignified, discreet; in fact it is sometimes mistaken for a bank.

First Congregational's terra cotta Corinthian columns and its thoughtful Baroque envelope suggest the financial solidarity of downtown San Francisco.

St. Mark's Lutheran Church

1111 O'Farrell Street, at Franklin Street
Founded in October, 1849

Among the German Americans arriving in the fall of 1849 was the Reverend Frederick Mooshake, a graduate of Goettingen University. Although not sponsored by any ecclesiastical body, Mooshake had decided that it was his mission to spread the Lutheran faith in "this wicked city." At first he held services in various Lutheran homes and in the Second Congregational (Greenwich) Church; when that group went bankrupt in 1859, the Lutherans assumed the mortgage and welcomed some of the Congregational members into their own group, which they called the First German Evangelical Lutheran Church.

Meanwhile, the Missouri Synod of the Evangelical Lutheran Church had been debating the feasibility of a mission to Oregon and California ever since 1848. A San Francisco matron's unsigned letter, published in the December 13, 1859, issue of *Der Lutheraner,* may have provided the necessary impetus. "There are many Lutherans here, at least in name, but all we see are these 'united' churches," she wrote. She went on to mention the large number of German children attending Methodist Sunday schools in order to receive religious instruction in their native tongue. By the following June the Synod had commissioned a missionary to California. He was Jacob Matthias Beehler, twenty-three years old and the only English-speaking graduate of the St. Louis seminary, class of 1860.

Beehler arrived after a quick but financially disastrous trip via the Isthmus of Panama during which someone stole his travel money. Fellow passengers contributed funds to help him get established. A few days later he was filling the pulpit recently vacated by Mooshake; the grateful parishioners immediately invited him to become their pastor. From his room in the Meyers Hotel on Montgomery Street he wrote his professor in St. Louis describing his first weeks: "Spiritually, things look sad in this otherwise so richly endowed country. . . . Here are many churches with but little religion . . . the one so-called Lutheran congregation numbers about twenty members. . . . The most influential members of this congregation are either freethinkers or avowed rationalists." With this observation, the young minister perhaps unwittingly identified the theological conflict that was to cause his resignation from that pastorate a few years later. Beginning with this letter (excerpted in Richard T. Du Brau's *Romance of Lutheranism in California*) and for the rest of his life, he signed his name J. Buehler, no doubt in deference to the Teutonic accents of his parishioners.

The church prospered. A day school was started in 1861, and in 1862 the congregation bought one of the first organs in San Francisco. That same year they bought a building site on Geary Street facing Union Square, where Macys is now located. The congregation split for a time during the construction of the new building, but soon after the February 3, 1866, dedication of the basement level, they were reunited under the name St. Mark's Evangelical Lutheran Church. The grateful membership gave Buehler and his wife a leave of absence to visit Europe while the rest of the church was built, and he returned to dedicate the imposing new structure on December 30, 1866.

Within a few months, however, theological differences arose. The conflict focused on Buehler's unwillingness to conduct funeral services jointly with officers of various lodges popular among his parishioners. As the result of an ultimatum from the liberal faction of the church, Buehler tendered his resignation as minister on April 12, 1867. A group of parishioners asked him to start a new, confessional Lutheran church, and on Easter Sunday he preached the first sermon for what became St. Paulus Church.

St. Mark's had a succession of short-term pastors until 1893, when, under the leadership of the Reverend Julius Fuendling, the congregation sold the Geary Street property and bought the lots for the present church and other buildings. The present red brick church cost fifty-six thousand dollars to build, and was debt free when dedicated in 1895. During the earthquake and fire eleven years later, it sustained some damage—the east tower needed reinforcing, and the tower cross melted in the heat of the fire. But the building itself was [illegible] enough to be used as a refuge for people made homeless by the catastrophe.

[illegible]e church the Lutherans built was what they wanted in the 1890s, "a solid brick [illegible]g that looked like a neighborhood church." But eventually the homes in the sur[illegible] area deteriorated and people moved away to new neighborhoods. In the early [illegible] the congregation was faced with the difficult choice confronting many churches in [illegible]rancisco—whether they should move to a new area. They chose to stay.

[illegible]is Lutheran congregation emphasizes liturgical worship as a way of nourishing and [illegible]ing the spirit for the struggle of daily life. A publication of the church includes this passage: "This Christian congregation exists to be and to become people of God in the city . . . caring for people and their needs." St. Mark's is among the Lutheran churches having ordained women ministers among their clergy. The people of St. Mark's sponsor a summer youth program, a senior center, a tutorial program, and a center for adult education. Their Urban Life Center on Luther Square is used by other religious groups—Jewish and Unitarian—in the true ecumenical spirit of the city. Several members of the congregation helped sponsor a nineteen-story building of moderately priced condominiums, Martin Luther Tower. This structure forms a contrasting modern backdrop to the traditional red brick church.

Architect Henry Geilfuss designed St. Mark's in a mixture of Romanesque and such Gothic elements as pointed gables and arches, pier buttresses, and a rose window. The red brick is set off by details done in buff-colored brick and Bedford stone. Of the two towers, the west one is low and round on an octagonal base, with a conical roof; the other is high and squared, with four upper corner turrets and a pyramidal roof. The otherwise staid building has a few whimsical touches, including a diagonal cadenza of three stepped small arched windows on the east tower. This is echoed by diagonal wood moldings and fleur-de-lis patterns between stained glass windows in the west tower.

The interior of the church has eleven large stained glass windows. Done in red, blue, and purple, these windows depict religious symbols such as the Tablets of the Law and the word *Jehovah* in Hebrew. The interior of the oblong sanctuary is painted French ivory and gold. A German chandelier, gift of Claus Spreckels and originally equipped for gas, hangs over the middle aisle; today the church is equipped with both gas and electrical power to cover all emergencies. This chandelier and the Schoenstein organ were transferred from the Geary Street church. The new twenty-eight-foot altar with its imposing reredoes was installed in 1944. The figures on the reredoes represent Justice, Temperance, Fortitude, and Prudence. A three-manual Moeller pipe organ with chimes was added as a part of the same remodeling program, which was directed by architect Vincent Rainey. St. Mark's Lutheran Church is in pristine condition; its interior is one of the most agreeable in the city.

The richly patterned trussing of the nave and the outlining of implied vault forms of the side aisles is a dramatic climax to the layering of St. Mark's Lutheran's interior.

A high square and a low round tower provide elevation to the Gothic silhouette of St. Marks Lutheran.

Grace Cathedral

1051 Taylor Street, at California Street
Founded December 30, 1849

Early in 1848 a group of San Francisco Episcopalians petitioned their Board of Missions for a clergyman, and the Reverend Jean Leonhard Ver Mehr was appointed. Ver Mehr held a degree from the University of Leiden and completed his theological studies under Bishop G. W. Doane of New Jersey. Illness having delayed his departure from the East, he arrived in San Francisco to find Trinity Episcopal church already functioning. But the burgeoning city, with a population of twenty-five thousand, could support two Episcopal churches, so with the friendship and cooperation of the Reverend Flavel Mines and Trinity Church, Ver Mehr organized a second congregation only a block away at the corner of John and Powell streets. Ver Mehr selected the name Grace Chapel, apparently in reference to the nearby Trinity Church and the two main New York parishes of the time—Trinity and Grace. The little shingled chapel could accommodate 240 people. Ver Mehr wrote of his first service, on December 30, 1849: "I peeped through the canvas partition. Sturdy miners came in and took their seats on the rough planks . . . others came. A few ladies . . . very few. My first sermon was listened to with attention. . . . The plates went round; there was not one silver piece on them! I had nothing but gold to offer at the altar." A tin-plated chalice and a silver wine-coaster paten were pressed into service for that first Communion. The din from the adjacent gambling halls was clearly audible during services. Within six months, the chapel assumed official status as Grace Church, but like every other church in the turbulent frontier city, Grace had to struggle to survive. Heavy winter rains in the winter of 1850, followed by a cholera epidemic in the spring, greatly reduced attendance. Nonetheless, a new church, constructed of prefabricated pine units from the East, was set up next door to the original chapel, which then became a private dwelling.

In 1853 the Right Reverend William Ingraham Kip was appointed the first Episcopal Missionary Bishop of California. After sailing down the Atlantic coast by steamer, crossing the Isthmus of Panama on a burro, and surviving a shipwreck near San Diego, he finally arrived in San Francisco in January 1854 and was formally consecrated the following October. He assumed the rectorship of Grace Church until the arrival in 1857 of the handsome, multi-talented, high-church preacher, the Reverend Ferdinand C. Ewer, whose brilliant sermons attracted overflow crowds. On visiting Grace Church in 1859, Richard Henry Dana described it as similar in every aspect to prosperous Episcopal churches in the East, even down to the ladies' fashionable French bonnets.

Grace Church's next home, designed by the English Gothicist William Patton, was located at the corner of California and Stockton streets and was dedicated on May 4, 1860, by Bishop Kip. It was built of brick and granite, and decorated with playful gargoyles, including likenesses of the two pastors, Ver Mehr and Mines, and their wives, Bishop Kip, and the rook in the rhyme "Cock Robin": "Who'll be the parson? 'I,' said the rook, 'with my little book, I'll be the parson.'" An 1862 entry in the church registry refers to this as Grace Cathedral. This unofficial cathedral designation is the third in the history of the Episcopal church in America. The earlier building was sold to Bethel African Methodist Church, the first of three black churches to be established in San Francisco in 1852.

The Civil War years were tense ones for Grace Church, as many of the members had come originally from the South. Despite a series of short-term rectors, the church continued to flourish, becoming a major society church with such prominent members as Leland Stanford, H. H. Bancroft, and James B. Haggin. Three long-term rectors led the church into the twentieth century. The Reverend William H. Platt was a southern theologian who had conducted services for General Lee at the siege of Petersburg and whose particular interest was the ongoing debate between science and religion over immortality. He was followed in 1884 by another southerner, the Reverend Robert C. Foute, who had served in the battle between the *Monitor* and the *Merrimac*. The Welsh-born Reverend David J. Evans was rector in the spring of 1906, when the handsome church was reduced to smoldering rubble.

Bishop William F. Nichols, who had succeeded Bishop Kip, had envisioned a diocesan cathedral as early as 1892. In June 1906 the Crocker family donated the land on which their two mansions had stood before the fire, and planning was begun. Three marble panels salvaged from the burned-out church were used in the new building; one of them was inscribed, "After the earthquake a fire, after the fire a still, small voice." The cornerstone was dedicated on January 24, 1910, and two weeks later Grace parish was formally dissolved and Dr. J. Wilmer Gresham became the first dean of Grace Cathedral.

The original plans, by architect George W. Bodley of London, called for the cathedral to flank Jones Street, and the cornerstone was laid with that in mind, but the direction was changed in 1912. Then Bodley died, and building stopped for a time. The Founders' Crypt (basement level), opened in 1914, served as a temporary cathedral until 1931. Anglican and Episcopal bishops from around the world preached there; the first interfaith service took place in 1921; Helen Keller visited in 1925. Work on the cathedral resumed in 1928, using the plans of Lewis P. Hobart, who had taken over from Bodley. The north tower was built from 1936 to 1941; in 1938 forty-four bells were given to Grace Cathedral by Dr. Nathaniel Coulson. The bells had been cast in England, and the largest weighed six tons. Dr. Coulsen spent his life's savings on the bells, a lifetime dream. Today they hang in the north, or "singing," tower. Because of earthquake danger, the original plans for a stone church were revised to use steel-reinforced concrete. Concrete being more expensive than stone, the design had to be simplified. Even so, the cost rose from the anticipated $1.5 million to more than $5 million. Although begun in 1910, the great cathedral was not dedicated until 1964, in a ceremony performed by Bishop James A. Pike, the church's most controversial leader. Several factors contributed to this long building period—death of the first architect, World War I, the Great Depression, and finally World War II. Most of Europe's great cathedrals took even longer to build.

Grace Cathedral is the third largest Episcopal cathedral in the United States. Its gold-leaf cross rises 265 feet from the rocks of Nob Hill and can be seen by sailors outside the Golden Gate. The twin towers, flèche, high roof, and curved apse are, in general, traits found in Nôtre Dame of Paris, but it also contains features from other French cathedrals—for example, Chartres and Amiens. The small interior Chapel of Grace recalls in its splendid glass Sainte-Chapelle in Paris. There are other European Gothic features as well. The bronze doors at the east central entrance were made from "waste" molds of the famed east doors of the baptistry in front of the cathedral of Florence. These had been designed by Lorenzo Ghiberti in the earlier fifteenth century, with the assistance of many other famed younger sculptors of the period. The Florentine doors, called "The Gates of Paradise" by Michelangelo, were taken down and hidden during World War II in order to protect them. At that time the waste molds, so-called because only one casting can be made from them before their destruction, were made by Bruno Bearzi as a further safety precaution. Later Bearzi made the single casting, or replica, and personally finished and chased the bronze work.

The altar inside is of California granite, topped with a table of redwood. Benches for kneeling worshipers were designed by Mona Spoor, said to be America's foremost needlepoint expert. The "kneelers" took several years to complete and were done by the women of the diocese under the direction of Mrs. Dean Witter. Bishop Nichols' daughter, grand-daughter, and great-granddaughter all worked on them.

The cathedral has several outstanding stained glass windows and other fine works of art. The great rose window, *Canticle to the Sun,* was done by Gabriel Loire of Chartres, who also did the four great lancets in the west walls of the transept. The *Children of the Old Testament* window is a masterpiece by Charles Connick of Boston; most of the windows in the western part of the cathedral are by this remarkable artist. Connick is credited with reviving the medieval art of stained glass making in this country and with creating the famous "Connick blues" in glass; he used thirteenth-century French glass as his model, with its extraordinarily large number of small pieces of intensely glowing glass and intricate leading. Some of his finest work is in this cathedral, notably in The Chapel of Grace. Of the twelve great windows in the lower walls of the side aisles, the six to the west (three on either side) are by Connick and the six to the east, in the newer part of the building, are by Willett of Philadelphia. The twelve clerestory windows, by Gabriel Loire, honor human endeavor and include such major figures as Jane Addams, Albert Einstein, and Frank Lloyd Wright. The window symbolizing achievement in letters depicts the poet Robert Frost, who was born a few blocks away from the site of Grace Cathedral. The window dedicated to agriculture shows Luther Burbank of Santa Rosa. In the east wall of the north transept is the most recently added window, designed by the renowned San Francisco artist, Mark Adams; it depicts the great Old Testament figure of Joshua.

The fine murals in the church were painted by the Polish-American artist John de Rosen and honor many church figures, including Saint Francis of Assisi, Sir Francis Drake, Bishop Kip, and Saint Augustine; others depict scenes from San Francisco history, like the fire of 1906. Along the lower sides of the aisles is a series of murals by Antonio Sotomayor on the history of Grace Cathedral. The eagle-topped lectern was made by Gutzon Borglum, who worked at Mount Rushmore. The cathedral contains many old and contemporary works of art, including a collection of fine tapestries. Excellent marbles and woods are used throughout, and all details of craftsmanship have been carefully executed.

Grace Cathedral is open to visitors and receives guests from all over the world. A visit suffices to convey the character of this almost European cathedral. It is in buildings such as this that stone, wood, metal, and cloth have been skillfully wrought by people to express the infinite.

San Francisco Registered Landmark #170

With its lofty pointed arches separating nave and aisles, a triforium and ribbed vaults, Grace Cathedral recalls the glory of medieval Europe.

Occupying the site of the former Charles and W. H. Crocker homes, Grace Cathedral adds a special medieval flavor to central Nob Hill.

The only full scale copy of the famous Ghiberti "Gates of Paradise" for the Florence cathedral's baptistry now provides a majestic entrance to Grace Cathedral.

T'ien Hou Temple

125 Waverly Place, between Washington and Clay Streets
Founded 1848–1851

Shortly after their arrival in San Francisco, a group of Chinese established a temple dedicated to T'ien Hou, Queen of the Heavens and Goddess of the Seven Seas, who is considered to be the protectress of all wanderers—fishermen, sailors, fallen women, travelers, and wandering minstrels—and hence of great importance to those who came to America. She is also called Tou Mu, and her tantric form is the Goddess of Light holding the sun and the moon in her hands.

A small altar and statue of T'ien Hou are believed to have been brought to San Francisco by one of the very first arrivals of 1848. Like many of the temple treasures, they came from the mother temple dedicated to this goddess in the Sue Hing district of Kwangtung. A house at the corner of First and Brannan streets served as a temporary temple until a larger, brick structure could be erected on Waverly Place. When that building was damaged in the earthquake of 1906, quick-thinking devotees rescued the temple furnishings before the fire destroyed all of Chinatown, taking them to Oakland for safekeeping until the temple could be rebuilt.

This one-room temple reflects the syncretic nature of Chinese popular religion, which incorporates elements of Confucianism, Taoism, Buddhism, reverence for one's ancestors, and other beliefs. T'ien Hou stands at the back of the temple, behind the main altar, guarded by smaller figures of Moi Dii, god of military affairs, and Hip Lung, goddess of motherhood. In front of her are two massive pewter urns, overlaid with Cantonese enamel, inset with semiprecious stones, and filled with prayer sticks. Beside them are paired standards bearing symbols of the attributes of this faith. There are shrines to Buddha, to Confucius, and to the unknown gods. Family altars along one side wall hold household gods. A myriad of paper lanterns hang above the altars, which have offerings of food and fruit, especially oranges, on them. Incense burns constantly, filling the room with its pungent aroma. The tiny altar light is never allowed to go out. The great bell, buried in the rubble in 1906, was discovered by workmen the next year and restored to its place in the rebuilt temple.

Westerners came to refer to Chinese temples as "joss houses," a corruption of the Portuguese *deus* (god) houses. Traditionally there are no fixed times for religious services in Chinese temples. No congregation meets for united prayer or sits together to listen to a priest. The worshiper comes when he or she feels the need, or has something to pray about. Each worshiper bows upon entering the temple.

The structure itself, constructed in 1911 on the original foundations reusing charred or "clinker" bricks salvaged after the earthquake and fire, is of a type sometimes called "Chinese Renaissance." This usually refers to a building of Western construction with roof and columns having Oriental detailing. Like most Chinese temples, T'ien Hou Temple is on the top floor, closest to heaven.

Almost bewildering in its multiplicity of parts is the colorfully oriental interior of the T'ien Hou Temple.

Although often called Chinese, the architecture of much of Chinatown is functional brick design of a plain form with decorative enrichments of oriental character.

New Liberation United Presbyterian Church

1100 Divisadero Street, at Turk Street
Founded September 15, 1850

San Francisco's second-oldest Presbyterian church traces its beginnings to a carpentry shop at Second and Minna streets. This district, called Happy Valley, was described in a city directory of the period as "destitute in religious privileges." The church was founded by the Reverend Samuel Hopkins Willey, one of the missionaries who left the East Coast in November of 1848, as yet unaware of the discovery of gold. Upon learning that the Reverend Timothy Dwight Hunt was already preaching in San Francisco, Willey left the Pacific Mail steamer *California* in Monterey on February 24, 1849. There he taught school, studied the Spanish language, served as Protestant chaplain for the Monterey garrison and also the Constitutional Convention of 1849, and established California's first public library. The following summer he was moved to San Francisco where additional churches were now needed.

On September 15, 1850, Willey, ten adults, and a few children gathered to organize a church in San Francisco. William D. Howard donated two lots facing the street that now bears his name, and in appreciation the new church was named Howard Presbyterian. Almost at once the congregation found the neighborhood too muddy. Selling that building to the newly formed Howard Street Methodist Church, they moved to a new building at Natoma and Jayne (now New Montgomery) streets. A city almanac described this new building, dedicated June 15, 1861, as "the best in the city" and "the first public building in the city with hard-finished plaster walls."

The members of Howard Presbyterian were New Englanders. They had come to San Francisco to make it their home and to help transform the turbulent seaport into a proper American city. Willey was an energetic and able leader. During the years 1849–1855 he served as the California agent for the American Home Missionary Society, promoting the interdenominational New England front. As one of the founding editors of *The Pacific,* founded in 1851, he wrote crusading articles which eventually caused two thugs to invade the offices of the publication and attack him. Perhaps as a result, Willey was among the ministers who supported the Committees of Vigilance of 1851 and 1856.

Education was among the causes for which Willey campaigned. In September 1851, he organized a parade of a hundred children down Montgomery Street to demonstrate the need for a public school system, and by the end of the month San Francisco had passed the necessary legislation. After working for nearly ten years toward the establishment of the College of California, he resigned his post at Howard Presbyterian in 1862 to serve as acting president of the new college. He remained in that position until 1869, when the college merged with the State University of California to form the University of California.

Enlarged and remodeled, Howard's second building served the congregation until 1896, when a new stone church was erected at 1321 Oak Street, facing the Panhandle of Golden Gate Park. Howard Presbyterian continued as a fashionable and prestigious congregation through World War II. Neighborhood changes in the turbulent 1960s brought a new kind of membership, but the historic congregation proved equal to the times. After reorganizing under the name New Liberation United Presbyterian Church, they sold their Oak Street building to the Mount Zion Baptist Church (whose previous home had been condemned by the urban redevelopment program). The move was undertaken during the ministry of the Reverend Hannibal Williams, whose wife, a fellow graduate of San Francisco Theological Seminary, is a great-granddaughter of the Reverend William A. Scott (the founder of both Calvary Presbyterian Church in 1854 and St. John's Presbyterian Church in 1870). New Liberation's present church complex at the corner of Divisadero and Turk streets, starkly contemporary in design, is well adapted to an active program of community involvement.

First Unitarian Church

1187 Franklin Street at Geary Street
Founded October 20, 1850

Unitarianism is a liberal, essentially ecumenical religion that rejects the traditional doctrine of the Trinity, supports the right of individual judgment in theological matters, and recognizes the universal truths taught by the great prophets and teachers of humanity in every age and tradition. The denomination was formally established in England in 1774 and in Boston, Massachusetts, in 1785. Most early American Unitarian societies grew out of Congregational institutions; by 1810 a majority of early Congregational churches had become Unitarian, and Harvard University was becoming known as a training ground for Unitarian preachers.

Like those of every other faith, Unitarians followed the lure of the gold to California. Twenty-five men, attracted by a newspaper item inserted by the Reverend Charles Andrews Farley, gathered in Athaeneum Hall on California Street on October 20, 1850, for a service. Someone produced a tune book. Joseph Coolidge took out his violin and led an impromptu choir in hymns learned in the Eastport, Maine, church where Farley had been minister until he had heeded an inner call to venture to California without any official commission. The First Unitarian Society of San Francisco, formed that day, met in the Museum Building on Sacramento Street, the United States district courtroom, and finally, the Armory Hall at Washington and Sansome (then the largest hall in town) until July 17, 1852, when they dedicated their first church, a Classical Revival temple on Stockton Street near Sacramento. By this time, the congregation included women and children. Farley stayed in California but a year, and the only Unitarian church west of St. Louis had a succession of short-term ministers until April 1860.

The Golden Age of California Unitarianism began with the arrival of the Reverend Thomas Starr King, a nationally known Boston clergyman. During his first year, he filled the church every Sunday; soon the pews were all sold (as was the custom in New England Congregational churches of the time) and the accumulated debt paid off. King preached an ethical universalism, and he practised it too. He exchanged pulpits with his close friend, Rabbi Elkan Cohn of Congregation Emanu-El, and participated in the educational and cultural fund-raising efforts of the city's three black churches.

With the secession of the cotton states in February 1861, followed by the outbreak of hostilities, King undertook a strenuous crusade to save California for the Union, lecturing and preaching all over the state until the vote was in. During 1862, he canvassed the entire West Coast as far north as Vancouver Island, raising a million and a half dollars for the Sanitary Commission, formed to care for sick and wounded soldiers. By 1863, the old church had become inadequate. A magnificent new Gothic church was built at 133 Geary Street and dedicated on January 10, 1864. Exhausted by his labors, King fell victim to diphtheria and pneumonia and died suddenly only eight weeks later at the age of thirty-nine. The city was draped in mourning. The state legislature recessed for three days, and cannons were fired on Alcatraz in tribute to his patriotic service. A monument bearing his likeness was dedicated in Golden Gate Park in 1892; he and Father Junipero Serra are the two Californians memorialized in the nation's Statuary Hall in Washington, D.C.

First Unitarian found a worthy successor to King in the Reverend Horatio Stebbins, who served for thirty years. During this period, the new church (designed like Temple Emanu-El and Grace Cathedral by the celebrated English architect William Patton) was host to a series of lectures by Ralph Waldo Emerson. Stebbins instigated the move to the present location, and the congregation used Temple Emanu-El's facilities while construction was under way. He was a major force in developing the University of California, a regent of Stanford University, and a trustee of the California School of Mechanical Arts. Memorial tablets for both King and Stebbins can be found on the south wall of the present sanctuary.

The Reverend Brad Leavitt was minister at the time of the earthquake and fire. Damage was relatively minor; the bell tower was destroyed and the church bell split in two. During repairs, services were held at the nearby Century Club. Leavitt was a leader in the citizen-based movement to prosecute city politicians (including Boss Abe Reuf) who were heavily involved in graft.

President William Howard Taft spoke at First Unitarian Church during the Panama-Pacific Exposition in 1915. Jack London attended services there, as did Governor and Mrs. Leland Stanford; the writer Ambrose Bierce was married in the church. Visiting speakers have included Julia Ward Howe, author of "The Battle Hymn of the Republic," Edward Everett Hale, author of "Man Without a Country," Harvard University President Charles Eliot, and Stanford University President David Starr Jordan.

The architects responsible for the present building were George W. Percy and F. F. Hamilton, designers of numerous other well-known San Francisco buildings such as the Children's Playhouse in Golden Gate Park and the first Academy of Sciences on Market Street. The gray stone Gothic-style building is of strong and simple proportions; the structure resembles a proper English parish church on a busy American city street. Brass handrails lead up to the massive, pointed double-arched portico, and then on to similarly shaped doors made of wood laid in herringbone patterns and bound in wrought iron. A facade gable is dominated by a striking traceried rose window filled with colored glass and set within a large, recessed pointed arch. The church's belfry was destroyed in 1906, and today the lower part of the tower provides an assertive strength to the overall design.

The interior is commodious and quietly dignified. It has an elaborately blocked and patterned wood ceiling with multiple cusped trusses of lively pattern. Behind the Gothic-style wood pulpit is a plain white wall with three tall and nobly proportioned pointed arches. In the center is a modern metal sculpture (by Norman Craig) which serves as a wall sconce. This, like the textured concrete revisions to the building, adds a reassuring note of compatibility of old and new. Indeed, the particular lesson of this church is its harmonization of past and present in religious and architectural unity. Also from an earlier time are the fine Oriental rug on the chancel floor (a gift of the Allyne sisters) and the wondrously rich late Gothic carved wood canopy over the baptismal font (a gift of First Congregational Church in New York). Bruce Porter's painting, *Lo, at Length the True Light,* was removed in the 1960s and Arthur Putnam's fine plaster angels in oval frames were placed in the choir and organ loft.

More recently a group of additions were made that both increase the usability of the old structure and relate it to its contemporary San Francisco setting. Given the general name of the Unitarian Center, these new additions, dedicated in 1968, were made possible by a gift from the Allyne sisters and designed by the firm of Callister, Payne, and Mosse.

They are constructed of textured concrete, stone, and wood, and are linked to the old church (which underwent some exterior revisions) by the use of glassed porticoes with Japanese-influenced wood posts. Grouped around a serene atrium with a cooling fountain and a metal abstract sculpture by Aristides Demetrios, the facilities include a new chapel with fine stained glass windows, offices, and nursery, kindergarten, and meeting rooms. At the end of the gallery on the Franklin Street side is the Starr King Room, which adjoins the Martin Luther King Room—an unusual example of homage paid to a member of another faith. On the lower level are a garage and choir practice room or theater.

This complex of buildings, remarkably harmonious though representing different styles and periods, seems particularly appropriate for this church. The congregation is concerned with doing service to God and to humanity; this often takes the form of concern with civic affairs. Unitarians have been well-known leaders of social causes. The present structures embody this relationship of religion to modern life with particular aptitude.

San Francisco Registered Landmark #40
California Registered Landmark #691
(sarcophagus of Thomas Starr King)

The noble rose window with bar tracery dominates the Gothic facade of First Unitarian.

Congregation Sherith Israel

2266 California Street, at Webster Street
Founded April 8, 1851

Without a rabbi or even a Torah, nearly a hundred Jewish pioneers gathered in the Hotel Albion in April 1849 to celebrate the ancient Hebrew Seder (Passover) recalling the exodus out of Egypt. In the fall they came together again to observe the High Holy Days. Records are scanty and somewhat conflicting, but there appear to have been two services—one at the Louisiana Hotel on Montgomery Street and another in a tent store on Jackson Street.

Although the Jewish population of California was still small, they brought a rich cosmopolitanism to the new territory. A few were Sephardim, descendants of aristocrats who had advised Spanish royalty before the Inquisition; their families had been in the United States since Colonial times. Most were European born—Bavarians, Englishmen, Frenchmen, Poseners, and Poles—who had spent a few years on the East Coast of America before joining the mass exodus to the West. Like other Europeans, they had come to America in response to the economic decline of the mid-1830s and the failed revolutions of 1848. As their numbers increased, they began to form associations along national lines. Polish and English Jews formed the First Hebrew Benevolent Society in April 1850, and bought the first Jewish burial ground, a half-block between Broadway, Vallejo, Franklin, and Gough streets, in 1851.

In the fall of 1850 a much larger group, including "many dark-eyed daughters of Judah," came together for High Holy Day services organized by Leon Dyer, the first leader of San Francisco's Jewish community. Lewis Franklin, who had been a business associate of Dyer's in Baltimore, delivered the Yom Kippur sermon, amplifying his theme—the folly of greed—with quotations from Ecclesiastes. At this meeting the group determined to erect a synagogue, but no further services were held until the following spring. By March 16, 1851, 182 contributors, representing more than half the Jewish households in San Francisco, had collected forty-four hundred dollars toward the establishment of a synagogue. But there was disagreement as to whether the German or the Polish customs would prevail, and as a result not one but two congregations were officially founded on April 8, 1851.

Forty-two Poles, Englishmen, and Poseners organized Congregation Sherith Israel. The name, taken from the book of Isaiah, means "loyal remnant of Israel," and they followed the Polish *Minhag* or ritual. Their first meeting place, in the Merchants' Court on Washington Street between Montgomery and Sansome streets, was destroyed by fire a scant two months later. The same thing happened to their next quarters on Kearny Street between Washington and Jackson. On August 6, 1854, the congregation laid the cornerstone for a permanent synagogue on Stockton Street between Broadway and Vallejo. This temple served them well for sixteen years. In August 1870, under the leadership of Dr. A. H. Henry, Congregation Sherith Israel dedicated a larger synagogue at the corner of Post and Taylor streets.

Rabbi Jack Nieto led the congregation from 1893 to 1930. He was active in many social movements, including women's rights (unusual for the time). Under his leadership Sherith Israel modified their ritual to join the reform movement.

The cornerstone was laid for the present temple on Washington's Birthday, February 22, 1904; the building was consecrated on September 24, 1905. This imposing structure, built at a cost of nearly a quarter of a million dollars, was one of the few public buildings to come unscathed through the earthquake and fire. Equally important, the temple's extensive library and collection of pioneer records was saved. The congregation offered the sanctuary, auditorium, and schoolrooms for use as an interim hall of justice. It was here that the mayor, the board of supervisors, and Boss Abe Reuf were tried for graft. Ruef, himself the son of French Jewish immigrants, was found guilty and sentenced to fourteen years at San Quentin. Eugene Schmitz, or "Handsome Gene" as he was called, the "Bassoon Mayor" who had led an orchestra before leading the city, was acquitted. Rabbi Nieto watched the proceedings daily from the gallery of the temple, looking like "a reincarnation of Michelangelo's Moses . . . gloomy, inscrutable, as he beheld this daily profanation of Jehovah's temple," according to a newspaper of the day. Congregation Sherith Israel was host to other groups as well, but none produced anything so dramatic as the graft trials.

Rabbi Morris Goldstein came in 1932, leading the congregation until 1972. During his tenure the temple was host to a founding session of the United Nations. Today Sherith Israel is a house of prayer, a house of study, and a house of fellowship. The building includes an especially fine library.

Sherith Israel is a temple in the Romanesque manner with Eastern overtones—a square building with a large central dome. It was designed by Albert Pissis, a graduate of L'École des Beaux-Arts in Paris, who also designed the Hibernia Bank, the Parrott Building (The Emporium department store), and the James Flood Building, as well as the Little Sisters of the Poor complex on Lake Street (recently demolished). Pissis was the only Mexican-born architect practicing in California at that time.

The masonry building is now painted in two tones of tan. The entrance is below and behind a massive stepped arch that curves above a rose window. Three large, multiple-molded arches form the entrance, with a modest glassed arcade between portals and a twelve-cusped rose window filled with stained glass. Stepped bracket modillions crown the upper gabled facade. Interiorly, the building is striking with decorated walls and ceiling that show the Sephardic Jewish heritage from Spain and Portugal. A great circular dome rises eighty feet above the floor of the temple and shows a blazing sun in the midst of traditional designs. The brightly colored interior is still fresh; walls are decorated with a stenciled design, a practice common in Victorian times. The intricately carved woodwork in the temple is of Honduras mahogany; the stained glass windows are Italian. The ark, built in 1854, has been used in every temple built by the congregation.

California Registered Landmark #462

(Bronze plaque on Montgomery Street between Washington and Jackson streets, commemorating the first Jewish religious services held in San Francisco.)

Staged areas of cusped circles and arches lead the eye ever higher at Sherith Israel.

Arches and pendentives support a large dome in Sherith Israel's interior.

Congregation Emanu-El

Arguello Boulevard, at Lake Street
Founded April 8, 1851

Attendance at the 1849 and 1850 Jewish High Holy Day services had been almost entirely male, but by March of 1851 the San Francisco correspondent could report in *Asmonean,* an Anglo-Jewish journal, "of late there has been quite an accession of ladies with their children. This will tend to improve and consolidate society, for when I first arrived the community was nearly destitute of the fair part of creation; you may be assured it was in a terribly disorganized state." So many had brought their families, he went on, that "public feeling has decided on erecting a permanent building for a synagogue."

As was generally the case in new American communities, congregations grew out of societies already existing for purposes of mutual aid or burial, and organized along ethnic or national lines. Two such societies were already in existence: the First Hebrew Benevolent Society organized in April 1850 by Jews of Polish and English ancestry, and the Eureka Benevolent Society formed in October 1850 by those from Bavaria. Meetings were held in March 1851 to plan the proposed synagogue, and it was agreed that because of the variety of cultural backgrounds two separate synagogues would be formed.

Congregation Emanu-El, meaning "God is with us," was officially founded on April 8, 1851, with sixty charter members, primarily Bavarians but including a few Sephardim. Their leader was Emanuel Berg. It was stipulated in the constitution that services should follow the *Minhag Ashkenaz* (traditional German ritual); other Orthodox customs would also be observed. Cantor Max Welhof was appointed Torah reader, and congregant Louis Cohn offered to serve without compensation as a teacher for the children of the members. The congregation rented space on Bush Street between Montgomery and Sansome until a synagogue could be built.

In 1854, Emanu-El bought nine thousand square feet of land on Broadway between Powell and Mason and selected the plans submitted by William Craine and Thomas England (designers of Old St. Mary's Church at California and Dupont). Emanu-El's first rabbi, Julius Eckman, who had earned his doctorate in classics at the University of Berlin, arrived in the city in July, just in time to perform the ceremonies of laying the cornerstone for Emanu-El and, two weeks later, nearby Sherith Israel. Eckman, a scholarly and ascetic man, consecrated the handsome Broadway Synagogue on September 14, 1854, and served as rabbi for a little over two years. He established the *Hefzibah* (people of Israel) school and published his own *Prayer-book for Children and Vocabulary of the Hebrew Tongue;* beginning in January 1857, he also co-directed a secular day school and published a newspaper, *The Weekly Gleaner,* which was the most influential Jewish journal in the western states for the next decade.

By 1856 Emanu-El had modified the ritual somewhat, and in 1860, under the skilled direction of their second rabbi, Elkan Cohn, the congregation joined the liberal reform movement which was then rapidly spreading from Germany to America. As might be expected, not all the members favored the change; in 1864 some sixty families withdrew to form a new congregation, Ohabai Shalome. There were roughly five thousand Jews in the city in that year—nearly ten percent of the population—and two newer synagogues—Shomrai Shabbes and Beth Israel, both Orthodox. Emanu-El was already committed to a building program, having bought property at the location that would later be known as 450 Sutter. Though handicapped by the loss of twenty percent of their membership, the congregation raised the necessary funds by various means—holding fairs, issuing bonds, selling lifetime seats in the new sanctuary, and selling the Broadway synagogue to the Board of Education.

The new Sutter Street temple, dedicated on March 23, 1866, was designed by Englishman William Patton, who had left a flourishing practice to seek his fortune in the California gold mines but returned to architecture after a short time. His creation of First Unitarian's imposing church on Geary had established his reputation as one of the finest architects in the West, and the new Temple Emanu-El was to become his *magnum opus*. The building incorporated Gothic features in its construction just as they would have been in a medieval church. Patton made use of Jewish symbols as well—a Star of David in several locations and stone Tablets of the Law above the central gable. The twin bronze-plated domes, 165 feet high, were designed to symbolize the headpieces of the Torah. The sanctuary, one of the largest vaulted chambers ever constructed in California, seated twelve hundred worshippers. This temple, considered by many the most impressive building on the Pacific Coast, was, like all other construction around Union Square, demolished in 1906 but was then rebuilt, to serve another twenty years.

Any listing of influential San Francisco clergy would have to include Cohn. He enjoyed deep friendships with several non-Jewish clergymen—Unitarians Thomas Starr King and Horatio Stebbins, Presbyterian John Hemphill, and Catholic Archbishop Joseph Alemany. Through precept and example, he worked for a synthesis of ancient Jewish values and modern American ideals. Under Cohn's leadership, writes Fred Rosenbaum in *Architects of Reform,* "the Emanu-El elite established itself as a philanthropic group. *Noblesse oblige* became a chief concern of the leading families inaugurating a tradition that was to become proverbial for its munificence and generosity." Many of the city's major institutions—museums, symphony, opera, ballet, parks, zoo, and hospitals—were made possible in substantial part by the generosity of Jewish San Franciscans.

It fell to Rabbi Jacob Voorsanger, an outstanding graduate of the Amsterdam Jewish Theological Seminary, to lead Emanu-El into the tumultuous events of the twentieth century. He led services bare-headed, performed intermarriages, and introduced a revolutionary new prayer book, mostly in English. His successor, Martin A. Meyer, the congregation's first San Francisco–born rabbi, showed great skill in developing young leadership and consolidated the various Jewish benevolence societies to provide more effective services for throngs of Jewish immigrants arriving from Russia. The rabbis and cantors of Congregation Emanu-El continue to play important roles in both religious and community life. The congregation has a strong commitment to the arts; every five years Emanu-El commissions an original liturgical work.

The present temple, dedicated in January 1927, was named the finest piece of architecture in Northern California by the American Institute of Architects. It was designed by architects Arthur Brown, Jr., John Bakewell, Jr., and Sylvain Schaittacher. Arthur Brown also designed the Opera House, City Hall, and Coit Tower. Consulting architects were G. Albert Lansburgh, Bernard Maybeck, and Edgar Walter, with Bruce Porter as interior designer.

The L-shaped domed building at Arguello and Lake is Near Eastern in feeling, a fusion of themes based on Byzantine-Roman and early medieval traditions. Building materials are steel and concrete faced with a warm-toned stucco and cast stone; the roof is red tile.

One enters the temple house and sanctuary through a courtyard surrounded by a colonnade with Romanesque style capitals and a porch with vaulted ceiling. The courtyard is quiet and often sun-dappled; the tall fountain with mosaic trim recalls the ancient Fountain of Oblation in the courtyard of the Temple of Jerusalem. Mosaics in a circle around a Star of David, set in the travertine floor before the entrance, symbolize the twelve tribes of Israel.

After passing through a wide narthex, or vestibule, with resplendent polished stone floor and vaulted ceiling, one enters the temple proper. The main focus of the temple interior is the ark and its pyramidal roofed canopy, supported by green marble columns. There are similar columns behind the ark and all around the interior. Hanging from the canopy is a *ner tamid* (everlasting light). Menorahs on either side of the ark, a gift of the Zellerbach family, are of the same design as the one in Solomon's Temple in Jerusalem. The ark itself was created by the California artists Frank Ingerson and George Denison. It is gilded, with enamel enrichments, and resembles an enormous jewel box, its sides covered with symbols of the twelve tribes of Israel. This ark, a gift of Mrs. Marcus Koshland, has the same dimensions as that which the children of Israel were told to build in the wilderness and which they carried to the Promised Land (see Exodus 25:10). The temple's stained glass windows were designed by Mark Adams in 1972 and 1973; they were donated by the Haas family of San Francisco. They are abstract and without images, yet they suggest the power and brilliance of such natural phenomena as fire and water. The organ, a four-manual Skinner with 4,500 pipes, is comparable to a symphony orchestra of eighty musicians. Corbeled balconies and a repeated theme of arches above the columns along the temple back and sides are picked up in the design of the temple wall behind the ark. On the pulpit, handwoven tapestries of rich blues and purples, designed by Yael Lurie and made at Aubusson, France, intensify similar hues in the immense glass windows that irradiate the temple. The effect is a lively aesthetic tension created by an overall austerity with well-chosen opulent objects here and there—such as the handsome lucite sculpture by Jacques Schnier in the vestibule.

The small Reuben R. Rinder chapel, executed in dark Australian mahogany and red fabrics, was designed by the architect Michael Goodman; it has lustrous red and yellow glass windows. The quotation at the entrance is from Isaiah: "My house shall be called a House of Prayer for all peoples." This temple complex houses the Martin A. Meyer Auditorium, cases and a museum for Jewish art, and the Jacob Voorsanger Library, with its fine collection of rare works of Judaica.

The subtle arch modulations of a Temple Emanu-El entrance leads the eye up to the sky-piercing dome.

Splendidly spacious, Temple Emanu-El's interior has overtones of Byzantine in a modern interpretation.

St. Patrick's Church

756 Mission Street, between Third and Fourth Streets
Founded June 9, 1851

On May 20, 1851, Bishop Alemany authorized Father John Maginnis to start a new parish, St. Patrick's, in the section of the city designated as Happy Valley. Maginnis, born in County Meath, Ireland, was well suited to serve the predominantly Irish congregation. During the first summer, services were held in a rented hall at the corner of Fourth and Jessie streets, but by September a simple wooden building had been put up where the Sheraton-Palace Hotel now stands. In 1854 this was replaced by a new wooden church of plain Classical Revival style, with an orphanage adjacent. In later years, as the city expanded toward the sea, many congregations found new locations. St. Patrick's Church, however, remained in the same neighborhood while the second little building, removed to make way for the Palace Hotel, moved westward twice. From 1873 until 1921, located on Eddy Street between Laguna and Octavia, it was known as the Church of St. John the Baptist; since that time it has served as the parish hall for Holy Cross Church, at 1822 Eddy Street near Scott. It is the oldest wooden religious building in San Francisco.

Ground was broken and construction begun on the present St. Patrick's in April 1870. The district was residential, but it was also the cultural and social center of the young city. Many prominent citizens lived nearby, including the pioneer lumbermen Pope and Talbot, Robert B. Woodward of the famous Woodward's Gardens, and Lloyd Tevis, head of Wells Fargo Bank. Other well-known Irish Americans in San Francisco included the so-called silver kings—Mackay, Fair, Flood, and O'Brien. At the other end of the social panorama was the Irishman Dennis Kearney, a prime mover in the beginnings of organized labor in the city and something of a rabble-rouser as well. When St. Patrick's was dedicated on March 17, 1872, the Catholic population of the parish numbered about thirty thousand people.

The first work of the Daughters of Charity on the West Coast was carried out at St. Patrick's parish, where they established a convent, schools, and an orphanage. Five years after the discovery of silver in the Comstock, they established a convent in Virginia City, which they described as a place where "dust was as abundant as sin" and "laundry was dirty before it was dry." The sisters operated a school and an orphanage there, under the leadership of Sister Frederica McGrath, who became known as "The Angel of the Mining Camps." Today the Daughters of Charity operate Cathedral High School on Ellis Street.

Each year around St. Patrick's Day, the so-called Mystery Tapestry is displayed at St. Patrick's Church. For years its origin was unknown; finally Father John Daly discovered that it had been made in 1877 in the Virginia City orphanage. It shows Saint Patrick with a charming church in the background. The church has been identified as St. Mary's in the Mountains, often called the Cathedral of the Comstock. Although the name of the tapestry's creator is still undisclosed, her family did write to the church with its story.

The brick church of St. Patrick's was severely damaged in the 1906 earthquake and fire, but it was eventually restored after being used to shelter and aid victims of the disaster. The makeup of the original congregation—mostly Irish—changed over the years to become first Mexican and then predominantly Filipino, with many business people attending today. The ten o'clock mass on the first Sunday of the month is in Tagalog, and the eleven o'clock mass is in Latin. St. Patrick's operates Alexis Apartments for the elderly and handicapped and St. Patrick's Family Center, which has a gymnasium, a well-baby clinic, and a child care center. The church also helps many of the unfortunates who live in the nearby area.

This church is yet another example of Gothic Revival or Victorian Gothic with its pointed windows, pier buttresses, and finialed front tower. After 1906 its original spire was not replaced, and the restored building had additional buttresses, steel girders, and rafters added to make it as substantial and earthquake-proof as possible. Delicate crocketed spirelets crown the tower today, and a traceried canopy covers a statue on the wall above the portal. The towers and walls survived the 1906 fire, and some of the original bricks were used in the new building. The fire scars are still visible. Monsignor John Rogers, who was pastor from 1905 to 1935, oversaw the restoration.

Inside the bronze doors, the interior glows with materials from around the world, using the Irish national colors—green, white, and gold. Green Connemara marble and white bottincino marble are lavishly used throughout the church. Green marble pillars, each surrounded by four smaller columns of white marble, are the most distinctive aspect of the nave, with a rib-vaulted ceiling above; the clerestory windows have Tiffany glass and show the pre-Christian beliefs and traditions of the Irish people. Other stained glass windows depict Saint Patrick and the Evangelists Matthew, Mark, Luke, and John. The coats-of-arms of San Francisco, Scotland, England, South Africa, and Australia, as well as those of four Irish provinces, are displayed in the church. St. Patrick's is the Irish National Church in San Francisco.

The main altar, set in a high apse, is made from white Carrara marble; the walls are botticino marble up to a height of about eight feet, with inserts of Connemara green. The pulpit was carved by Albert Bernasconi, who did the Pulgas Water Temple. Bernasconi was one of San Francisco's great craftsmen and the teacher of many others. Irish artist Mia Cranwill designed the metal crucifix on the main altar and the vestments, which are done in cloth of gold and embroidered with ancient Gaelic patterns. There are statues of many saints throughout the church, notably those of Irish background. The lower windows show scenes from the life of Saint Patrick.

St. Patrick's Church and a fine post-fire Pacific Gas and Electric Company power station nearby are the only remaining buildings in the proposed Yerba Buena redevelopment project. Many visitors to the city, especially those who are Irish, visit the venerable old church. On weekdays there is always a scattering of worshipers—the church is there to offer solace and a place for reflection away from the rush of the city outside its doors.

San Francisco Registered Landmark #4
California State Point of Historical Interest #SFr 002
(St. Patrick's Church)
San Francisco Registered Landmark #6
California State Point of Historical Interest #SFr 001
(Holy Cross Parish Hall)

The crocketed finials of St. Patrick's provide a lively rhythm against the vertical thrust of nearby high rises.

2

A City on Many Hills

1852–1875

During the 1850s, fortune seekers from all over the world continued to converge in San Francisco, bringing with them a kaleidoscopic array of cultural and religious traditions. A scant four years after the discovery of gold at Sutter's Mill, the city directory listed foreign consuls representing Austria, Bremen, Britain, Chile, Denmark, France, Hamburgh, Hanover, Hawaii, Mecklenburg-Schwerin, Mexico, Netherlands, and Norway-Sweden. The city had acquired a distinctly heterogeneous culture within the short span of five or six years, and the uniquely American opportunity for people to affiliate with the churches of their choice—or with no churches at all—had produced a spontaneous, voluntary attitude toward religion that was to modify all the faiths flourishing here. By the mid-1850s it was becoming clear that the Protestant dream of a Puritan City on a Hill was evolving into something even more promising—a multifaceted City on Many Hills.

As early as 1852, the San Francisco black community established three churches. The congregations included both freemen from the North and former slaves, originally brought by their masters from the deep South, who had bought their freedom by working in the gold fields or boom towns. The Pioneer Meeting House (now Bethel African Methodist Episcopal Church) opened its doors in February and soon thereafter welcomed the official A.M.E. Missionary Elder for the Pacific Coast, the Reverend Thomas Myers Decatur Ward. The month of August saw the founding of two more black congregations—First Colored Baptist (now Third Baptist) and African Methodist Episcopal Zion. Already two generations old in the East, the black churches provided their congregations with not only spiritual sustenance but also an institution for developing the educational, social, and political skills useful in working toward a full participation in American society.

Also in 1852, the Presbyterians recalled the Reverend William Speer, a medical missionary, from China to minister to the rapidly growing Chinese population of San Francisco. Dr. Speer established a Sunday school, a free dispensary, and classes in English as a Second Language. In November 1853, he formally founded the Chinese Presbyterian Church with a membership of four, all previously converted in China.

On July 23, 1853, the Holy See established the Archdiocese of San Francisco, elevating the Right Reverend Joseph Sadoc Alemany to the rank of archbishop. By this time, Roman Catholics could attend services in several languages at St. Francis of Assisi; and the rapidly growing Irish population had their own parish at St. Patrick's. The city's first cathedral, St. Mary's, celebrated Christmas mass in 1854; the Jesuit order began offering both educational and religious programs in 1855. Within the next few years, citywide "national" parishes were established to serve French-, German-, and Spanish-speaking Catholics, and additional neighborhood parish churches were opened as the city moved to the south and the west.

January 1854 saw the arrival of the Right Reverend William Ingraham Kip, newly consecrated as the Episcopal Missionary Bishop of California. The Yale-trained prelate brought to his work not only dedication but also a rich awareness of the new state's cultural and aesthetic potential. He immediately set out to establish Episcopal congregations throughout California. During these years, various other denominations added new parishes as well, and by 1860 there were at least thirty-eight Christian churches and two synagogues as well as several Chinese temples serving a city of nearly seventy thousand people.

During the 1850s there were more newspapers in San Francisco than in metropolitan London of the same period. Among those published by religious leaders were Sam Brannan's *California Star* (1847), William Taylor's *California Christian Advocate* (1850), Mifflin Gibbs' *Mirror of the Times* (1855), Dr. William Speer's *The Oriental* (1855)—America's (and probably the world's) first newspaper printed in Chinese and English. Rabbi Julius Eckman started *The Weekly Gleaner* in 1857. The Reverend John J. Moore of First African Methodist Episcopal Zion Church first published his combination magazine-newspaper *The Lunar Visitor* in 1858. In 1862, Phillip A. Bell, a black leader, and Samuel Hopkins Willey, founder of Howard Presbyterian, jointly founded the *Pacific Appeal*.

San Francisco has been called the Phoenix City because, like that mythical bird, it has repeatedly risen from the destruction of fire. The best-known fire occurred following the 1906 earthquake, but during the 1850s, large and small portions of the city burned several times. The first shelters, including churches and other public gathering places, were either tents or wooden buildings. Eventually, buildings in downtown San Francisco were built more substantially, and the city hired its own firefighters, but before that happened, repeated losses from fires inspired the formation of volunteer fire companies. During the 1850s, these companies dominated the social life of the city. Each had a nickname and number—the Knickerbocker Five, the Proud Ten, the Big Six—and most citizens belonged, usually to a company with members from the same hometown or state.Several conflagrations were known to have rampaged unhampered while two companies fought over the privilege of putting them out. On the other hand, contemporary accounts note that both Archbishop Joseph Sadoc Alemany and Bishop William Ingraham Kip proved themselves capable firefighters, assisting various companies on several occasions.

The first known temperance organization of the young city was formed by Howard Engine Company Number Three—the Social Three. This group of Bostonians early on discovered the need for their organization, and they named it the Dashaway Society, building a hall by that name as well. Dashaway Hall became the first meeting place of the original St. James' Episcopal Church and was used by other young congregations too. St. James' eventually built a church of its own but then sold it and disbanded when the minister decided he wanted to become a Catholic priest. Changes like this were commonplace during the city's early days. The Social Three changed allegiances, too, becoming Brannan Number Three when San Francisco's first millionaire, Sam Brannan, gave the company a gold trumpet to accompany its twenty-thousand-dollar silver-plated fire engine.

Churches, volunteer fire companies, social clubs—everyone got involved in everything, including vigilante groups. The Committees of Vigilance of 1849, 1851, and 1856, as they named themselves, were formed by people who felt that the legal authorities could not or would not uphold the laws. The members were average citizens, and several ministers gave at least unofficial blessings to their activities. Only one minister, the Reverend William Anderson Scott, spoke out against the vigilantes, and he was hanged in effigy for speaking his convictions. Those accused by the vigilance committees of wrongdoing were run out of town, or, in a few famous cases, hanged. Controversies persist about who was guilty and whether the vigilantes were justified in their extralegal actions.

In 1859 Richard Henry Dana returned to the "village" he had visited twenty-four years earlier, and wrote in "Twenty-four Years after *Two Years before the Mast*":

> I could not complain that I had not a choice of places to worship. The Roman Catholics have an archbishop, a cathedral, and five or six smaller churches—French, German, Spanish, and English; and the Episcopalians have a bishop, a cathedral,

and three other churches; the Methodists and the Presbyterians have three or four each; and there are Congregationalist, Baptist, a Unitarian, and other societies.

Dana also noted a curious effect the move to California had on people. Visited in San Francisco by a man he had last known as a deacon of a Congregational society in New England, he remarked:

> Gone was the downcast eye . . . the non-natural voice, the watchful gait, stepping as if he felt responsible for the balance of the moral universe! He walked with a stride, an uplifted countenance . . . his voice strong and natural. . . . In short, he had put off the New England deacon and become a human being.

Three new forms of Christian worship arrived in San Francisco in 1859. Seventh Day Adventists, members of one of the faiths developed in America, started holding services in a courtroom even before their national denomination was officially established. Silent Quaker worship was formalized in July when two well-known British Friends on a mission to America conducted a series of meetings in the home of James Neal. And the Greek cross of Eastern Orthodoxy made its first official appearance in the city as the chaplain from a Russian naval vessel in the bay came ashore to conduct services and baptize several Serbian and Russian children. This event led, within the space of five years, to the establishment of the first permanent Orthodox parish in California. The United States bought Alaska from the Russians in 1867, and in 1870 San Franciscans welcomed Archimandrite John Mitropolsky, the bishop of the newly established episcopal see of the Orthodox Church in America.

Several historic events shaped the city's growth in the 1860s and 1870s: the discovery of silver in the Comstock Lode, the Civil War, and completion of the transcontinental railroad in 1869. News of the immense silver deposits in Nevada must have seemed too good to be true coming only a decade after the Gold Rush. Though the silver was in Nevada, the great outpouring of wealth started another building boom in San Francisco. Hotels, commercial buildings, banks, and churches were all built with silver money, and a new generation grew rich and influential.

California eventually decided in favor of the Union cause in the Civil War. Before this decision was reached, however, there was dissension and controversy. Many people had come to California from the South. Calvary Presbyterian's outspoken minister, William A. Scott (from Tennessee) was again hanged in effigy during this period because he included the men in gray in his congregational prayers along with the men in blue. He left town with his family, but years later returned to found another pioneer church. Another minister, the Reverend Thomas Starr King of First Unitarian Church, is credited with almost singlehandedly saving California for the Union. A staunch abolitionist, King conducted a strenuous statewide campaign on behalf of the Union cause. He was also instrumental in the success of the U.S. Sanitary Commission, forerunner of the Red Cross, inducing Californians to contribute a fourth of the national fund, an extraordinary amount considering the state's relatively small population.

Congregations responded to the conflict in various ways. Bethel A.M.E. sponsored a series of scientific lectures by a Dr. Johnson, sending the proceeds to the wounded black soldiers of the 54th Massachusetts Regiment. Members of the congregations signed up with the recently established Company A, California Colored Volunteers, and, when not called to active service, contributed the funds raised for that group to the Sanitary Commission. First Congregational was the first church in the city to unfurl the Union flag over its building, and the first to sing Julia Ward Howe's *Battle Hymn of the Republic* during worship services. Another ardent abolitionist was Rabbi Elkan Cohn of Congregation Emanu-El. Like King, he campaigned vigorously against slavery, and is credited with playing an important part in assuring California's loyalty to the Union. One of his few sermons that have been preserved is the eulogy he delivered only moments after learning of the death of President Abraham Lincoln. It concludes, "Oh, he served God in his love to man, the most glorious worship on earth."

The transcontinental railway, completed in 1869, brought California into the mainstream of American life. Materials, mail and ideas, as well as people, became more easily accessible, ending the state's geographical isolation but probably some of its unique qualities as well. Four Californians, especially, achieved wealth and power as a result of this great continental roadway—Huntington, Stanford, Hopkins, and Crocker—the Big Four. The last-named gentleman was also responsible for bringing many Chinese to this country to build the railroad. He began this practise when other immigrants or local workers wanted what was considered to be too much for their labor. Six thousand Chinese workers were hired in 1865 and fifteen thousand by 1869. *Hired* may be too courteous a word; the Chinese were paid a dollar a day, for which they would work hard and feed, clothe, and shelter themselves, and, it is said, never be heard to complain.

In 1869, as the Chinese population continued to increase, the Methodist church opened a mission house under the direction of the Reverend Otis Gibson, a veteran of several years' service in China. Methodists met immigrants at the boat, clearing away red tape and helping them to find housing. The mission house included an asylum for Chinese women and children as well as a chapel, several classrooms, and housing for the missionaries. Presbyterian women, meanwhile, were developing a highly successful program to help Chinese women caught up in enforced prostitution. The Reverend William C. Pond, minister of Third Congregational Church, invited Chinese people to attend services there, but found the directors and membership hostile to the idea, so he resigned that pastorate and started Bethany (now Chinese) Congregational Church in October of 1873.

At first welcomed, the Chinese became the focus of much animosity during the 1870s. By then the economy had slowed down. The Bank of California closed its doors for a while, and there was widespread unemployment. Dennis Kearney, the most famous of the so-called sandlot orators, incited workers against the wealthy silver and railroad magnates, but especially against the Chinese. During a three-day "reign of terror" that began on July 23, 1877, a mob broke through a police barricade and destroyed several Chinese-owned buildings, but the rowdies met their match when they threatened the Methodist Mission House. Anthony's *Fifty Years of Methodism* recounts the event: "The conduct of Dr. Gibson was dignified and fearless. He was ready to die at his post, but not ready to surrender the rights he held as an American citizen to the claims of foreigners [nearly half of San Francisco's population was foreign born at this time] who never learned in their country, or from the church in which they were raised, the first lesson of civil liberty."

There is little doubt that San Francisco would eventually have become a major western seaport, but the Gold Rush had pushed the young community through a quick infancy and adolescence. By the 1870s San Francisco had become a metropolis, a fully developed city like its eastern cousins. In 1871 the city started to build itself a suitable city hall, and in 1873 Andrew Hallidie's ingenious invention, the cable car, began moving people up and down the steep hills. Golden Gate Park, now an internationally recognized civic treasure, was then an optimistic plan laid out in the shifting sand dunes on the city's border. The park, designed as a woodland retreat for beleaguered city people, was developed according to the visionary plan of William Hall. Legislative authorization for the acquisition of parklands was achieved in part by the efforts of Father Gallagher of St. Joseph's Church. The bay window came into widespread use during the 1870s and 1880s; it lets in more light than a conventional window, an advantage in the endless rows of new houses with no side windows. The bay window appears rarely in churches but frequently in hotels and apartment buildings. It is almost universal in the period's residential architecture—the Victorians that are so admired and renovated today.

The city center had moved from its original location around the old plaza (Portsmouth Square) to the Union Square area, where several of the oldest congregations built imposing new churches designed by famous architects and seating a thousand or more worshipers. Meanwhile, the railroad and silver kings had built themselves fine new houses, as had many of the prosperous merchants, in the city's new residential districts. Stanford and Crocker built on California Street, at the top of Nob Hill. Less wealthy people built houses to the west, creating new neighborhoods and hence new parishes. The area south of Market Street was a well settled working-class neighborhood, with churches of all denominations located along both Howard and Mission streets and as far west as Mission Dolores. Within a ten-year period, the city's population had more than doubled, reaching nearly a hundred fifty thousand by 1870, and the number of churches doubled as well. Among the sacred places available to San Franciscans were four synagogues and a selection of churches including six Baptist, four Congregational, seven Episcopalian, fourteen Methodist, ten Presbyterian, sixteen Catholic (eleven churches and five chapels), two Swedenborgian, four German Lutheran, and one congregation each representing the German Evangelical, German Reformed, Unitarian, Disciples of Christ, Mariners', Friends, Spiritualist, and Eastern Orthodox religious traditions. In addition, there were at least four Chinese temples, not yet listed in the city directory.

Swedenborgian Church of the New Jerusalem

2107 Lyon Street, at Washington Street
Founded February 15, 1852

San Francisco followers of the teachings of Emanuel Swedenborg were holding services in private homes as early as February 14, 1850, but it was not until Sunday, February 15, 1852, that the resident members of the various New Church societies of San Francisco officially formed the Society of the New Jerusalem. This meeting took place in the Superior Court Room on Dupont Street (now Grant Avenue). Thereafter, the regular meetings were held in the rooms of the Twelfth District Court and communion at the home of Robert L. Smith, who conducted services in the absence of an ordained minister. Their first building, erected in 1863, was a simple small Gothic Revival structure designed by the architect S. C. Bugbee and noted as "one of the neatest little churches in the city." This was on O'Farrell Street between Powell and Mason. By this time the church had a regular minister, the Reverend John Doughty, who had come to California for his health but had nearly lost it while crossing the plains. Attacked and captured by Indians, he had pushed his sleepy guard into the fire and dashed away on his horse amidst a shower of arrows.

By 1890 attendance had grown to such proportions that the congregation built a new and larger church farther out on O'Farrell, but three years later Doughty died and gradually the members affiliated with a second congregation of the same faith, the San Francisco Church of the New Jerusalem. That congregation was started by the Reverend Joseph Worcester, whose father, the Reverend Thomas Worcester, had founded the New Jerusalem Church in Boston. Joseph Worcester, who was an architect as well as a minister, started his work in San Francisco in 1867. In 1894, the joint congregation bought a lot and planned a church to express the religious philosophy of Emanuel Swedenborg (1688–1772).

Swedenborg, the son of a Lutheran bishop, wrote several works of theology. In the course of his long life he also did original work in metallurgy, biology, physics, and the medical sciences. He was a devoted family man and interested in social causes as well. Among his main ideas was a focus on the interweaving of the spiritual and material worlds. The denomination that bears his name started a few years after his death, and though small, soon became influential. Several famous Americans were followers of his teachings, among them Helen Keller, the novelist Henry James, and John Chapman, better known as Johnny Appleseed.

In San Francisco, Joseph Worcester lived in a cottage near the Vallejo Street cul-de-sac, behind that group of distinctive houses that are considered the earliest example of the Shingle Style in the Bay Area. He counted among his friends many of the painters, musicians, and writers who lived on Russian Hill; accordingly, many of them helped design and build the Swedenborgian church, or contributed something to it. The building, which was dedicated in 1895, strives to reduce the separation between the inside and outside worlds. An attractive walled garden outside, filled with flowers and a verdant lawn, symbolizes both international and universal truths with trees from all over the world—

cedars of Lebanon, Irish yew, English hawthorne, and Japanese maple. Natural objects from the woods are used to decorate the church.

The exterior of the now-famous brick and stucco church, with its wall belfry and low roof, was designed from drawings done by Bruce Porter of a small church in the Po Valley near Verona, Italy. A young draftsman working in the office of A. Page Brown drew up the plans; his name was Bernard Maybeck. The roof is supported interiorly on heavy beams of madrone with the bark left on. These madrones were brought by wagon from Glen Ranch, a farm in the Santa Cruz mountains.

The plans include some elements of Mission Revival, such as a red tile roof—to pay homage to California's original religious tradition. The cross in the garden is from Mission San Miguel. Inside, the coffered-effect ceiling shows the simple design of the low gabled roof. The church is simply furnished with eighty handmade maple chairs designed by Bernard Maybeck. The chairs are pegged (they have no nails), and the seats and backs are woven from tule rushes that grow wild in the Sacramento Delta. At the front of the church is a high carved wooden lectern and a fine carved stone communion table. A tall wrought iron candelabrum echoes similar iron wall sconces. There is a large brick fireplace at the back of the church to warm parishioners on foggy mornings.

The well-known California painter William Keith did a series of paintings for the church. The four works in oil, depicting the seasons of the year, hang on the north wall. He also gave the church an old Japanese temple bell that had been in his studio. Reportedly, he would ring the bell from time to time to clear his head for painting. Bruce Porter made two windows, all in blue tones, for the church. One shows the fountain of life, and the other depicts Saint Christopher and the Christ child, whose head is surrounded by a halo of light. Porter also contributed some glass that had once been a part of England's Westminster Abbey, and this was made into a narrow window under the brick bell tower. Worshipers are called to service by a bronze bell from Western Pacific's steam locomotive No. 318. During Worcester's pastorate, many artists attended services at the Swedenborgian church. Today it is a church favored for weddings.

Like a Scandinavian meeting house, Swedenborgian's interior has the spare and ascetic character of its founder. The rough, almost crude beams that sustain the roof attest to interest in honest workmanship and native materials.

The calm garden of Swedenborgian offers an oasis for meditation, appropriate to this faith.

Bethel African Methodist Episcopal Church

970 Laguna Street, between McAllister and Golden Gate Streets
Founded February 22, 1852

Bethel African Methodist Episcopal Church, the oldest black congregation in San Francisco, is affiliated with Methodism's original black denomination. The A.M.E. Connectional came into being in 1787 when Richard Allen withdrew from Philadelphia's St. George Methodist Episcopal Church and bought a small blacksmith shop (possibly the first real estate purchase by a black person in the United States) in which the African Methodist Episcopal Church was born. Denied ordination by the Methodist bishop, Allen went to court to secure official sanction for the new church. Since that time the A.M.E. Connectional has become a worldwide denomination.

The first A.M.E. church in San Francisco, a small building called the Pioneer Meeting House, was dedicated on February 22, 1852, by the Reverend George Taylor of Boston. A few months later the small congregation had engaged the Reverend Joseph Thompson, a white clergyman, to serve as pastor, and by August of that year they had erected a new building, St. Cyprian's A.M.E. Church, at the corner of Jackson and Stone streets. St. Cyprian's next pastor was the Reverend Thomas Myers Decatur Ward, who came to California in 1854 as the Missionary Elder for the Pacific Coast of the A.M.E. church. The congregation continued to worship at this location until 1856, when financial difficulties caused them to reorganize in a Scott Street carpentry shop as Pilgrim A.M.E. Church.

Because Ward's duties required extensive travel, he appointed a Sacramento minister and teacher, the Reverend Jeremiah B. Sanderson, as pastor of Pilgrim A.M.E. in 1857. Sanderson had a strong interest in education, becoming a teacher at the colored school in 1858 and principal in 1859—just in time for a confrontation with the Board of Education over the allocation of facilities and supplies. By 1867 Sanderson was the director of the Evening Adult School, one of the earliest such schools in the city. In 1861 Pilgrim bought the Grace Episcopal Church on Powell Street and took the name Union Bethel A.M.E. They kept the Scott Street building, renting it to the Board of Education for eight hundred dollars per year for use as a school for black children.

Ward was reappointed Missionary Elder of the Pacific Coast in 1861. He published articles on religious and social themes, worked to obtain full citizenship rights for black people in the courts and in the voting box, and became almost as revered as his contemporary, Unitarian pastor Thomas Starr King. In the area of civil rights, Ward's approach tended towards optimism; he stressed understanding and love among all races of men. In 1868 the A.M.E. Connectional established the Bishopric of the Pacific Coast, appointing Thomas Myers Decator Ward the first bishop.

During the 1860s Union Bethel was host to a statewide conference of the A.M.E. Church in California; members also participated in the several statewide Colored Citizens' Conventions. Union Bethel was widely known for its compassionate care of the hungry and the homeless in the years following the Civil War. The old church building was demolished and replaced in 1894; however, the events of 1906 left the congregation homeless once again. Members quickly constructed a temporary church which they dedicated on July 15, 1906. On June 5, 1913, the cornerstone was laid for a new Bethel at 1207 Powell Street; the congregation remained there for 32 years.

Population shifts following World War II made it advisable to find a location more accessible to the membership; conferences were held, resolutions passed, money raised, and property purchased. The congregation moved to its present location on January 21, 1945. With the arrival of the Reverend J. Austell Hall in 1958, Bethel extended its ministry to the larger community. Pastor Hall was president of the Urban League, chairperson of the Anti-Poverty Program, and a member of the Police Commission. Under his leadership a new sanctuary was erected and plans laid for Fellowship Manor housing for the elderly. The Reverend Jerry Ford was appointed to Bethel in 1977. His ministry included utilization of church properties to provide alternative schooling for black youth during a community dispute over public school policies. The ministry of the Reverend Howard S. Gloyd, appointed to fill the vacancy caused by the death of Ford, has included completion of the Fellowship Manor housing complex, which provides housing for senior citizens.

Third Baptist Church

1399 McAllister Street, at Pierce Street
Founded in August 1852

Although lacking a minister, a group of nine devout Christians gathered in August of 1852 at the home of William and Eliza Davis to organize the First Colored Baptist Church of San Francisco. For the first few months, communion services were conducted by various ministers from neighboring white Baptist churches, and on October 11, 1852, a special recognition council of the San Francisco Baptist Association gave the church official status. In 1854 First Colored Baptist bought the old First Baptist building and moved it to Dupont Street between Greenwich and Filbert, at the same time changing their name to Third Baptist Church. The first black minister, the Reverend Charles Satchell, was called in 1856; he was succeeded by a white minister, the Reverend Thomas Howell, in 1865.

During the 1860s, Third Baptist conducted a weekly Sunday school and maintained a library of some three hundred volumes, available to parents and students. Under Howell's direction, Sunday school children presented a number of church benefits in which they demonstrated their knowledge of music, public speaking, and religion. Like the other churches, Third Baptist sponsored a wide variety of fund-raising affairs—lectures, concerts, fairs, dances, and parties—to provide money for church-sponsored activities. Noteworthy among these affairs was the lecture given in 1863 by the Reverend Thomas Starr King, minister of the First Unitarian Church, on the poetry of Hosea Bigelow.

By 1866, Third Baptist was able to buy the old Howard Presbyterian Church for ten thousand dollars. That building served until 1868, when the congregation dedicated a new church on Powell Street near Bush (present location of San Francisco State University Extension Division). That building was lost in the 1906 earthquake and fire, and for two years thereafter the congregation held services in a member's home, meanwhile buying property and beginning a new church at Hyde and Clay streets.

The Reverend Frederick Douglass Haynes, Sr., became pastor in 1932, remaining for thirty-nine years, during which time the congregation increased its involvement in civil rights, education, social welfare, health care, and city government. More recent pastors—the Reverends Frederick Douglass Haynes, Jr., and Amos C. Brown—have continued this involvement in community life. Third Baptist operates an apartment complex for tenants with low to moderate incomes, a remedial summer school for grades one through twelve, a skills network referral service, and an outreach program for the prisoners at Vacaville. The church provides financial aid for college students and a vocational training program for refugees from Ethiopia and Haiti. Third Baptist has about three thousand members at present, and has sponsored the formation of several additional Baptist churches. Internationally known leaders who have addressed the congregation include Adam Clayton Powell, Jr., W. E. B. DuBois, Tom Mboya, Martin Luther King, Jr., Andrew Young, Jesse Jackson, Ralph Abernathy, Benjamin Mays, and Benjamin Hooks.

The present church, completed in 1966, was designed by the architect William H. Gunnison. The white stuccoed modern building with a graceful pillared circular entry portico and lofty rectilinear tower contrasts with the surrounding Victorian homes. The complex includes a large sanctuary, a youth center, and an administration building.

The church has purchased the block bounded by Fillmore, Turk, Steiner, and Eddy streets, and announced plans for a complex of buildings including offices, an elementary school and gymnasium for three hundred sixty students, a convocation center including a banquet hall for one thousand people, and a new church to accommodate two thousand worshipers. Architects Jack Robbins and Jim Ream have prepared a model of the proposed complex, which will combine African and San Francisco architectural motifs as required for the area by Redevelopment Agency guidelines. Robbins has traveled through Kenya, Tanzania, and Ethiopia studying architectural patterns.

Prismatic clarity of a modernist design gives Third Baptist its precise simplicity.

First African Methodist Episcopal Zion Church

2159 Golden Gate Avenue
Founded August 1, 1852

The African Methodist Episcopal Zion Church was founded on August 1, 1852, by the Reverend John J. Moore. Services were held in a building on Stockton Street between Vallejo and Broadway. In addition to his religious duties, the pastor participated in the founding of the Athaeneum Society in 1854 and in the 1855 statewide Colored Citizens' Convention as both the chaplain and a prominent member of the education committee. After the convention he accepted a position at the San Francisco Colored School as principal and teacher. The school, located in the basement of St. Cyprian's Church at the corner of Jackson and Virginia streets, prospered under Moore's direction. During this same period, A.M.E. Zion Church opened a highly successful Sunday school with fifty pupils, six teachers, and a library containing some two hundred fifty books.

Between 1858 and 1862, while Moore was in Cariboo, British Columbia, the Reverend Adam B. Smith served as pastor. On his return to San Francisco, Moore participated even more extensively in civic affairs, giving a long oration at the Emancipation Celebration on August 1, 1862, and supporting black attempts to change laws restricting black participation in court cases and in elections. Moore differed from his counterpart in the Bethel A.M.E. church, Thomas Ward, in viewing civil rights problems with less optimism. In his own publication, the San Francisco *Lunar Visitor,* Moore called for "unity of sympathy . . . of purpose . . . of particular interest in our own race . . . of confidence in ourselves . . . and of self-respect"—concepts later expressed by Stokely Carmichael and Malcolm X. In 1868, at the general conference of the A.M.E. Zion church, Moore was appointed Bishop of the South Episcopal District, which required him to move to Washington, D.C.

In 1864, A.M.E. Zion was able to buy the Graeco-Egyptian temple being vacated by First Unitarian Church, for which they paid fifteen thousand dollars. Within less than a year the debt had been reduced to seven thousand dollars. For the next decade they called themselves the Starr King Methodist Church in acknowledgment of the support given all black churches by First Unitarian's outstanding minister. Also during 1864, A.M.E. Zion played a leading role in contributions to the underprivileged, sponsoring a Freedmen's Relief meeting in June and an Indian Protection meeting in December.

Like other black churches both in San Francisco and throughout the northern United States, Starr King Methodist continued to provide a focus for educational, cultural, social, and political activities during the 1870s and 1880s, and the clergy played prominent roles in the community. In the mid-seventies the church adopted the name First African Methodist Episcopal Church. In January 1878 their pastor, the Reverend W. H. Hillary (a member of the Colored Citizens' Equal Rights League delegation to a local convention of the National Labor Party) was elected to represent San Francisco at the party's national convention. Like Moore, Hillary was eventually made a bishop of the A.M.E. Zion church.

The handsome church was completely destroyed in the earthquake and fire of 1906. For three years the congregation continued to meet in a worship hall at Powell and Pacific streets, although they had no minister. The Reverend W. J. Byers, arriving in 1909, reactivated the congregation. Between 1911 and 1919, under a succession of pastors, the congregation erected a new church at 1669 Geary Street. Byers was then reassigned to San Francisco; his ministry included establishing a Christian Endeavor (young people's) society and the Booker T. Washington Center, San Francisco's first black community center. During the pastorate of the Reverend E. J. Magruder, A.M.E. Zion realized a long-standing ambition to construct an apartment house adjacent to the church, and in 1945 they were able to burn the mortgage on the Geary Street property.

A.M.E. Zion dedicated the present church at 2159 Golden Gate Avenue in 1965, and nine years later that property too was mortgage-free. Future plans include the erection of an educational building. The church provides for its members a balanced program including musical, athletic, cultural, and missionary activities. A.M.E. Zion clergymen continue the denomination's tradition of community service, participating in such groups as the Model Cities Board of Directors, the Urban League, the National Association for the Advancement of Colored People, and the Interdenominational Ministers' Alliance.

Calvary Presbyterian Church

2515 Fillmore Street, at Jackson Street
Founded July 23, 1854

As the city expanded, first to the south and then to the west, many if not most congregations built new churches or temples close to the newer residential areas. But Calvary Presbyterian is the only San Francisco church to be dismantled, stone by marked stone, and re-assembled in another location.

The congregation was founded on July 23, 1854, by a group from First Presbyterian who felt that church had grown too large. They made contact with one of the nation's foremost clergymen, the Reverend William Anderson Scott, once chaplain to Andrew Jackson at The Hermitage in Nashville, Tennessee, and at the time pastor of the First Presbyterian Church of New Orleans. A meeting in May convinced all present that the choice was a good one, and within two months Calvary Presbyterian Church began its congregational life in the Unitarian Church building. Their own first church edifice—"an impressive Roman Corinthian building"—was soon built on Bush Street between Montgomery and Sansome.

Scott brought a cultured urbanity to the pulpit and the lecture platform. A graduate of Princeton Theological Seminary, a world traveler, and a published biblical scholar, Scott was a man of principle and courage. He preached tolerance and pluralism and opposed the enforced reading of the Bible in the public schools. His outspoken opposition to the actions of the Second Committee of Vigilance resulted in his being hanged in effigy from a lamppost at Bush and Montgomery on October 5, 1856. Scott's offer to resign his pastorate was not accepted, and two years later he achieved national recognition when he was elected moderator of the Old School Presbyterian Assembly, the highest honor his church could bestow. In 1861, however, he disregarded the mandate of the Presbytery of California to "preach . . . the awful crime of rebellion" by including Jefferson Davis, president of the Confederacy, in his public prayers. A week later he was hanged in effigy again—this time outside his church. Nervous elders spirited their pastor and his wife out a back door and into a waiting carriage. A few days later the Scotts were on a steamer bound for Panama, and Calvary was without a minister.

An eloquent and forceful Philadelphia preacher, Dr. Charles Wadsworth, came with his wife and young son to be Calvary's next pastor, apparently breaking the heart of the poetess Emily Dickinson. One of her biographers, Richard Chase, wrote that she "worshipped Calvinist Wadsworth above all men," dressed herself only in white after his departure, and sometimes referred to herself in her poems as the Empress of Calvary. Wadsworth's hold on San Franciscan audiences proved to be equally strong, and the church began looking for room to expand. For thirty-five thousand dollars they bought a fifty-vara lot "farther out," at the corner of Powell and Geary. Even after selling part of the property they were able to erect what the press described as "one of the largest and most elegant structures for the worship of God on the Pacific coast." Shortly after the May 16, 1869, dedication, Wadsworth decided to return to the East and submitted his resignation.

Soon the Reverend John Hemphill, a tall, black-bearded Irishman with a rich Celtic voice, arrived in San Francisco on a preaching mission from the Presbyterian church in his homeland. Offered the Calvary pulpit, he accepted; by April 1870, a weekly paper commented on the "fervor with which the services of the young pastor are received. . . . Many prayers are offered that . . . he may be the instrument in battling the powers of darkness, in advancing the cause of Christ on this coast."

After thirty years on Union Square, Calvary moved west again, this time to make way for construction of the St. Francis Hotel. Property was bought at the corner of Fillmore and Jackson streets. Both fireworks and hymns were featured at the laying of the cornerstone on July 4, 1901. By popular consent every brick and stone of the old building was marked and reused; even the pews were saved. The new-old church was dedicated on February 7, 1904.

Fortunate in being beyond the sweep of the great fire of 1906, Calvary became host to Old First Presbyterian and St. Luke's Episcopal churches, Temple Emanu-El, the Loring Club concerts, and (in the basement gymnasium) the Superior Court, while the city was rebuilding. Calvary has remained a vital force in the city of San Francisco throughout its long history. The church represents a large community of faith that includes a diversity of fellowship groups, and sponsors programs for singles, married couples, families, and seniors as well as youth guidance and tutorial activities. The church has three ministers and says of itself, "Together we try to discover the purpose of life in God's world and try to live in harmony with it."

Reconstruction of the former Union Square church was supervised by architect Charles McDougall. The main sanctuary was enlarged in 1928 to accommodate what was then one of the finest organs in the country, gift of Mr. and Mrs. John McGregor; the adjoining educational and social halls were extensively renovated at the same time. In the late fifties another addition provided a five-thousand volume library and the Kit Stewart Chapel. In the late 1970s an anonymous gift from a third-generation member, matched by congregational contributions, facilitated the razing and replacing of the antiquated social and educational annex. The new wing, designed by architects Robinson and Mills, provides a social hall, Sunday school, church offices, and a roof-top playground.

The main building shows Roman and Italian Renaissance influence in the rounded arches over the tall composite columns as well as in the roundels of the frieze beneath the strong pediment. Tall arched windows with tracery and colored glass impart a slight medieval look, but the overall Mannerist-Baroque effects of the design, with high narrow shapes grouped around a projecting center, suggest a public building such as a library or a bank as much as a church.

San Francisco Registered Landmark #103
(sanctuary)
National Register of Historic Places, May 3, 1978

The design of the present Calvary Presbyterian repeats faithfully parts of the original at a downtown site.

Presbyterian Church in Chinatown

925 Stockton Street, between Clay and Washington Streets
Founded November 6, 1853

This, the first Christian mission to the Chinese in North America, actually began on New Year's Day, 1853, when the Reverend William Speer, an ordained minister who was also a physician and a veteran of five years' prior service in China, began providing formal preaching services in English and Cantonese, classes in the English language, and free medical services to the Chinese population, who numbered about five hundred at that time. The Presbyterian Board of Foreign Missions had sent him in response to requests from the Reverend Albert Williams, pastor of the First Presbyterian Church, and the officers of the Synod of the Pacific. Within the year, Dr. Speer formally organized the Chinese Presbyterian Church with four members, all of them previously converted in China. (Similar missions to the Chinese were started in 1877 in Hawaii and in 1878 in New York City.) The church's first home, a two-story building at 800 Stockton Street, housed the chapel, several classrooms, Dr. Speer's study, and his family. Speer campaigned actively for better treatment of the Chinese. In 1855 he started a weekly bilingual newspaper, *The Oriental* or *Tung Gnat Sam,* which helped to allay prejudice between the races. This is thought to be the first Chinese language newspaper, since journalism was unknown in China at the time.

Under the subsequent leadership of the Reverend A. W. Loomis (1859–1866) a Sunday school and regular prayer meetings were established, followed by a publicly funded evening school—the first American public school to admit Chinese people. As the program expanded, an additional missionary was supplied. He was the Reverend A. W. Condit, who, having worked in Canton, knew the language and customs of the Cantonese. During his twenty-five years' ministry, he sent Chinese Christian *colporteurs* to visit groups of Chinese people all over the West—in towns, mining camps, ranches, and villages. Several of the church's early members became ordained ministers. The best known was the Reverend Ng Poon Chew, the first Chinese graduate of the San Francisco Theological Seminary, who founded the first Chinese daily newspaper in this country, *Chung Sai Yat Po*.

Mrs. Condit, meanwhile, was distressed at the number of Chinese women caught up in enforced prostitution. In 1874 she called together a group of women from various Presbyterian congregations to find ways of helping them. The church had no agency to handle such programs; out of the women's efforts grew both the Presbyterian Board of Occidental Missions and the community center later known as Cameron House. Donaldina Cameron came in 1895 planning to work in the mission for one year; she wound up staying for forty. During that time she and her staff rescued many young Chinese women from one form of slavery or another. She has been described by those who knew her as soft-spoken and ladylike but notably courageous in her resolve. At first the tongs opposed the mission, making her work dangerous, but she seemed impervious to such perils. Early in her life Donaldina Cameron adopted some young Chinese children. Later she came to be called

Lo Mo, originally a somewhat derogatory term for "mother" in the Chinese tongue. As time went on, *Lo Mo* (in San Francisco, at least) became a term of respect and endearment.

In 1882 Chinese Presbyterian Church bought the Gothic church on Stockton Street as it was vacated by First Presbyterian; they replaced it with the present Neoclassic building a few doors away after 1906. The church's evangelical emphasis produced a growing corps of missionaries who established Chinese churches throughout California and in China as well. David Ng became the first Chinese pastor of the local church, followed by Wilbert Tong, Harry Church, and Gordon Lam. In 1947 Cameron House and Chinese Presbyterian Church were officially combined, sharing facilities, resources, and staff.

The Donaldina Cameron House building at 920 Sacramento Street was designed in 1907 by Julia Morgan, first woman to graduate from the University of California in engineering (1904), first woman to receive a master's degree from L'École des Beaux Arts, and the first woman architect licensed to practice in California. She also designed William Randolph Hearst's retreats, Wyntoon in Shasta County and La Cuesta Encantada at San Simeon, as well as another Presbyterian-sponsored community center, the Potrero Hill Neighborhood House. Cameron House is a utilitarian, multiwindowed structure with an overhanging cornice, strongly and simply built of bricks recovered from the previous building on the same site. It is well adapted to the steep hillside; four stepped windows filled with colored glass echo its physical and spiritual upward movement. The four-square character of the structure suits both the mission and Donaldina Cameron.

San Francisco Registered Landmark #44
(Donaldina Cameron House)

Old St. Mary's Church

660 California Street, at Grant Avenue
Founded December 25, 1854

San Francisco's first cathedral was dedicated at the midnight mass on Christmas 1854. Twelve hundred eager worshipers filled the beautiful brick church to capacity, and another thousand were left standing in the streets outside—this in a town of from thirty-five to forty thousand people. The interior was lacking a few finishing touches—workmen had laid down their tools only a few hours before the service—but the music was splendid and the response of the people joyful. It must have been a proud moment for Archbishop Joseph Sadoc Alemany. San Francisco's new cathedral had the distinction of being the first in the entire world dedicated to the Immaculate Conception of the Virgin Mary after the solemn proclamation of that dogma only three weeks earlier in Rome.

The young prelate had first arrived in California four years earlier, shortly after his consecration in Rome as bishop of the newly created diocese of Monterey (until 1850, that city and port had remained mission territory under Mexico's diocesan administration despite the fact that the stars and stripes now flew over the thirty-first American state). After a survey of his overwhelming diocese—from the Mexican border to Oregon, and east to Colorado—Alemany determined that San Francisco should be his headquarters. In 1853, after being named archbishop of the San Francisco diocese, he began preparations for the new cathedral.

Money was no longer plentiful in the city by that year, as the gold mines were less productive and there was widespread unemployment. Nevertheless, contributions poured in from Catholics, Protestants, and Jews. All shared the prelate's hope for a proper religious edifice. Irish-born John Sullivan provided a lot. Sullivan had never left the city for the gold fields, but had earned his money as a teamster and by investing in real estate; he later became the founder and first president of the Hibernia Bank.

Within the next three years a grammar school, a high school, and an adult school were opened by the church. In 1884 Archbishop Alemany retired to his native Spain. A new St. Mary's Cathedral was built on Van Ness Avenue in 1891 under the leadership of Archbishop Patrick Riordan. By then the neighborhood around Old St. Mary's Church had deteriorated. Archbishop Riordan invited the Paulists to take over the church in 1894. New programs instituted by the Paulists succeeded in building up church membership. Although the church was gutted in the earthquake and fire of 1906, it was rebuilt. Enlarged in the 1920s to accommodate new social service programs, used as a servicemen's center during World War II, and rebuilt after being damaged by fire in 1966, the old church continues as a valuable asset to the city today.

One of St. Mary's most loyal and well-known parishioners was Jack Manion, who attended early morning mass at the church each working day and Sunday of his thirty-nine-year career in the San Francisco Police Department. Manion was in charge of the Chinatown Squad formed in 1921. He succeeded in stopping the killings that occurred during the tong wars and is credited with saving at least fifty Chinese girls from being sold into slavery. Over time he won the respect of most of the Chinese, including the Chinese Six Companies. The Chinese finally felt safe on their own streets. While on the Chinatown Squad, Manion used to visit the local schools and talk with students who were reported to be getting out of line. He had a positive influence on these children, and many of them later came as adults to visit him during his retirement years. On his retirement in 1946 he was honored by the Chinese as the "Guardian of Peace, Protector of Chinatown."

Old St. Mary's, located on the edge of the financial district and within Chinatown, is one of San Francisco's best-loved ecclesiastical landmarks. It is well used by people in the nearby office buildings and by the Chinese community. There is a popular noon mass, and the church is known for its tradition of excellent liturgical music, its library, lectures, and concert series. The sturdy brick and stone Gothic Revival building, with its big wide-balconied interior, was designed by the architects William Craine and Thomas England, who also designed Congregation Emanu-El's Broadway Street temple. The high ceiling is rib-vaulted and supported with grouped colonnette pillars; the windows are filled with pictorial stained glass. White marble is used lavishly on the high altar; the original organ, termed "first rate," was from the East Coast, as were some of the fittings and ironwork shipped around Cape Horn. Granite used in the foundation was quarried in China and brought here ten years before large numbers of Chinese immigrated to work on the railroad. The Madonna of the Immaculate Conception behind the altar is a copy of a work by Murillo. With elements of many countries, the building and its fittings reflect the diverse populations it has served over many years. The inscription on the four-faced clock tower—"Son, observe the time and fly from evil"—was meant to influence the young people of the early city.

John McLaren, the longtime superintendent of Golden Gate Park, landscaped the original courtyard between the rectory and the church. Mayor James Phelan, who later became a senator, gave the window of Saint Paul the Apostle and a fifty-thousand-dollar trust fund to support the work of the church where his parents had been married and where he was baptized in 1861. The use of excellent materials and workmanship throughout the building proved worthwhile when the church shell withstood the 1906 earthquake and fire.

As one pushes through the doors of the sanctuary with their beveled glass windows, the rush of city noises fades and one feels in a place of stillness, a shelter. At the entrance, the Chapels of Remembrance and Forgiveness glow with colored glass and mosaics. The interior has a chaste quality, cool and serene. Old St. Mary's is the tranquil grandmother of San Francisco's churches.

Stylistically, it is an excellent example of American Gothic Revival, favored in eastern ecclesiastical circles in the 1840s and 1850s. The main portal has a high, pointed stone arch with hood mold above, typical of Victorian Gothic. Paneled pier buttresses line the flanks of the clock tower. On the sides, more salient buttresses rise to crenellated parapets. Although the spire was never constructed, the building has the aspirant, vertical quality so typical of this style. A crisply contemporary four-story brick and stone parish house, on the site of the 1854 rectory, provides a pleasing transition to the high rises nearby.

San Francisco Registered Landmark #2
California Registered Landmark #810

St. Mary's prickly tower shows the sharp silhouette of the mid-nineteenth century Gothic Revival.

A rich pattern of lancet arches and panelled pier buttresses harmonizes with the exoticism of Chinatown at Old St. Mary's—now buffered by neutral high rise windows.

St. Ignatius Church

650 Parker Avenue, at Fulton Street
Founded July 15, 1855

From every approach to San Francisco the twin towers of St. Ignatius Church impel an upward look, whether rising out of a sea of fog or glistening in the sunshine of a perfect day. This magnificent church and the surrounding campus of the University of San Francisco herald the achievements of one hundred thirty-five years of Jesuit service to religion and education in California.

It was an urgent appeal from Father Antoine Langlois, pastor of St. Francis of Assisi Church, that brought the first two Italian Jesuits to San Francisco. Foreseeing the educational needs of the exploding San Francisco population, he contacted two Oregon missionaries, Father Michael Accolti and Father John Nobili, who arrived aboard the brig *Raymond* on December 8, 1849. Accolti's first impression of the city was vivid, if uncomplimentary. "We were able to set foot on the longed-for shores of what goes under the name of San Francisco," he wrote in his *Memorial of the Journey to California,* "but whether it should be called a madhouse or a Babylon, I am at a loss to determine—so great in those days was the disorder, the brawling, the open immorality, the reign of crime which, brazen faced, triumphed on a soil not yet brought under the sway of human laws." Accolti was soon recalled to become superior of the Jesuit missions in Oregon, but Nobili was assigned to the Santa Clara mission, where in 1851 he founded the College of Santa Clara. That same year, Bishop Alemany asked Nobili to assume responsibility for an abandoned college that had been started near Mission Dolores, but despite strenuous efforts that school had to be closed again in 1856.

Accolti, meanwhile, realizing that the Jesuits working in the eastern United States were hard-pressed to supply the schools and churches needed there, had gone to Rome in search of support. His efforts were successful; a decree of August 1, 1854, made the Turin, Italy, province of the order permanently responsible for the Jesuit missionary apostolate in Oregon and California. Several priests from Turin were ordered to go to California. Among them was Father Anthony Maraschi, who was assigned to San Francisco after the Archbishop of Baltimore received a letter from Alemany wishing for a "good college in San Francisco for the education of male youth." He arrived on November 1, 1854.

Maraschi was faced with a real challenge. While the city was beginning to emerge from the chaos engendered by the Gold Rush and attendant population explosion, the Catholic church was struggling to catch up. Mission Dolores, dilapidated but functioning, offered morning services in English, French, and Spanish, as did St. Francis of Assisi Church. St. Patrick's Church, then located on the future site of the Palace Hotel, ministered to the Irish constituency, and ground had been broken a year earlier at the corner of Dupont and California streets for a new cathedral. But twenty-three Protestant churches were already serving their people. For the first six months after his arrival, Maraschi served, at Alemany's request, as assistant pastor in two of the city's pioneer parishes.

By April of 1855, Alemany and Maraschi had agreed upon a suitable location for the new church and college. A lot was purchased from former U.S. Consul Thomas O. Larkin on Market Street, at the present-day site of The Emporium. That section of town was then called the Valley of Saint Anne and was beyond the confines of the central town. Nobili, assisting Archbishop Alemany in the dedicatory services on July 15, 1855, said, "Here let us build and wait, for someday this will be the center of a great city." Proclaimed among a collection of tents and shaky wood buildings, the statement was visionary, though prophetic. By October the first students of St. Ignatius Academy were attending classes in another small frame building behind the church, and a third two-room structure with a kitchen housed the Fathers.

By the early 1860s the location was becoming more accessible, as a new steam train ran along Market Street. In 1862, both the church and the academy were replaced by substantial brick structures which served them well for another fifteen years. During this time, the college achieved considerable fame by virtue of the presence of two outstanding professors. Father Joseph Bayma, a philosopher, scientist and mathematician of international reputation, served as president of the college from 1869 to 1873. Among his publications were a three-volume work on rational philosophy, a treatise on molecular physics, and a series of textbooks for the entire college course of mathematics. Perhaps even better known is Father Joseph Neri, whose early research and demonstrations in the field of electricity brought considerable fame to the school. He designed for the college a system of outdoor electrical lighting, which was unveiled on the evening of July 4, 1876, in connection with San Francisco's and the nation's Centennial Year observances—three years in advance of Thomas Edison's first commercially successful incandescent lamp. During August and September of that year, Neri's entire collection of apparatus for teaching and research in all the branches of physics was displayed at the Eleventh Industrial Fair sponsored by the San Francisco Mechanics Institute. Neri gave lectures and demonstrations, assisted by his students, and the exhibit was among the fair's most popular attractions.

A new and spacious St. Ignatius Church, which with the college occupied the entire block bounded by Grove, Franklin, and Hayes streets and Van Ness Avenue, was dedicated on February 1, 1880. Between three and four thousand persons crowded into the church (with as many more waiting outside) as Archbishop Alemany offered the Pontifical Mass and Bishop James A. Healy delivered the sermon. Many society weddings were held in this church, among them that of Frank Sullivan and Alice Phelan, whose brother James D. Phelan (an 1881 graduate of St. Ignatius College) went on to become mayor of San Francisco and then a California state senator. These facilities were destroyed in the earthquake of 1906, and temporary buildings at the corner of Hayes and Shrader streets served while the choice of a future site was under discussion.

John H. Pope, a civil engineer, proposed the concept of the present church, "with its towering outline in view from all parts of the city." And so it was that the fifth St. Ignatius Church came into being off the drawing board of the architect Charles J. Devlin and was dedicated on August 2, 1914. St. Ignatius Church is an elegant, classicizing English, French, and Italian design in a style sometimes referred to as "Jesuit Baroque." In the present instance, however, the inspiration is more from Alberti's San Francisco at Rimini, St. Paul's in London, and seventeenth- and eighteenth-century French sources than from the Gesù in Rome. The material is buff-colored brick with rich architectural details of classicist Renaissance form in cream and yellow terra cotta. The building has twin towers, a campanile, and a dome with lantern. There is a six thousand-pound bell, brought from the original church, which was purchased from a volunteer fire company that had ordered the bell from England but was then unable to pay for it. The twin-staged towers rise above tabernacle-like windows to a height of 312 feet, and the facade features large Corinthian columns above Ionic columns—both noticeably bowed. A statue of Saint Ignatius gestures between the two central columns of a temple-front motif on the upper center. The floors of the portico and vestibule are in colored marbles. Woods used in the building include mahogany and white cedar.

The interior, based on early Christian types, is majestic not only in size but in execution. The painted ceiling is deeply coffered, as is the extended half dome over the altar. Lofty Corinthian columns are repeated throughout the interior, with coffered arches above the side aisles to complement the coffered ceiling. The auditorium of the church seats seventeen hundred people, and another three hundred can be accommodated in the upper gallery over the organ and choir loft.

The main altar contains relics of Saint Ignatius, Saint Bobola (a Polish Jesuit who won Lithuania to the faith), and three North American martyrs. One was Jean de Brebeuf, called the Apostle of the Hurons. The altar murals were done by Tito Ridolfi, and the altar itself is made of white marble. Richly colored stained glass lights the clerestory, and throughout the church dramatic spotlighting aids the architectural effects. There are many portraits in the church. Each of the smaller shrines and confessionals that line the sides of the nave is topped by a small dome, an unusual feature of this church. Each shrine is lighted by a colored glass window at the apex of the dome. The church interior is painted gray-white and gold, and the coffered ceiling is picked out in blue and dark red. St. Ignatius is both stately and serene. The interior almost suggests a royal court and is admirably suited to music and the mass.

The lofty staged towers and high dome and campanile of St. Ignatius are a focal point for much of western San Francisco.

Suggesting a more elaborate form of an Early Christian basilica, the interior of St. Ignatius rises to a coffered ceiling and half dome.

Nôtre Dame des Victoires Church

566 Bush Street, between Grant Avenue and Stockton Street
Founded May 4, 1856

Frequently called simply the French Church, Nôtre Dame des Victoires has served as the focal point for French Catholicism in San Francisco ever since its founding. Like Old St. Mary's Church nearby, Nôtre Dame still occupies its original site, on a slope originally called Frenchmen's Hill because the French miners pitched their tents here as they came in from the camps for supplies and to sell their gold. By the mid-1850s French-speaking people could attend services in their own language at either St. Francis of Assisi Church or the then-new St. Mary's Cathedral, but in November of 1855 they petitioned for a church of their own. Abbot Dominique Blaive, at that time pastor to the French-speaking worshipers at the cathedral, was appointed to lead them. A member of the Diocese of Rouen in France, he had arrived in California early in 1854 and served for the first year as pastor of two parishes in Calaveras County.

Jubilant over the recent victory of the western European powers in the Crimean War, they named the new church Nôtre Dame des Victoires. A former Baptist church, purchased in April and adapted to the Catholic liturgy, was solemnly blessed by Archbishop Alemany on May 4, 1856. Faced with a fifteen-thousand-dollar debt, the new congregation organized subscriptions and charity festivals, but the results were discouraging. To avoid the expense of a separate dwelling, Blaive chose to live in the damp church basement; he contracted acute rheumatism which is thought to have contributed to his early death in 1862.

The second pastor, Abbot Jean Molinier, organized more festivals, appealed to the French government and the Society for the Propagation of the Faith, and gathered resources for his church in other ways. Though he is said to have died of exhaustion in 1867, he left the church debt-free, with a newly purchased organ and a treasury containing two thousand dollars.

In 1885 Archbishop Riordan asked the Marist fathers to take charge of the French parish. This order, founded in 1816 by Father Jean-Claude Colin, had already established six colleges and twenty parishes when called to Nôtre Dame. The French government gave 25,000 francs toward the erection of the school, which was built under the direction of a Breton priest, Father H. Gerard. Instruction in the French language has been offered from kindergarten through high school since its beginnings.

After the devastation of 1906, the congregation worshiped first at the Lake Street facilities of the Little Sisters of the Poor (recently demolished), and then in the reconstructed basement of the church during rebuilding. The congregation is no longer exclusively French, and in the ecumenical spirit of the times, a sister from Nôtre Dame does volunteer work at Presbyterian-sponsored Cameron House nearby. Many of the ten thousand French residents of the Bay Area make arrangements with their parish priests to observe such special occasions as baptisms, weddings, and funerals at the church of Nôtre Dame des Victoires. In 1956 the French government presented the church with a plaque commemorating the centennial of its founding.

The architect for the present building, finished in 1908, was Louis Brouchoud. Some say the church was modeled after Nôtre Dame de Fourvièr in Lyons, France, which was begun in 1870; other French sources have also been noted. Though sometimes mistakenly referred to as Byzantine, the exterior is actually Romanesque with Baroque massing. Built of gold colored brick and terra cotta, it has twin octagonal towers with open belvederes. Between the towers a rounded area with high-arched, many-colored glass windows projects like a second apse onto Bush Street. The long, barrel-vaulted interior has richly colored imitation marble (*scagliola*) columns with Romanesque-style capitals and a ribbed ceiling. The windows, with French legends, are memorials to past members of the congregation. The main back altar has an unusual combination of copper and brass in the canopy and torchères. The organ loft, at the rear of the church, still contains the fine old organ, one of the few ever built in San Francisco.

San Francisco Registered Landmark #173

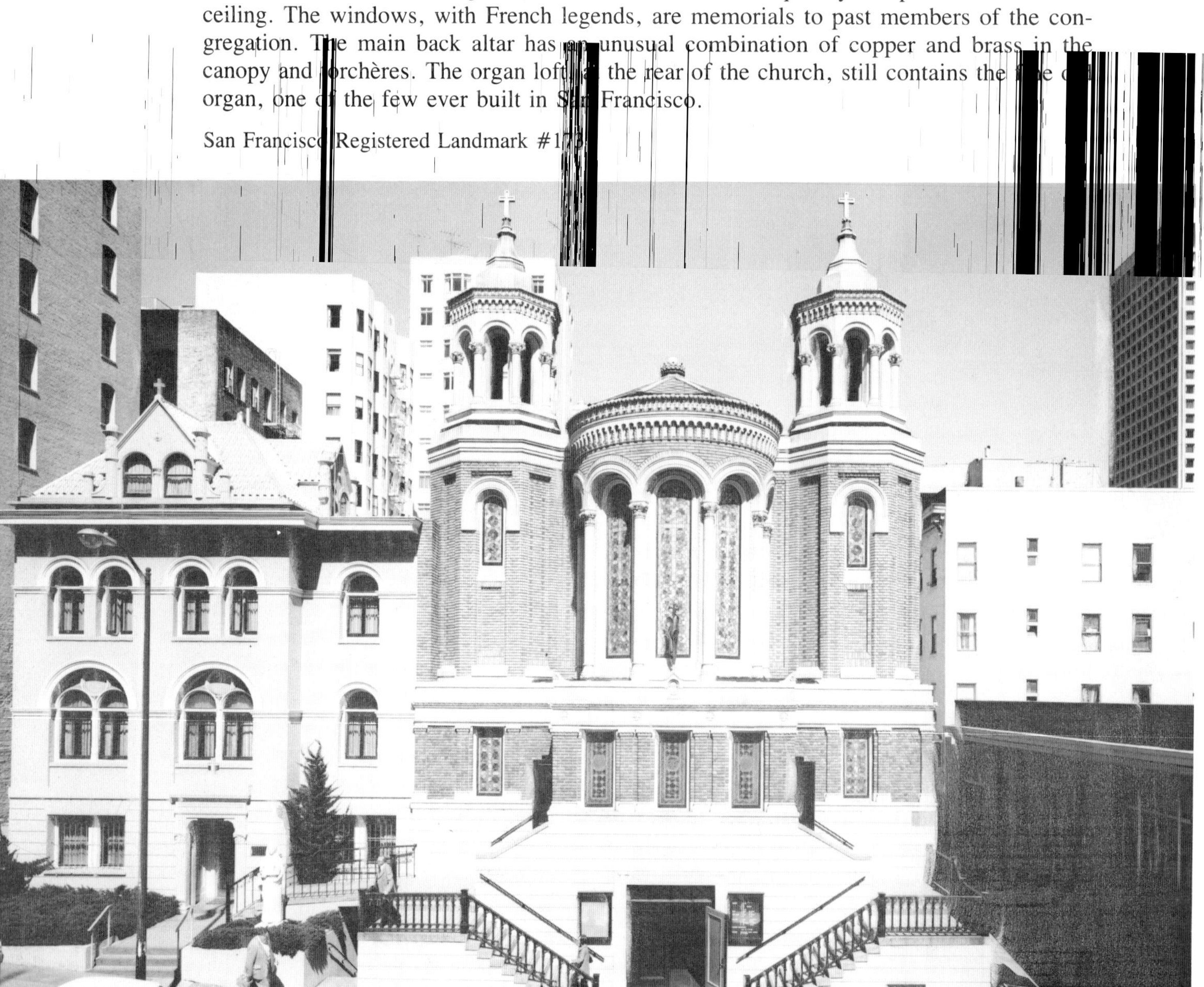

Adapted from Romanesque sources, but with Baroque focus, Nôtre Dame des Victoires serves a largely French congregation.

The altar and tabernacle of Nôtre Dame des Victoires are richly resplendent with marble and stained glass.

San Francisco Monthly Meeting of Friends

2160 Lake Street
First services in July, 1859

Friends, or Quakers, worship silently, believing that the light of God's presence confronts and instructs each one directly without the intervention of ordained clergy. Worshipers may speak of their revelations; the assembled group listens but does not comment. There had been a few American Friends among the early gold-seekers, but most of them, uncomfortable in the boisterous city, either returned to their former homes or settled in quieter parts of California.

The earliest Quaker meetings in San Francisco were called by two well-known British Friends on a mission to America in July 1859. Announcements in the newspapers attracted a diverse group that increased in size from twenty to one hundred fifty within a month. Sarah Lindsay's diary (quoted in David C. LeShane's *Quakers in California*) describes the third meeting, held at the Town Hall on the last day of the month: "The assembled multitude included many who might truly be called the off-scourings of the earth—Chinese, Indians, Africans, Mexicans, and I suppose, other nations, suffering the penalties of the law; and the clanking chains with which some were loaded impressed my mind with mingled feelings." The Lindsays later moved to San Jose, where California's first Society of Friends was established in 1861 and incorporated as the College Park Meeting House in 1889.

In San Francisco, Friends held weekly services in various courtrooms of the city hall from the early 1860s until 1901, when they established a headquarters at 570 Harrison Street. By 1905 they were operating a day and night mission at 928 Harrison. But it was not until 1940 that the San Francisco Monthly Meeting was formally established. Peter Gilbrandsen, a Danish member of the Berkeley Friends Meeting, and Josephine Duveneck of San Francisco were instrumental in convening a group at the Presidio Open Air School on Washington Street.

Quakers have a testimony against all wars, but customarily find ways of alleviating the suffering resulting directly or indirectly from war. Early in 1942, as the Japanese-American community was being evacuated from the Pacific Coast, the Friends assumed responsibility for maintaining the headquarters of the Japanese Young Women's Christian Association at 1830 Baker Street until the regular tenants could return. Shortly before the war's end Milton Eisenhower, Associate Director of the Office of War Information, asked the Quaker-related American Friends Service Committee to help with the relocation of Japanese-American college students. The Committee immediately budgeted $25,000 for this effort. On July 4, 1945, John R. Bodine of the San Francisco office received an order from Eisenhower authorizing the immediate release from the Tule Lake relocation center of a young nisei, an honor graduate of the University of California who had been admitted to the medical school at Washington University in St. Louis provided he could matriculate on July 6. No doubt speed laws were broken as Bodine drove the 350 miles north to the camp. There he was told that since the commanding officer was on holiday, nothing could be done. But Bodine's Quaker resolve must have prevailed, for soon he was driving a bewildered young man to Klamath Falls. The train was late, and the first Japanese-American to be released from any relocation center barely made the deadline to St. Louis.

During the 1950s members of the San Francisco Monthly Meeting assisted with the establishment of the Marin Meeting, and also participated in writing "Faith and Practice," the guide to religious discipline used by the Pacific Yearly Meeting of Friends. The present Friends Center, a Georgian residence remodeled to accommodate the Monthly Meeting, a library, and the programs of the American Friends Service Committee and the Friends Committee on Legislation, was dedicated on January 3, 1960.

Friends believe in the power of love to bring about change through nonviolent means. In order to pursue their goals more effectively, members attend adult religious education classes during the week in addition to worship meetings on First Day (Sunday). Friends actively work on behalf of such causes as inner-city youth, Native Americans, abolishment of capital punishment, ethical political concerns, and good legislation, and have a history of willingness to be imprisoned for their convictions.

Church of the Advent of Christ the King

261 Fell Street, between Franklin and Gough Streets
Founded March 7, 1858

By 1858 the districts of Rincon Hill and South Park had become fashionable, and the residents included many members of Trinity Episcopal Church. Feeling that the long walk across town to their church was a burden, they informally organized a new parish on February 25, seeking and receiving Bishop Kip's canonical consent the following day. The congregation of the nearby Second Presbyterian Church offered the use of their facilities, and the following Sunday the bishop officiated at the first service, baptizing one adult and seven infants. Various local rectors conducted services until the Reverend F. Marion McAllister arrived from Georgia in September. By 1859 his diocesan report showed 101 communicants, 37 Sunday school teachers, 323 pupils, 39 baptisms, and 25 confirmations.

In 1861 the congregation consecrated a new brick church on Howard Street opposite the present New Montgomery Street. In 1878 the building was enlarged to accommodate the thriving congregation, and the second rector, Father Lathrop, resigned because of ill health. Bishop Kip assumed the responsibilities of rector, assisted by an outstanding priest who devoted most of his time to social welfare projects. With the help of young lay readers he provided weekly services at the County Jail, the Seamen's Home, the Old People's Home, and other institutions.

By the time a new rector arrived from Colorado in 1885, the city offered public transportation—horse cars—and residents were moving farther out as business houses became established in the Rincon Hill area. The original property was sold and an expensive red brick church built on Eleventh Street just off Market. But this was a sparsely settled area, and the few homeowners appeared indifferent to religious efforts. Several rectors tried to increase the membership and reduce the building debt, but without success. By 1899, it seemed that the only solution was to sell the church and satisfy the creditors. Suddenly the Reverend Herbert Parrish, at that time rector of St. Mary the Virgin, offered to try revitalizing the church "if given a free hand in regard to finance and conduct of worship." Almost overnight The Advent became an Anglo-Catholic Episcopal parish. Father Parrish took up living in the church basement, adjusted expenses to meet the current income, and began to pay off the debt. Membership increased as "Catholic-minded people," attracted by the high church liturgy, joined the congregation, and by 1906 the debt had been reduced to four thousand dollars.

When the raging fires of 1906 threatened the church, members quickly packed up ceremonial robes and appurtenances and took them to what seemed a safe place. Soon that, too, was enveloped in flames, and everything was lost. Father Charles N. Lathrop, the rector, was the first of many clergymen to care for the injured and dying who had been taken to the Mechanics' Pavilion. A layman's ingenuity enabled The Advent to become the first of the burned-out churches to reopen in its own building. He contacted a Seattle firm that made portable wooden structures and convinced them to redirect a building that was already enroute to South America. The congregation celebrated communion using a beautiful silver chalice saved by the parishioners of the Russian Orthodox Cathedral of the Holy Trinity and presented to them by Bishop Tikhon, a close friend of their priest. That chalice is among the church's treasured possessions today.

With its allotment of relief money the vestry bought a new lot on Fell Street and moved the portable building to where it now stands as the parish house. The name of the congregation was changed to The Church of the Advent of Christ the King in 1920. Although the church had a series of short-term rectors during the 1940s and a rotation of retired priests and chaplains in the 1950s, services have been held continuously. This is an inner city parish, consisting mostly of single adults and childless couples, but members remain intensely loyal, often returning for services after moving as far as a hundred miles away.

The Church of the Advent, built in 1946, is one of San Francisco's garden churches. An elegant wrought iron gate in black and gold leads past a circular fountain in the quiet, green-lawned court to the rose garden. The exterior and interior of the small church suggest Mission Dolores—a Mission-style facade with a long, narrow, rectangular interior. The facade has double paired composite half-columns with gilded capitals below and one pair above. The roofline rises in a gentle Baroque curve of emphasis. Windows of gold-colored glass cast a warm light throughout the simple interior, with its dark wood ceiling and elegant altar. The simplicity in no way detracts from the feeling of sacred space one has on entering the sanctuary.

A chalice and paten are at the heart of all Christian ritual, as in the Church of the Advent of Christ the King. This silver chalice was given by the Russian Orthodox cathedral of the Holy Trinity to the Church of the Advent of Christ the King to replace ceremonial appurtenances destroyed in the fire of 1906.

A simple altar, framed in a stepped floriate molding, suggests the overall serenity of plain effects in Church of the Advent.

Seventh Day Adventist Central Church

2889 California Street, at Broderick Street
First services in 1859

Adherents of the Seventh-Day Adventist teachings were active in San Francisco even before the denomination was formally established. The movement started in New England in the late 1830s as members of several Protestant denominations began interpreting the Book of Revelations in new ways. Various groups of converts formed an informal association in 1844 and formally established the denomination in 1863. Seventh Day Adventists observe the Sabbath, or seventh day of the week, and attach great importance to the second advent of Jesus, which is believed to be imminent.

The western history of the Adventists started in 1859, with the arrival in San Francisco of Merritt G. Kellogg, the elder brother of Dr. J. H. Kellogg of Battle Creek Sanitarium in Michigan, a man famed for developing special breakfast foods. Merritt Kellogg obtained a room in the courthouse where he lectured once a week for a few months, then he rented a hall and gave three lectures a week. Shortly after that fourteen persons organized a temporary congregation which lasted two years. After a hiatus during the Civil War, the congregation resumed meeting and asked the church's General Conference to send a pastor. This was in 1865, but no one wanted to undertake the far western assignment. The congregation tried again in 1867, and finally the next year Kellogg sold his home to finance a trip to the next general conference in Battle Creek. Although the five-year-old denomination still had no money for a mission to California, there were two volunteers. One was named Bordeau and the other was J. N. Loughborough. Nothing further is known of Bordeau, but Loughborough officially founded a congregation in December of 1871. Loughborough and a second elder, M. E. Cornell, conducted services at the Excelsior Hall on Mission Street for several years.

Traditionally the Seventh Day Adventists do not build impressive houses of worship, but concentrate their considerable energies on working toward the spiritual and physical betterment of their fellow human beings. In 1875, under the leadership of Elder E. C. Israel, Central Church dedicated a small edifice at the corner of Laguna and McAllister streets. In 1923 they bought the present church, built by the California Street Methodist Episcopal congregation in 1893. This building survived the events of 1906 only to have its steeple topple in the less-famed earthquake of 1957. The handcarved walnut lectern from their original church now stands in the narthex, holding a guest book for visitors to sign. The walls of this Romanesque Revival church are of red Arizona sandstone below and painted brick above. Much of the sandstone, including the cornerstone inscription, has been partially eroded. The main west tower is squared; the east one is rounded. Under a gable motif with circular carved medallions are two entrance arches. A foliated capital above a plain stone central column leads the eye back to reveal handsomely wrought iron and wood doors. The cross vaulted ceiling of wood is one of few in the city. Pews were especially built to conform to the clover shape of the interior, with its pulpit at the end of the stem. The church has a special glass-enclosed mothers' room, making it easier for mothers with young children to attend services.

St. Boniface Church

133 Golden Gate Avenue, between Jones and Leavenworth Streets
Founded April 15, 1860

St. Boniface, the seventh Roman Catholic Church to be founded in San Francisco, has a citywide parish for Catholics of German birth or descent. The first pastor was Father Sebastian Wolf, a Benedictine monk sent from Germany. Various priests had been offering religious services in the German language since 1852, but it was not until 1856 that the new parish was authorized. On April 15, 1860, Archbishop Alemany blessed the new church, a reconstructed iron building bought from a jeweler for $1,530 and moved to a lot on Sutter Street between Kearny and Montgomery where the Bank of America's French-American branch now stands. Within a week the congregation celebrated its first marriage and first baptism and enrolled eight pupils in a parochial school.

Eight years later, in October of 1868, San Francisco was shaken by a severe earth tremor, the worst damage occurring in the vicinity of St. Boniface. Immediately St. Ignatius Church offered the use of their old frame church, the Sodality Chapel, on Market Street (present site of The Emporium) as the Jesuits had by this time moved into their new, larger church across the street. The offer was accepted gratefully and services held there until late February 3 1870, when the property was sold.

After selling their Sutter Street property to the Mercantile Library Association, St. Boniface had bought the present site on Tyler Street (now Golden Gate Avenue). But their new church—a frame structure with school, priests' residence, and meeting rooms on the ground level—was not yet finished. The congregation then received a remarkable invitation to share the facilities of Nôtre Dame des Victoires, in spite of the fact that the mother countries of the two congregations were at war. Mrs. Herman Burhans, a member of St. Boniface, had been governess to Prince Eugène Louis, son of Napoleon III, for many years in Paris. She came from a German family in Aix-la-Chapelle, where the French and the Germans had intermingled for years. In San Francisco she and her husband had close friends among the extensive French community, hence the generous invitation that overrode national loyalties and disputes.

On February 10, 1887, at the invitation of Archbishop Patrick Riordan, the Franciscans took over the administration of the parish. Ten days later they celebrated their first masses in St. Boniface Church, which was packed to the doors with fervent worshipers. St. Joseph's Hospital was opened in 1889 under the direction of the Franciscan Sisters of the Order of the Sacred Heart. Five years later a second church, St. Anthony's, was established to serve another developing area of the parish.

As the congregation continued to grow, a larger plant was needed. A splendid new church, friary, and school were dedicated on June 22, 1902, by Archbishop Riordan, only to be destroyed, like so many others, on that April morning in 1906. Franciscan Brother Adrian Wewer, assisted by Brother Ildephonse Lethert, was the architect responsible for both the original structures and the rebuilt church complex, which was undertaken immediately. The new St. Boniface Church, built more substantially than before but similar in design, retained the original cornerstone from 1900. It was dedicated on the Feast of All Saints, 1908, by Archbishop Riordan, with a Pontifical High Mass celebrated by Bishop Silva of Portugal. A local news story described the church as "the most beautiful in San

Francisco," while an editorial in the *San Francisco Star* observed that "The Fathers could easily have made one and one-half million by selling what had now become exceedingly valuable property had they not felt in the heart, instead of love of riches, 'that sweet desire for souls that is the very essence of the true brotherhood of man.'" That observation applies even more strongly today, not only to St. Boniface but to several historic churches located in the downtown area.

To the public St. Boniface is probably best known for its "Miracle of Jones Street," or St. Anthony's Dining Room, founded in 1950 on the Feast Day of Saint Francis, who protects the destitute. The kitchen, which feeds up to a thousand needy people a day, is considered a good economic indicator: when times get harder, the lines get longer. Thanksgiving and Christmas dinners, when the guests may number as many as three thousand, have become traditional San Francisco events when citizens of many ranks and professions, ministers of every faith, the young and the middle-aged don caps and aprons to carve turkeys or pour the coffee. The dining room was founded by Father Alfred Boeddeker of the Order of Friars Minor, who became pastor of St. Boniface in 1949. To supply the kitchen, he established a farm in the countryside near Petaluma. The best product of the farm, he says, is men. More than six thousand have been restored there. "We offer them work and a home. We have no psychiatrists or social workers. There is just a chance for men to think it out, sweat it out, talk it out, and learn a trade."

Other charities closely allied to the church include an employment service and medical clinic for the poor, a thrift shop, and a residence for elderly women with meager incomes. Many refugees from Southeast Asia have settled in the neighborhood, and the church is constantly developing new programs to meet their needs. Describing it as primarily an "action church," Boeddeker acknowledges that the complex charity functions performed by St. Boniface are built on public support—ecumenical public support. And in spite of what he sees every day, he says, "I don't despair for the human race. Deep down there is a fundamental goodness."

The St. Boniface building is a German Romanesque design. The double-doored entrance along the side of the nave leads to a richly ornamented church interior. Like its sources in Europe, this type of church has a monastic origin; its elevation features a triple-towered, corbeled center and helmet domes. A unique feature of this church is the rib-vaulted ceiling and lofty apse covered with murals hand painted in meticulous and loving detail by Father Josaphat Kraus. The columns that support the ceiling are a tan- and cream-colored scagliola. The high, arched windows are filled with colored glass; a large organ dominates the rear organ loft. Fine carved wood pews line the interior; they are often occupied by the "down and out," quietly meditating or resting.

San Francisco Registered Landmark #172

Reminiscent of German Romanesque churches, St. Boniface uses corbel tables to rim its various parts.

St. Joseph's Church

1415 Howard Street, at Tenth Street
Founded July 1861

Motorists driving on the crosstown freeway are sometimes startled by sunlight deflected from the twin golden cupolas atop the towers of St. Joseph's Church. This stately church with its spacious garden is the third edifice on the original property—a sandlot next to an abandoned waterworks—that was donated by an early philanthropist, Horace Hawes, as the site of the future cathedral of the San Francisco Archdiocese. That civic-minded citizen later received a medal from Pope Pius IX for his gift, but as it happened, the second St. Mary's Cathedral was ultimately located farther north, on Van Ness Avenue at O'Farrell.

Archbishop Alemany established the parish of St. Joseph to serve the people in the district south of Market Street. After having a meeting early in the month, they sponsored a concert in Platt's Hall on July 18, 1861, to start the building fund. Father Hugh Gallagher, their new pastor, had been the first to respond in 1852 when Alemany had appealed to the Plenary Council of Baltimore for clergymen willing to serve in the California mission field. He took a year's leave (which extended to a lifetime) from his position as rector of a seminary in Pennsylvania, arriving in San Francisco in 1853. Gallagher's first assignment was as assistant pastor to the English-speaking Catholics of the city. In the fall of 1854 he was sent to Rome to bring back the Archbishop's pallium and, while in Europe, to solicit both financial support and additional clergy to serve the rapidly growing California population. He was received in audience by Emperor Franz Joseph in Vienna, who sanctioned his request for German-speaking priests by sending two Austrian fathers to San Francisco. After returning from Europe, Gallagher established new churches in Humboldt and Siskiyou counties, California, as well as Carson City and Virginia City, Nevada.

Under his leadership, St. Joseph's soon became the most populous and prosperous parish in San Francisco. A larger church was built in 1865; two years later it was necessary to add two large galleries and extend the transepts to accommodate the crowds. There were almost no schools in the area south of Market at that time; to meet this need Father Gallagher established schools for both girls and boys. Lay teachers administered the schools from 1867 to 1871, when the Sisters of the Holy Names arrived.

Father Patrick Scanlon, second pastor of St. Joseph's, was also committed to the cause of education. He called the Brothers of Mary to take charge of the boys' school; soon its graduates, known as the "South of Market Boys," began to assume leadership positions in all phases of city life—political, business, educational, and religious. By the time of his death in 1904 the schools attached to St. Joseph's had an enrollment of eleven hundred pupils.

Under the leadership of its third pastor, Father Patrick E. Mulligan, St. Joseph's reached its highest membership, three thousand families (a total of fifteen thousand members), mostly Irish—the largest parish west of the Mississippi. Mulligan immediately started construction of a new and larger school, with a convent above. But it was never to be occupied, for the raging fires of April 1906 left St. Joseph's parish, like so much of the city, in piles of charred debris. Church, parochial residence, brothers' home, convent, and schools all had to be rebuilt. The advent of the automobile was changing the patterns of city life, influencing most of the members to resettle in other parishes. But the loyalty of descendants of old families and the income from early investments made it possible for the church to rise again. The cornerstone of the present church was laid in 1913.

Father James McGee came to St. Joseph's in the mid-twentieth century after serving thirty years as police chaplain. An associate described his coolness under fire: "One time he gave an officer last rites when the man was lying on the street and people were shooting all around him. It didn't faze Father McGee one bit!" McGee enjoyed a close spiritual relationship with his largely Mexican congregation, saying "You're with 'em from when they're born until they die. You baptize 'em; you marry 'em; you bury 'em." One of his highly visible contributions is the Lourdes shrine in the Howard Street garden. Asked how he happened to have it built, he replied simply, "I thought it would give them comfort."

Toward the end of McGee's pastorate the ethnic makeup of the parish changed again. Today the congregation is ninety percent Filipino, the largest Filipino church in the United States. On April 22, 1979, one thousand parishioners celebrated the dedication of a replica of the Miraculous Image of Santo Niño de Cebú in St. Joseph's. The original image is believed to have been brought by Magellan to Cebú, Philippines, in 1521. A marble shrine was erected to hold the image in 1980, and in August of 1981 the church received the Apostolic Blessing from Pope John Paul II for the Fiesta of the Santo Niño de Cebú planned for the following January.

Among the many religious and civic projects initiated by the pastors of St. Joseph's Church are the Young Men's Institute and St. Mary's Hospital. The official diocesan publication, *The Monitor,* started by Father Gallagher, was published continuously until 1984. The presence of a large woodland park within the city can also be traced, in part, to the efforts of St. Joseph's first pastor. Working with both city and state officials, he helped to secure passage of the legislation necessary to acquire the land on which Golden Gate Park was built.

The present building, designed by architect John J. Foley, has an early steel skeleton. The style is Romanesque, with corbel tables along the roof line and Baroque massing, somewhat like Nôtre Dame des Victoires. Twin staged towers are topped with gold cupolas and crosses, and rose windows grace the facade, towers, and transepts. In the green-lawned garden next to the church is the grotto modeled after the famous grotto at Lourdes in France, making St. Joseph's another of San Francisco's garden churches.

A triple portal leads to the interior, which contains six marble altars. St. Joseph's was the sixth church in the world to have the altar table facing the congregation, bringing the priest closer to the people, after the Second Vatican Council made such an arrangement permissible. The chastely columned nave, with barrel vault above and a profusion of consoles, leads to a high, coffered-ceiling apse. The stained glass windows, German-made in muted yet colorful tones, tell the life of St. Joseph.

San Francisco Registered Landmark #120
National Register of Historic Places, January 15, 1982

The sober classicism of columns and pilasters in St. Joseph's interior forms a dignified setting for the Gothic stained glass windows.

A rocky grotto in the garden of St. Joseph's recalls the Virgin's shrine at Lourdes.

St. Brigid's Church

1615 Broadway, at Van Ness Avenue
Founded September 10, 1863

Archbishop Alemany was a man of vision. By 1863 there were seven Roman Catholic churches ministering to the already settled neighborhoods of the city. Now, looking to the future, he declared a new parish bounded by Larkin and Bush streets (later changed to Jones and California), San Francisco Bay, and the Pacific Ocean. The area was then an immense expanse of sandy hills sparsely covered with brush and scrub oak. A government road meandered from the Presidio to Portsmouth Square. There was a Jewish cemetery at the corner of Gough and Vallejo and a cluster of slaughterhouses at the foot of Buchanan. Not more than five or six houses had been built. The Dominicans were put in charge of the new parish. Because it was expected to serve a mostly Irish congregation, the church was given the name of a saint of Eire.

The first pastor was Father James Henry Aerden, from the province of St. Rose in Belgium. He designed the first church, a simple wood building on top of a sandy knoll that rose fifteen feet above the southwest corner of Van Ness and Broadway. The archbishop dedicated the new church on February 14, 1864. Under successive pastors the church was enlarged and a parish house added. In 1875 the Dominicans were assigned to a new parish, St. Dominic's, on Pine Street. St. Brigid's, by then free of debt, was transferred to Father Timothy Callaghan of the diocesan clergy.

By the 1880s the area was well developed, with graded streets and many new houses. St. Brigid's had become the center of a busy city parish. In 1888 a school was opened under the direction of the Sisters of the Charity of the Blessed Virgin Mary (an Irish order founded in Dublin in 1831). Opulent Victorian residences were rising alongside the broad boulevard, Van Ness Avenue, and the congregation began to feel the need for a larger church.

In 1889 Father John E. Cottle was appointed pastor of St. Brigid's, a post he was to hold for thirty-seven years. He immediately began planning the new edifice. The crypt was finished and opened for services in June of 1897. In 1900 the then Archbishop Patrick Riordan dedicated the imposing new superstructure built of granite blocks that had served as curbstones in pioneer days. Six years later, on the dreadful morning of April 18, 1906, the former curbstones were once more in the street; within days, two-thirds of the parish was in ashes. However, the church was rebuilt and reopened for services in December of the same year, with "no scar remaining to remind the people of its wounding." In the years that followed, the old wood school and convent were replaced.

The building is simplified and modernized Romanesque, with richly carved symbolic details around and above the arched doorways. The complex decorations of the double-paneled central entryway and tympanum are in terra cotta rather than granite. The work of the Gladding McBean Company, they show the high quality of workmanship in terra cotta common in the city at the time the church was built.

The stained glass windows were made by the Harry Clarke Studios of Dublin. There are three rose windows. The major one, over the main entrance, has sixteen cusps with insert panels of stained glass. Each transept of the church has a smaller rose window. St.

Brigid's was enlarged and renovated in 1947. Two new sacristies, a new west wall, lighting, and decorating were added to the church. The sanctuary carpets of many colors were handwoven by the Dun Emir Guild of Donegal, Ireland. Fine gilded-work ornaments the interior. In the 1950s the tall, squared corner tower with its upper corbel table was crowned with a metal pyramidal spire and gilded cross. The architect of the basic structure was H. A. Minton.

A portion of the main portal at St. Brigid's reveals Celtic and stylized Romanesque details with a myriad of symbolic motifs.

A mixture of medieval ideas and modern materials sparks the richly repeated arched bands of ornament at St. Brigid's.

Holy Trinity Orthodox Cathedral

1520 Green Street, at Van Ness Avenue
Founded on Easter, 1864

Eight Russian missionaries settled on Kodiak Island in 1794, thereby establishing the ecclesiastical jurisdiction of the Patriarchate of Moscow over future Eastern Orthodox churches in North America. By 1809 Russians were settling in the Bodega Bay area, where they built Fort Ross with its modest church (now several times restored). Although the Russian government sold Fort Ross to Captain John Sutter in 1841, many Russians remained in California. During the Gold Rush, Russian traders brought Alaskan glacial ice down to sell in San Francisco. Many of the gold mining companies were owned and operated by Slavonians (those from the area of present day Yugoslavia).

Followers of the Eastern Orthodox faith who settled in San Francisco had no priests to serve them at first. In 1857 they established the Slavonian Illyrian Benevolence Society to help one another in tending the sick, sustaining the aged, and burying the dead. The first Orthodox service in California after the closing of Fort Ross took place in San Francisco in 1859, when a priest came ashore from a Russian vessel anchored in the bay to baptize several Russian and Serbian children. Religious services were provided intermittently by Russian naval chaplains for another five years.

The Russian-Greek-Slavonian Church and Philanthropic Society, the first permanent Orthodox parish in California, was formed on Easter night, 1864. Admiral Popov, whose fleet of six Russian vessels had arrived in San Francisco after visiting Japan, invited a group of Orthodox faithful to a service at the home of the acting Greek consul, George Fischer (actually a Serb who had anglicized his name). The services were conducted by Archpriest Cyril, a chaplain from Popov's fleet. The sixteen founding members of the new parish included Serbs, Russians, and Greeks. Furnishings for the church were supplied from one of the Russian Naval Ministry's field chapels. The church was formally registered at the San Francisco City Hall in 1867, with several additional members, including a Syrian. Martin Klinkovstrem, the Russian consul, was the first president. In response to a request from the San Francisco community, the Holy Synod of the Church of Russia appointed Father Nicholas Kovrygin dean of the new parish, underwriting his salary for the first two years, and also sending the money to build a new church. This House of Prayer of the Orthodox Church was erected at 504 Greenwich Street, and services were offered in Old Slavonic, Serbian, and Greek.

On June 10, 1870, San Francisco became the cathedral city of the newly established episcopal see of the Orthodox church in the U.S.A. Archimandrite John Mitropolsky, former Inspector of the Moscow Theological Seminary, was the first bishop. The tall, bearded figure of Father Fedor Pashkovsky, first dean of the cathedral, became a familiar sight not only in San Francisco, but nationally. In later years he was named Metropolitan Theophilus of the United States and Canada. Although he maintained a home in Long Island, he returned each winter to his beloved city by the Golden Gate.

At a time when much of the city's population was moving to the south and the west, the Orthodox community settled in the north, overlooking the bay, on the slopes of what soon came to be called Russian Hill. The cathedral was moved to 915 Jackson Street in 1872 and to Pierce Street in 1874. Between 1876 and 1881 the diocese was administered from St. Petersburg. With the arrival of Bishop Nestor in 1881, the church, offices, archives, and school were moved to a remodeled house at 1715 Powell Street near Columbus Avenue, the present location of the Pagoda Palace Theater. During these years the cathedral was consecrated to various saints—Saint Alexander Nevsky, Saint Nicholas, Saint Basil the Great—before receiving its present name, the Holy Trinity Orthodox Cathedral, on November 16, 1897.

Not all the clergy were Russian. In 1892 Sebastian Dabovich was ordained as the first American-born Orthodox priest. Father Sebastian had been among the Serbian infants baptized by a Russian chaplain in 1863. While serving as missionary priest to California he founded the state's second Orthodox congregation, St. Sava Serbian Church, in Jackson, Amador County, in 1894. After several years of service in Alaska, he was named Archimandrite Sebastian, head of the Serbian Mission to North America, in 1905. A Greek priest, Father Andreadis, served at Holy Trinity Cathedral from 1905 until 1918, when he joined the newly formed Greek diocese.

The year 1899 marked the arrival of Bishop Tikhon, one of San Francisco's most illustrious clergymen of any faith. He introduced the use of English as a liturgical language in the Orthodox church service, which proved to be effective in reaching the younger generation. The cathedral, with its seven onion domes, was totally destroyed by the earthquake of 1906. By a stroke of good fortune, the church belfry was in the process of being repaired, and the cherished bells, temporarily stored in a wagon, were saved. The present cathedral at 1520 Green Street was dedicated in 1909.

In 1907, Bishop Tikhon moved the administrative center of the Orthodox Church in America to New York, to be more accessible to the large numbers of Slavic, Greek, and Arabic Orthodox Christians who were beginning to settle in the eastern and midwestern sections of the United States. On his return to Russia in 1917, Tikhon was named Patriarch of Moscow and all Russia, a post that had gone unfilled for more than two centuries. Although the Bolshevik Revolution succeeded in suppressing the Orthodox church within Russia, it had the effect of spreading the faith throughout the western world. More than a million Russians left their homeland, and emigration from surrounding areas increased accordingly. In November 1920, Tikhon authorized the bishops outside Russia to establish temporary ecclesiastical jurisdictions, to function until such time as the Patriarchate of Moscow could again assume control. Several such groups were formed. Tikhon defended the church against the new state regime and was eventually sentenced to prison for a time. After his release he retired to a monastery. Holy Trinity Cathedral in San Francisco has several treasured mementoes of Patriarch Tikhon's service here, including his vestments, which are used in special services.

The Orthodox Church in America, already established in New York with a resident bishop, continued to administer the churches under its jurisdiction, after 1926 functioning as a *de facto* autonomous body. In 1970 the Patriarchate of Moscow declared the Orthodox Church in America to be autocephalous (independent). The San Francisco parish also includes Christ the Saviour Church at 490 Twelfth Avenue—a modern structure designed by Joseph Esherick after he had studied traditional forms in Russia.

San Francisco's Holy Trinity Cathedral resembles Chicago's cathedral of the same name, designed in 1900 by Louis Sullivan. The present building (designed by an unknown architect) was built in 1909, with additions in 1934 and 1979–1984. This rambling structure is both recognizably Russian and turn-of-the-century American Period Revival. Distinctively Russian components include the kokosniki-decorated base and gilded finial of the bell tower and main dome, the various gilded crosses, and the minor polygonal dome. The flat pedimented main door, rusticated surfaces, block-outlined cornices, and rich Georgian balustrade reflect American influence. Holy Trinity Cathedral occupies the main floor, and the St. Innocent Chapel the lower level. The downstairs chapel is dedicated to a seventeenth-century missionary bishop of Irkutsk in Siberia (at one time both Alaska and California were included in the diocese of Irkutsk).

Among the cathedral's treasures are the seven bronze bells, cast in Moscow in 1888 at the request of Bishop Vladimir of San Francisco. An inscription on the largest commemorates the miraculous escape of the Russian Emperor Alexander III and his family when revolutionaries bombed the train on which they were passengers. Such bells are exceedingly rare because most of them were melted down for the metal during the Russian Revolution or World War II. The open bell tower was rebuilt in 1979, giving it the extra height characteristic of churches on the flat Russian steppes; the original, more Serbian tower is to be reused on a chapel the parish is building at Point Reyes.

As is traditional for Orthodox churches, Holy Trinity is built in the form of a Greek cross with the altar in the east. The dome, representing heaven, has stained glass windows in the drum, and a massive brass chandelier hanging from its groined center. Many Oriental rugs and brass stands holding candles give a rich warmth to the church. The congregation is separated from the altar by a screen, or iconostasis, covered with sacred images or icons. Originally an iconostasis was an openwork barrier, but in later times it became the almost solid wall it is today. Doors in the iconostasis afford glimpses of the altar as priests pass through during services. Icons—two dimensional representations of saints—are considered to be windows into heaven. The icons and murals throughout the church were done by the artist Gleb Ilyn. Poetry and music, chanted and sung without accompaniment, give Orthodox worship its distinctive character. Early Orthodox congregations were led by cantors, but in America most congregations westernized their worship services by adding choirs—at first male, and then mixed. There are no pews or benches in Holy Trinity Cathedral; worshippers stand or kneel in accordance with age-old custom.

A modest but sumptuous altar screen backs the many candles and chandelier of Holy Trinity Orthodox Cathedral.

St. Paulus Lutheran Church

999 Eddy Street, at Gough Street
Founded May 15, 1867

St. Paulus Church, San Francisco's second German-speaking Lutheran congregation, was founded on May 15, 1867, by the Reverend Jacob M. Buehler and some former members of St. Mark's. For the first two years they met at the Dashaway Hall on Post Street. While meeting in these temporary quarters they established a flourishing Sunday school, the first in the Missouri Synod. In 1869 they bought a handsome Classical Revival church (formerly Second Presbyterian) on Mission Street between Fifth and Sixth.

St. Paulus became the center and headquarters for confessional Lutheranism on the Pacific Coast. Lutherans came from all over California to have children baptized and marriages solemnized in the San Francisco church. Many of the candidates for the mission fields in California, Oregon, Nevada, and Washington were ordained there. At Christmas time the entire congregation including from six to eight hundred children gathered at the church to march for several blocks along Mission Street singing Christmas carols. St. Paulus German-American School, established in 1873, taught the standard curriculum, grades one through four, in both English and German.

By 1890 the Mission Street church was too small and its location unsuitable for the active congregation, so they bought the present property overlooking Jefferson Square. Buehler lifted the first spadeful of dirt at the groundbreaking on September 7, 1892, and the new church (their present building) was dedicated on the first Sunday in Lent, February 11, 1894. The building cost sixty-five thousand dollars, a huge debt in those days. The debt felt especially taxing as some members did not make the move to the new location, and there was no immediate buyer for the Mission Street property. The Women's Aid Society helped substantially to reduce the debt, which was not paid off until the old building was sold ten years later. By 1900 the church had almost fifteen hundred parishioners. The Reverend G. A. Bernthal became pastor in 1901.

During the citywide fire following the 1906 earthquake, St. Paulus was doubly threatened. The fire was racing toward the ornate wood structure, and city firemen were determined to dynamite the building as they had others around the area in the hope of heading off the fire. Sticks of explosive had already been laid to the church when Bernthal pleaded with the firemen to at at least try the nearby hydrant. None of the other city hydrants had any water pressure, as the earth tremors had broken the mains. The firemen tried the hydrant, as much to humor the distraught pastor as anything else. Water gushed forth—either by luck or by miracle—as this particular hydrant had a separate connection to the city reservoir. The church was saved.

In gratitude the congregation offered the building for use as an emergency hospital. Over the next two months, the Red Cross, the United States Army, and the National Guard hospitalized more than three thousand persons there and gave first aid treatment to ten thousand more. St. Paulus, like many other churches, lost members after the disaster, as many decided to move to outlying neighborhoods rather than rebuild in the old location.

Beginning in 1883, St. Paulus had offered occasional services in the English language, although this was frowned upon by the Missouri Synod; but it was not until 1920 that the weekly early service was given in English. After 1936 all services were in English. The church building was restored in 1940, but a large fire during the restoration caused a loss of fifty thousand dollars, only half-covered by insurance. Somehow, the church was rebuilt in spite of the loss. In 1971 a forty-nine rank organ was installed. Built by Werner Bosch of Kassel, Germany, it cost sixty thousand dollars, almost the same as the cost of building the entire church in 1894. The organ produces a brilliant and authentic Baroque sound.

The emphasis of Lutheran congregations is on preaching the Bible. Members of St. Paulus have every reason to be proud of their graceful church, yet a congregational history emphasizes the focus of the parishioners: "The church's greatest beauty is not so much the architecture, but in the use to which this building had been put."

There is a question about whether St. Paulus Church is somewhat vaguely inspired by an old Berlin church or by the Cathedral of Chartres in France. At Chartres, the heights of the facade spires are reversed, the proportions of parts are quite different, and the magnificent stone cathedral is much more complex structurally. Julius A. Kraft, the architect, put three spires on the church, each of a different height—175, 125, and 100 feet. The church has a brick basement, a redwood superstructure, and slate roof. The only stone used is in the steps and the spur walls leading up to the entryway, and yet the effects created in the wood suggest masonry. Late Victorian Gothic, St. Paulus is an elegant rendering in wood of what is usually done in stone on the European continent.

The church was built in the overall shape of a cross in the basilica tradition. The triple-arched portal has multiple colonettes and fleurs-des-lis in the tympana. Above is an openwork arcade or gallery. A particularly graceful rose window rises in the upper level over the entrance; there is a smaller rose window on each transept. With pride, the architect said of St. Paulus, "The original idea has been developed and carried out in the style of the noblest Gothic at the height of its creativeness." The ornate detailing of the painted, creamy white exterior with its pier buttresses, tracery, galleries, pinnacles, finials, and crockets have earned this church the sobriquet of the "Wedding Cake Church."

San Francisco Registered Landmark #116
National Register of Historic Places, February 11, 1982

One of the most complex of San Francisco's Gothic Revival churches is St. Paulus Lutheran.

St. Luke's Episcopal Church

1755 Clay Street, at Van Ness Avenue
Founded in March, 1868

By the mid-1860s there were enough people living in the Spring Valley district west of Nob Hill to support an Episcopal mission. Not one but two such missions began in 1866, both under the aegis of Grace Church or some of its members. Soon the two united, and Bishop Kip officiated at Christmas services in what he named the Church of the Nativity.

By November of 1867 the church's Martha Society had raised $775 toward the cost of buying a lot and erecting a much-needed building. In March of 1868 the church was incorporated under the name suggested by the Martha Society—St. Luke's Church. A new frame church building on the south side of Pacific between Polk and Van Ness was completed in time for services on St. Luke's Day, October 18, 1868.

As new residential neighborhoods developed in the Western Addition and Van Ness Avenue became a broad boulevard lined with stately homes, St. Luke's grew and prospered with the area it served. In 1872 the church opened a parochial school on Polk Street between Washington and Jackson. Three missions were also established: St. Stephen's Mission and Sunday School in the Hayes Valley District in 1871, the Mission of St. Mary the Virgin in Cow Hollow in 1888, and All Saints in the Haight Ashbury in 1904.

The second Pacific Avenue church was consecrated on Easter Day of 1873, when the building debt had been paid. As the congregation grew, the church was enlarged twice and finally moved on wooden rollers three blocks away to Clay and Van Ness. There it was enlarged once again to serve what had become the largest Episcopal congregation on the Pacific Coast. When the much-altered building could not be further enlarged, it was moved across the street to make way for the stone church that replaced it in 1898.

Eight years later the facade crashed across Van Ness Avenue in the thirty-five seconds of the 1906 earthquake. The beautiful edifice became the first victim of the dynamite that stopped the disastrous fire. Most of the parishioners lost their homes, and services were held in Lafayette Park for a while, and then by invitation in various churches outside the burned-out area. Today's building was started in 1909 and opened for services on St. Luke's Day, October 18, 1910. The church has more than fourteen hundred parishioners, mostly from the Pacific Heights district. It serves the community with a day school, an Alcoholics Anonymous Center, and, in cooperation with San Francisco State University, a rubella clinic.

The building, of painted stone, has been called a mini-cathedral, although in many ways it resembles an English collegiate chapel. Its staid exterior, with stepped, pointed pier buttresses and large traceried facade window under a pointed hood mold, provides a strong setting for the grace of the interior. A kind of narthex with pointed arch and cross leads the eye inward. There, the white marble altar, of simplified English Gothic design, reaches up to a stained glass window executed in a symphony of color. The walls are lined with high, pointed clerestory windows. This is a marriage of the simple, the repeated Gothic arches, and the rich, the many stained glass windows casting a rich play of colored light throughout the interior. The impressive fifty-five rank Aeolian-Skinner organ was dedicated by Bishop James Pike in 1960.

St. Luke's Episcopal draws on its basic English heritage for a superbly designed modern Gothic altar and fine stained glass windows.

Impressively scaled, the Gothic interior of St. Luke's Episcopal has still an American simplicity about it.

Chinese United Methodist Church

920 Washington Street, at Stockton Street
Founded 1869

By 1869, the number of Chinese immigrants on the West Coast had increased to seventy thousand, and with the completion of the transcontinental railroad, many of them returned to San Francisco to find work. As their numbers increased, so did racial animosities. The only Caucasian institution actively concerned with their welfare at this time was the Protestant church. Nineteen or twenty congregations were operating Chinese Sunday schools, and Chinese Presbyterian was conducting an evening English school partially supported by public funds—important because the Chinese were not allowed to attend American public schools at the time.

In 1868, the Reverend Otis Gibson, just back from ten years' service in China, was appointed Methodist missionary to the Chinese community in California. After mastering a new language—the Cantonese dialect spoken by West Coast Chinese—and surveying the San Francisco situation, Gibson determined that only a permanent mission building would suffice to sustain and guide the Chinese immigrants in a hostile land.

His request for funds was granted by the Methodist Board of Home Missions, but only on condition that he raise five thousand dollars locally. By appealing to all the city's Protestant congregations he was able to raise eight thousand dollars, and the new thirty thousand dollar mission house at 916 Washington Street was dedicated on Christmas day, 1870. In his *History of the Mission* Gibson described the building as containing "four fine school rooms, an asylum department for Chinese women and girls, parsonage for the superintendent, and rooms for the assistant missionary and teachers, besides the basement designed for rental purposes." The graded evening school taught reading, writing, spelling, grammar, arithmetic, geography, history, music, and the Bible. Chow Loke Shee, the first convert, was baptized in October of 1871. Beginning in April of 1872 a small chapel known as the Foke Yam Tong (Gospel Temple), located at 620 Jackson Street, offered religious services in the Chinese language every afternoon.

As the economy faltered in the 1870s, the tide of opposition to the Chinese rose to a fury, culminating in "Riot Night," July 23, 1877. A mob marched on Chinatown; police held them at bay at Pine and Dupont, but a second group approached from Broadway to the north, broke through and raced down Stockton, surrounding the mission house. Only the determined and fearless stand of Gibson and his followers saved the building. The church history reports that he was ready to die rather than let the rabble destroy the very religious and racial freedoms he believed his country was based upon.

Beyond preaching the gospel, the main concerns of this mission have been the education and assimilation of Asian immigrants. Methodists met new arrivals at the docks, helping them through the bureaucratic red tape of admission; they taught English to immigrants and Chinese to their American-born descendants. This Chinese language school became an interdenominational project, the Hip Wo School, in the 1920s. Not only the Chinese but other Asians benefited from the work of the United Methodists. Japanese converts met here until they could establish a church of their own, as did the first Korean Protestants. The Native Chinese Missionary Society began sending representatives back to China in the early years of the twentieth century. The Reverend Kwai Ku, Miss Caroline Lee, and the Reverend Theodore Chew went to Canton in 1917.

The mission house burned to the ground after the earthquake of 1906, and the present Chinese United Methodist Church, dedicated in 1911, took its place. The Reverend Tso Tim Taam, born in Canton, China, and educated in the United States, served as pastor from 1938 to 1968. Taam ministered to three generations of China-born immigrants as well as to the American Chinese community. He served as dean and later principal of the Hip Wo School, three times as president of the Chinese Benevolent Association (Chinese Six Companies), and as president of the National Conference of Chinese Churches in America.

Chinese Methodist Church, whose congregation is ninety-nine percent Chinese, is proud to have the only Christian church in Chinatown with Oriental architectural features. The present building was built under the direction of Dr. Edward James, who had been a missionary in China. The Chinese-style structure in stucco is said to resemble buildings at Nanking's Ginling University. As the building neared completion, Mah Moon, the elderly caretaker, was unhappy to see a rough concrete slab at the entrance. A tiled foyer had been planned, but money had run out. Mah Moon took his life savings, sixty dollars, and paid for the tiling. It was a source of great pride to him; every day he polished the tiles, repeating Psalm 84:40 to the school children who entered: "I had rather be a doorkeeper in the house of my God than to dwell in the tents of wickedness."

Appropriately topped with a pagoda and with orientalizing balconies, Chinese Methodist fits its Chinatown setting.

St. John's Presbyterian Church

25 Lake Street, at Arguello Boulevard
Founded March 6, 1870

The tranquil appearance of St. John's Presbyterian Church gives no hint of the stormy events that led indirectly to its beginning. Its founder was one of San Francisco's most dynamic and controversial clergymen, the Reverend William Anderson Scott, who had previously founded Calvary Presbyterian Church. Scott had the distinction of being the only San Francisco pastor ever to be hung in effigy. It happened twice—in 1856, after he spoke out against the "cruelties and tyrannies of the Vigilantes," and again in 1861 when he included Jefferson Davis, president of the Southern Confederacy, in a congregational prayer. The following Sunday a screaming mob surrounded Calvary Church, and heeding the advice of his parishioners, Scott accepted a call to Birmingham, England, for the next few years. But by the late 1860s, his correspondence with friends in Calvary led them to believe he would like to return to San Francisco.

A group of Scott's supporters began considering the need for an additional Presbyterian church, and at a meeting held on November 29, 1869, they formalized an overture to Scott to establish a church named for John, the beloved disciple. The new church, with sixty-one communicants, was formally organized at the Pacific Hall on Bush Street on March 6, 1870. Scott, then fifty-seven years of age, vowed "each year to do two years' work to compensate for the lost and vagrant days away."

Within three weeks, the trustees had found a new sanctuary. St. James' Episcopal Church, on Post Street between Mason and Taylor, was vacant, as that congregation had disbanded when their rector decided to become a Catholic priest. In an era when most Protestant churches resembled austere lecture halls, St. John's moved into a Gothic Revival structure designed and furnished for "high church" services and accommodating a thousand people. Most of the interior appointments have been retained and incorporated in subsequent churches.

In a little over a year Scott had demonstrated his ability to do two years' work in one by founding the San Francisco Theological Seminary (later moved to San Anselmo). Some of the students, who were given living quarters in the church basement, were called "church mice," and "were as poor as," according to church records. Scott became the seminary's first elected professor, first trustee, first president, and the first to occupy an endowed chair. The following year the church installed a Johnson pipe organ purchased for ten thousand dollars and shipped around Cape Horn from Boston. Perhaps the most famous marriage performed by Scott was that of Robert Louis Stevenson and Frances Matilda Van de Griff Osbourne, on May 19, 1880. Scott died in 1885, having served the longest pastorate of his career at St. John's.

The congregation built a new church at Octavia and California streets in 1888, but kept the same interior plan and furnishings. There was a rapid succession of young ministers in the 1890s, but none could fill the dynamic founder's place. Membership declined; and the church was burdened with a large debt. Then unexpected good fortune came their way. Calvary Church sold its Powell Street lot and moved west to make way for "progress" in the form of the St. Francis Hotel. Not only did the sale bring enough money to pay for the removal, stone by stone, of their large building and its reconstruction at Fillmore and Jackson streets, but there was a surplus which was loaned to St. John's. While Calvary was under construction, the two congregations worshiped together, their pastors preaching on alternate Sundays. This union proved so harmonious that some declared St. John's should be abandoned and the two churches continue as one.

Then the congregation received a remarkable proposal. Arthur W. Foster, who had married Scott's daughter Louisiana, offered to repay the loan from Calvary, buy land and build a new church, and guarantee the pastor's salary if fifty people would commit themselves to keeping the church debt free at the end of each year. Foster, probably one of California's wealthiest men, was president of the California Northwestern Railway, a developer of the San Francisco waterfront, a regent of the University of California, and the director and treasurer of the 1915 Panama-Pacific International Exposition. He had many interests, among them the sponsorship of Luther Burbank's experiments.

Foster encouraged the congregation to choose a site far to the west of the developed part of the city, reminding them that their founding pastor had predicted that one day there would be no vacant land on the San Francisco peninsula. The trustees selected "a sand lot north of the park, south of the Presidio, west of the cemeteries, and east of the race track"—their present location at the corner of Arguello and Lake. Groundbreaking was held in April of 1905, "solemnized with prayer, enshrouded in fog, and with the sounds of the Pt. Lobos train and moaning foghorns in the distance." The architects retained the interior appointments of previous buildings, adding a massive brass chandelier and, in honor of Foster's parents, the Elijah window. Services were held in the lower level until April 14, 1906, when the newly completed sanctuary was dedicated. Four days later came the earthquake and fire. The chimney toppled into the rear of the church, damaging many of the furnishings, but the building was still able to house a number of people whose homes had been destroyed. The church was repaired and rededicated on April 25, 1907, and additions have been made thereafter.

The church was active during the Depression, always keeping to the provisos of its deed. It was never in debt at the end of the year, although sometimes the minister's salary came out of the collection plates and there was nothing left over. The Johnson organ expired on Easter Sunday, 1948, and was restored by Otto Schoenstein. Still discernible are the carved initials of the many young men who hand-pumped its blower during the first sixty years of its service.

St. John's offers a multitude of activities to its parishioners and to the surrounding community. Special emphasis is now placed on multicultural programs. Members feel that their church has three basic functions—celebration, instruction, and involvement.

The present building, designed by George Dodge and J. Walter Dolliver, copies the original church at Post and Mason. In accordance with the custom of that time, the architects felt free to draw from many architectural and historical traditions in designing the church. The building is a Gothic-style wooden structure but with wider and squarer proportions than most Gothic Revival churches. Features include a simple crenellated squared tower at the corner and a smaller octagonal tower at the south end of the facade facing on Arguello. Over the main entrances are ogival hood molds above large, strap-hinged doors. The simple shingled exterior of the church links it to the general Bay Area use of that concept and gives it a quiet, rural appearance. The building is dominated by three high, arched stained glass windows. Several of its pointed windows date from 1870 and are excellent examples of old-school craftsmanship. The chancel arch has been in all three St. John's churches. The interior, with its elaborate and interlacing wooden timbering and hanging banners, suggests a medieval English hall. This English character is reinforced by the stained glass windows, which include light colors, much as those in English churches do.

San Francisco Registered Landmark #83

Handsomely shingled, St. John's Presbyterian suggests an English country church of the late Gothic era.

3

Where West Is East and East Is West

1875–1915

From its beginnings as a city, San Francisco had looked out toward the Orient as well as over its shoulder to America and Europe. As the mining industry declined, sea transport became a major economic factor, focusing attention on the countries of the Pacific basin. The Spanish-American war intensified Californians' awareness of their position linking the Eastern and Western worlds. European immigration to America reached a peak during this period, and large-scale Asian immigration was just around the corner. The period spanning the turn of the century was a time of growth and development for the entire country. Transportation, commerce, industry, foreign trade, agriculture, and politics came of age during these years. By 1880 the city had a population of roughly 234,000 people and 100 churches. One-half of all San Franciscans were foreign-born, and four out of five had parents born abroad. As new waves of immigrants established themselves, homes, schools, and churches proliferated, especially in the newer neighborhoods south of Market Street and west of Van Ness Avenue. By 1900 there were nearly half again as many people—343,000—and 175 churches.

Not all the city's sacred places are included in the above totals. By 1890, nearly 26,000 San Franciscans were Chinese, about a tenth of the population, and Chinese men outnumbered women by 27 to 1. As in other virtually all-male enclaves, this imbalance encouraged such enterprises as gambling, prostitution, and opium. Chinatown became a virtually autonomous area, governed by its own complex set of organizations based on surname, dialect, or region of origin. The most influential of these associations formed the powerful Chinese Six Companies.

Although religion was not as central in the lives of the Chinese as it was to most Westerners of the period, it provided a spiritual solace to lonely men living in a frequently hostile land. As their numbers grew, the various associations established temples to serve them. By 1892, there were fifteen Chinese temples in San Francisco, each dedicated to a particular god but including shrines to a number of other deities. These were mostly household and regional gods—actual people (ancient kings, statesmen, or warriors) apotheosized for their protection or benefaction of the people. The present Chinese New Year's parade, ending with an enormous dancing dragon, was initiated by the priests of the Yeung Woh Company temple to "scare away all evil influences from Chinatown streets and bring health and peace to the community."

Many of the Chinese became active in Christian churches, which were the only organizations actively working for better treatment of the Chinese at that time. Nearly all denominations sponsored evening schools; by 1888 the Congregationalists offered a choice of three locations. Baptists operated a boys' home; Methodists cared for Chinese orphans; and Presbyterians rescued Chinese slave girls and cared for delinquent girls. Old St. Mary's Church opened a Chinese Sunday school in 1903.

Among the city's European immigrants, the Irish (one eighth of the population) were well established in several residential areas, served by St. Patrick's, St. Joseph's, St. Brigid's, and St. Dominic's churches. The Germans, nearly as numerous as the Irish, included Protestants, Catholics, and Jews. For them the city offered St. Mark's, St. Paulus, and St. Matthew's Lutheran; St. Boniface and St. Anthony's Catholic, and several Methodist and Evangelical churches as well as at least two synagogues—Emanu-El and Ohabai Shalome.

In 1870, Scandinavians had banded together to establish Our Saviour's (now Ascension) Lutheran Church, with positions on its governing board divided equally among Norwegians, Swedes, and Danes. In 1882 the Swedish community broke away to found their own Swedish Evangelical Ebenezer Lutheran Church. Trinity, the first all-English speaking Lutheran church (sponsored by Our Saviour's) opened its doors in 1899. Other Swedish immigrants founded Swedish Evangelical (now First Covenant) in 1877, Hamilton Square Baptist Church in 1881, and First Swedish (now Temple) Baptist in 1889. Shortly after the turn of the century, St. Ansgar Danish (now St. Francis) Lutheran congregation dedicated its present church.

By direct order from Rome, SS. Peter and Paul was established in 1884 to minister to the growing Italian population of North Beach, already becoming better known as Little Italy. In response to a request for a local Holiness group, two Englishmen organized the San Francisco Salvation Army Post #1 in 1883. A group of Christian Scientists established that distinctive American faith in the Bay Area in 1889. Recent Jewish arrivals from Eastern Europe organized Chevra Thilim—a Society for the Recitation of Psalms—in 1893. San Francisco's second Eastern Orthodox congregation—Holy Trinity Greek Orthodox Church—held its first services on December 25, 1903.

Admiral Matthew Perry's visit to Japan in the 1850s had opened that part of the Far East to trade and communication with the West. The first Japanese workers were brought to California in 1869 to operate a tea and silk farm in the Gold Hill area. Although that enterprise was unsuccessful, other Japanese followed. Most were students seeking a Western education. Generally they studied the English language at the Methodist mission and then enrolled in one of the nearby schools. Some attended worship services at various Protestant churches and accepted the Christian faith. The earliest Japanese organization in the United States was the Japanese Gospel Society, founded on October 6, 1877, by ten students, evenly divided between Methodist and Congregationalist converts. As their membership increased, the society divided along denominational lines, each of which developed into a church: Japanese (now Christ United) Presbyterian in 1885 and Japanese (now Pine) Methodist in 1886.

The San Francisco City Hall was going up so slowly on pay-as-you-build financing that it might have been a giant sequoia. This municipal temple, riddled with graft, would take over twenty-five years to build; it was not totally finished when destroyed in the 1906 earthquake. The destruction of the building was, however, virtually complete despite the city directory's description of it as "the most durable structure in the city." Political corruption proved its undoing. During this period, "Blind Boss" Buckley came to power; he was said to run the city government from the back of his saloon. James Phelan ran for mayor on a reform ticket, ousted Buckley, and went to work to link San Francisco with the City Beautiful movement that was sweeping America after the World's Columbian Exposition in Chicago in 1883.

The elegant Baroque forms of the "White City" beside Lake Michigan influenced designers and architects from all over the world. San Francisco architects who felt the impact of this world's fair included Willis A. Polk, A. Page Brown, Arthur Brown, Jr., and Bernard Maybeck. Fine new buildings went up in the downtown area, among them the Ferry Building at the foot of Market Street and the Chronicle Building at the corner of Market and Kearny, perhaps the first steel-framed structure in San Francisco. The new Civic Center, built a little later, affords the most outstanding example of the City Beautiful influence. At a time when "urban sprawl" was becoming widespread, it reestablished the importance of monumental civic architecture.

In 1893, the whole world was looking at Chicago. The World Parliament of Religions, held in connection with the exhibition there, brought together leaders from all the world's living religions, giving Americans and many other Westerners their first exposure to the richly textured theological traditions of India, China, and Japan. Six years later Swami Vivekananda established the Vedanta Society of Northern California in San Francisco. Japanese Jodo Shinshu (True Pure Land Teaching) Buddhism arrived in the person of two missionaries from Kyoto in 1898. Within three years the Japanese Young Men's Buddhist Association was co-publishing the bimonthly magazine *Light of Dharma* with its companion organization composed of young Caucasian males. The first Moslems arrived in San Francisco around 1900, but they did not establish a worship center for some time.

Not to be outdone by Chicago, San Francisco put on the California Midwinter Fair the very next year. The name itself was chosen to call attention to California's mild winters, and the fair was scheduled to open on January 1. The buildings had an exotic, Near-Eastern appearance, emphasizing San Francisco's proximity to the Orient. The most popular attraction of that fair, and (except for two sphinxes outside the de Young Museum) the only part of it surviving today, was the Japanese Tea Garden. Among the flowers and shrubbery were two fine examples of Japanese temple art and architecture—a handsome five-storied pagoda and a large wooden statue of the Buddha. The garden was designed by George Turner Marsh, a dealer in Oriental arts, and lovingly tended by members of the Hagiwara family from 1894 until 1900 and again from 1907 to 1942. (Makota Hagiwara left an additional legacy; in 1909 he served a "fortune cookie" to his tea garden clientele. So popular was this confection that enterprising Chinese merchants copied the idea, and today the cookies are even exported from San Francisco to China.)

Protestant and Catholic churches continued to appear as fast as new neighborhoods were established. Three Episcopal missions were sponsored by St. Luke's—St. Stephen's in the Hayes Valley, St. Mary the Virgin in Cow Hollow, and All Saints in the Haight-Ashbury district. St. Anne of the Sunset, serving mostly Irish and German Catholics, appeared in that newly opened area. The second St. Mary's Cathedral rose at the corner of Van Ness and McAllister streets, and St. Vincent de Paul in Cow Hollow. The Swedenborgian congregation built their jewel-like church on Lyon Street. Trinity Episcopal dedicated its present impressive stone structure "in the suburbs" at the corner of Gough and Bush. Calvary Presbyterian dismantled its monumental edifice at the corner of Powell and Geary, moved the marked stones farther west, and reassembled the church in its present location at Fillmore and Jackson. It is a sad irony that this burst of ecclesiastical construction should be followed so soon by a natural disaster of such proportions. Some must have wondered about divine wrath as they saw their cherished churches become damaged, or worse, demolished—or about divine grace if their buildings were spared.

San Francisco is a dramatic city, shaped by distinct periods and events. The Gold Rush was the first such period, bringing the city in two decades to a level of development that often takes a century or more to achieve. The second climactic occurrence was an event rather than a period—the disaster that struck early Wednesday morning, April 18, in Easter week of 1906. People often assume that the destruction of the city resulted from the tremendous earth tremors. In fact, the bulk of the damage was caused by fires that swept the city to become the biggest combined blaze in the recorded history of cities. In an understandable attempt to allay fears, San Franciscans always emphasize the limited destructiveness of the actual earthquake, though it was severe. As Oscar Lewis says in his book *San Francisco: Mission to Metropolis,* "The earthquake demonstrated that no properly designed and soundly constructed building was likely to be severely damaged by another earthquake of the same magnitude."

This view is borne out by eyewitness accounts from that decisive morning. The first frightening tremor lasted almost a minute. The Reverend and Mrs. Philip Andreen, whose Swedish Ebenezer Lutheran congregation had dedicated their new shingled Gothic Revival church at Fifteenth and Dolores streets exactly sixty days earlier, stepped to the window of their third-floor bedroom. His recollections, published in the church history, describe the rising and falling of the parsonage and adjacent houses "like boats in a storm." The falling church chimney had broken through the wall of their kitchen, but they failed to hear the crash over the groaning noises made by the jerking and twisting of the parsonage. "We dressed quickly. Everything was quiet after the great noise. Birds could be heard singing as if nothing had happened." They were amazed to see the church still standing, but upon entering, they found that the interior was a shambles.

Other tremors followed, but none was as strong as the first, the big one. People gathered outside their homes with coats thrown over nightclothes, and waited. Eventually they returned to their homes to survey the damage. Dishes were broken, plaster cracked, and chimneys toppled, but the houses, virtually all wood frame, had ridden out the jarring without major damage. In most homes enough was intact that appetites returned to normal, and women started to cook breakfast for their families. But in addition to cracking the brick chimneys, the quake had broken gas lines, causing natural gas to seep out and provide fuel for any candle, lamp, match, or cooking fire. As people started breakfast preparations, the escaping gas was ignited and the dry wood of most houses caught fire quickly. In the downtown section broken electrical wires sent sparks flying into the gas-filled atmosphere, starting fires in that district. The earthquake also had broken the city's two main water supply lines, cutting off both the pressure and the supply in most areas. And finally, the city's primitive fire alarm system was destroyed. Even if there had been water, there was no way to locate the fires before they became too large to stop.

Beginning in small pockets all over the city, more than fifty small local fires joined and raced on about their destruction. Two, or possibly three, separate but huge conflagrations resulted. At first the townspeople were not aware of the fire danger. Most probably felt euphoric at being alive after the enormous earthquake. Arnold Genthe, a photographer, tells about taking pictures of the disaster rather than saving any of his lifetime collection of negative plates or artworks. One series of photos shows people "calmly watching the approach of the fire." Some brought chairs and made themselves comfortable for this singular spectacle. "When the fire crept up close, they would just move up a block." Eventually the fire pushed people to the edges of town or to the hilltops, where they gathered to watch the roiling, smoky monster consume their city. By Thursday morning, the entire central city was obviously beyond hope of rescue.

Here and there—mostly on the edges of the fires and the city—buildings were saved by hard work or good luck, most often a combination. After evacuating his family to Golden Gate Park, Reverend Andreen returned in time to save Ebenezer Church by organizing a bucket brigade composed of two parishioners, his brother, and a few total strangers. St. Paulus Lutheran church was saved when the Reverend A. G. Bernthal convinced the city firemen to at least try the nearby hydrant before dynamiting the building in an effort to head off the fire. Whether by luck or by miracle, that particular hydrant was working, and the church was saved. For the most part, though, everything in the fire's path went, either gutted by the fire or dynamited in an attempt—usually futile—to stop the conflagration.

When the blaze finally died out on Saturday morning, over four square miles and more than five hundred city blocks had been burned—an area representing four-fifths of the entire property value of San Francisco. The death toll is uncertain, but estimates range from four hundred to a thousand. At least twenty-eight thousand buildings were destroyed. Suddenly in this city of 350,000 urban dwellers, nothing worked. Even people whose homes were intact could not use their stoves or fireplaces. There was little food, only limited medical supplies, and no public transportation, but an abundance of smoke, rubble, and confusion. People were homeless, many were also injured. The city was vulnerable to looters and anarchy because of the complete devastation.

Mayor Eugene Schmitz quickly organized a Committee of Safety made up of fifty leading citizens and, rising above political differences, named as the head of the committee a man with the administrative experience to do the job—his political foe, former mayor James Phelan. Army troops stationed at the Presidio under the command of General Frederick Funston were put at the service of civil officials. The soldiers helped fight fires, maintain order, set up and run refugee camps, and aid the wounded. The effort was cooperative, and martial law was neither needed nor imposed on the ruined city. Tens of thousands of homeless left San Francisco to stay with friends or relatives, going by ferry to Marin County or the East Bay. Many stayed in the city and walked with their few salvaged belongings to one of the large camps at the Presidio, near Potrero Hill, at the foot of Van Ness Avenue, or in Golden Gate Park. The army supplied what extra rations it had, and food was donated from all over the country. Distributing stations were established throughout the city, and it is generally conceded that no one went hungry. By April 25, it was reported that *only* forty thousand people remained in Golden Gate Park. In July, the Presbyterian church sought permission to erect a tent in the park for church services, but the request was not granted.

Even more than the Gold Rush, this disaster mixed people socially. By 1906 the city had already established its rich, average, and poor classes of people and its well-defined ethnic neighborhoods. But after the fire, people from all backgrounds stood in the same lines for the same kind of food. Society was leveled along with the buildings, and though this equality lasted for only a while, its effects extended to a tolerance for which San Francisco is known far and wide.

The Chinese section was completely devastated, and for the first time the Chinese people were forced out of their enclave. One woman saw her grandmother hobble several miles to Golden Gate Park on feet crippled by having been bound when she was a child. Previously, the Chinese had kept to themselves and avoided the white population except during working hours, often with good reason. Strong anti-Chinese feelings and some actions served as intimidators. After the earthquake and fire, the Chinese were forced to mix with everyone else, face to face. In many cases mistrust was replaced by mutual respect. Chinese people started to deposit their money in American banks for the first time after 1906.

Some public officials wanted to use the devastation of the section as an excuse to relocate the Chinese in a less central part of the city, such as Hunters' Point. No one consulted the Chinese, however, and most of them quietly moved back to their original locations and started to "build all new." About a third of the Chinese people moved to Oakland. The ten thousand who stayed in San Francisco developed a Chinatown that became world famous. In an effort to construct an "Oriental City," architects and builders added structural and ornamental details to the new buildings, creating the style commonly called Chinese Renaissance.

Of the churches and temples, many were completely gone—destroyed by quake damage, fire, or dynamite. The elaborate St. Ignatius Church was leveled, as was the small T'ien Hou temple, although only the former was front page news in the combined *Call-Chronicle-Examiner* edition of April 19. Other churches sustained varying degrees of damage, and nearly all lost their steeples. (As an architectural by-product of the earthquake San Francisco churches were built or rebuilt either without steeples or with low steeples. Towers were topped with cupolas or pyramids, or were left without adornment.) The churches that were not badly damaged sheltered refugees or hospital patients and offered religious services. Homeless congregations met in the still-standing structures of other religions or denominations. Compassion for others was put into practice, and a strongly ecumenical spirit prevailed. Many churches lost their congregations in the relocation after the city was rebuilt.

Migration within the city was common. People who had been burned out relocated farther from the city center. Catholic churches tended to remain in or near the same locations and serve the new residents of the parish, while some Protestant and Jewish groups moved with their original constituencies to newer sections of the city. Before the fire, Van Ness Avenue had been an elegant residential area; afterward many burned-out merchants opened shops in the mansions that still stood along the west side of the avenue, and this began the transformation of Van Ness to the commercial area it is today. Many Japanese, who had previously lived south of Market, moved to the area of the present Nihonmachi, or Japantown, at this time. In the nine years between the earthquake and the Panama Pacific Exposition of 1915, a large number of ecclesiastical structures were built or completely rebuilt in San Francisco. The city directory for 1915 lists 245 churches and chapels in the city.

Rebuilding presented the city with both problems and opportunities. In an effort to establish property lines quickly during and immediately after the Gold Rush, the streets had been laid out following Jasper O'Farrell's plan of 1847 in the grid pattern used for all American cities at that time, making only minimal allowances for the steep hills that formed the natural geography of the area. During James Phelan's tenure as mayor, a far-reaching proposal for the "Improvement and Adornment of San Francisco" had been submitted by D. H. Burnham, a famous architect and city planner who had designed an impressive beautification program for Chicago. But the plan, which took the hills into account and created a new, more Baroque or Parisian street pattern, required major rebuilding at great expense, and although it was discussed in 1905 and again in 1906, the proposal seemed too costly. With the destruction of the city in 1906, there was a unique chance to bring Burnham's visionary plan into reality. But San Franciscans were in a tremendous hurry to rebuild. Business men were particularly eager to get back into operation, and as soon as they got materials and insurance money, they quickly rebuilt on the old plan. Some say that Burnham's plan would have made the city more convenient for traffic as well as more expansive and attractive. On the other hand, there are those who contend that the rectangular grid produces the wildly improbable vistas that make this hilly city irresistible.

Immediately before the earthquake, city politics had been dominated by Boss "Abe" Ruef, but with the destruction of their city—and their City Hall—the citizens saw it as a time to eliminate corruption in city government. A group of reformers started a campaign to bring Ruef, Mayor Eugene Schmitz, and many more to trial for graft. At first there was broad community support for the trials, which were held in Temple Sherith Israel, but public enthusiasm waned as the procedures dragged on for nearly six years and got closer to investigating influential citizens who were suspected of accepting bribes in exchange for political favors. Ruef was sentenced to fourteen years in prison for accepting bribes, and Mayor Schmitz was removed from office.

The San Francisco Russian community was enlarged in October of 1906 by the arrival of several Molokan families who had left their farms along the Don River to escape religious persecution and also to avoid conscription in the Russo-Japanese War of 1904–05. Their first impressions of the earthquake-ravaged city must have been less than reassuring. Police put the new arrivals in horse-drawn carts and took them to the camp near Potrero Hill (adjacent to the city dump), where they joined the thousands of people who were still homeless. Although they had originally planned to find farm lands in the new country, they stayed in the city and set about building shepherds' huts for themselves. The men found work in nearby shipyards and lumberyards. Additional Molokan families soon joined them, forming the close-knit community that still exists today. In 1908 the minister of the nearby Olivet Presbyterian Church began teaching English to the Molokan men, and the members of his Scottish congregation gave assistance of various kinds to the families. In 1919 the Presbyterian Board of Home Missions commissioned the architect Julia Morgan to design the Potrero Hill Neighborhood House to serve the community; in 1928, the congregation, working with hand tools, built their own church, the First Russian Christian Molokan Church, at 841 Carolina Street. Molokans observe strict dietary rules and a simple life-style. The sect derives its name from the custom of drinking milk during Lent. Molokan ministers serve on a volunteer basis.

James Rolph, Jr., became mayor of San Francisco in 1912, holding the office until becoming governor of the state in 1931. "Sunny Jim," as he was called, was a popular man who vowed to clean up the city, including the infamous Barbary Coast area. His early years in office were especially good ones for San Francisco. A municipal railway was built to provide public transportation to the Richmond and Sunset districts, and the Twin Peaks tunnel was opened in 1917, making it possible for people to live in the newer areas of the city and work downtown. A municipal water system was started in 1913 to bring additional water from the Tuolumne River, enabling the city to sustain a larger population. Then there was the development of San Francisco's Civic Center, acknowledged as one of the most impressive in the United States. Although the Burnham Plan had been bypassed, discussion about it had served to educate both city officials and the public, and in 1912 the voters approved the necessary bond issue for these civic buildings. The Civic Auditorium was the first to be built; then came City Hall. Arthur Brown's City Hall has a steel frame faced in granite and a dome that rises more than three hundred feet from the ground. The proud mayor took pleasure in telling visitors that this dome was higher by sixteen feet than the dome of the United States Capitol building in Washington, D.C. Both the auditorium and City Hall were finished by 1915 in time for the Panama-Pacific International Exposition.

This world's fair was a triumph for San Francisco, the "Phoenix City" that had been in ruins only nine years before. A citizens' group had started preparing to host the international event early in the 1900s when it was learned that an exposition would be held to honor the completion of the Panama Canal. A bill approving San Francisco as the site was already pending in Congress at the time of the earthquake. Despite the virtual destruction of the city, the committee formed a non-profit corporation in 1907 to pursue plans. Bonds for the project were voted in a widespread show of public support and civic confidence, and in January of 1911, Congress officially designated San Francisco as the site of the exposition. President Taft then extended invitations to the other countries requesting their participation.

The site chosen was an empty marshland. First a seawall was built; then sand and soil were brought in to fill the area. An exposition of this scope required the cooperative support of architects, artists, craftspeople, tradespeople, and many workers. Building began in 1914. Just as the fair was about to open, war broke out in Europe, causing several countries to withdraw completely or send smaller exhibitions than originally planned. But other nations increased the size of their exhibitions, feeling that their national treasures would be safer in far-off America while Europe was at war. Several religious groups held national or world conventions in San Francisco during the fair, among them the Unitarians and the Buddhists. During the exhibition, any distinguished guest of honor to visit the fair planted a tree. After the fair some of these trees, originally planted in the Presidio, were moved to Golden Gate Park; a group of palms went to Dolores Street. Of the ten main exhibit halls put up for the fair, only one remains: The Palace of Fine Arts, designed by Bernard Maybeck. Recently rebuilt in more permanent form, it now houses the Exploratorium and a performance hall for musical and theatrical events. The other buildings, courtyards, and gardens were carefully dismantled, leaving the city with a potential new residential area and a yacht harbor—today's Marina district. With the nearly total devastation of their city and a series of contentious graft trials so recently behind them, the citizens of San Francisco must have felt proud of their achievement—not only building a magnificent fair, but also rebuilding an entire city.

St. Dominic's Church

2390 Bush Street, at Steiner Street
Founded June 29, 1873

When the Dominican fathers were transferred from St. Brigid's on Van Ness Avenue to establish a new church even farther out in the Western Addition, they were faced with another pioneering situation. An article in *The Monitor* describes the new location—the entire city block bounded by Pierce, Steiner, Pine, and Bush streets—as almost impossible to reach from other sections of the city whether on foot or by horseback because of the shifting sands.

The first St. Dominic's Church, a rectangular hall described as "pure Tudor Gothic in the style of Henry VIII" (they planned to add the transepts later on), was blessed by Archbishop Alemany on June 29, 1873, and dedicated to Saint Dominic, founder of the order. Music was furnished by the choir from St. Brigid's, and a priest from St. Francis of Assisi delivered the dedicatory sermon. Two priests were assigned to the church, Father Benedict James McGovern and Father Thomas Aquinas Fitzsimmons, with a third priest from Benicia assisting on Sundays. The church soon had a full complement of activities and also a novitiate for the training of young priests. In order to help retire the building debt, the women of the congregation held a fair at Platt's Hall in July of 1875. Luncheons were served for fifty cents; among the items to be raffled were jewelry, silver tea sets, china sets, a ton of coal, a trotting horse, and a team of sorrel horses. The Honorable Peter H. Burnett, the first elected governor of California, was a member of the fair's executive committee.

The cornerstone of the second church was laid in 1883, but the building was not completed until a decade later because of a shortage of funds during a time of economic uncertainty. When completed, architect T. J. Welsh's imposing Gothic Revival structure with its high Baroque altar and allegorical frescoes was said to be "one of the most universally admired structures in San Francisco." The building's life was destined to be short, however, and after the earthquake the congregation met in a temporary structure until 1928, when the present church was completed.

St. Dominic's was the last Catholic church in the city to be rebuilt; construction moved along gradually throughout the twenties. Two thousand parishioners attended the dedication. Over the years, especially since World War II, the ethnic profile of San Francisco and of the area surrounding St. Dominic's Church has become infinitely more varied. St. Dominic's is now the center for the San Francisco Filipino Association and is the parish church for groups of Lebanese, Arabian, and Japanese Christians. St. Dominic's Church organized a mission that became St. Benedict the Moor Church and later evolved into the St. Benedict Deaf Center. Today the church is known for its outstanding boys' choir, weekly folk masses, and the Shrines of St. Jude and of the Holy Rosary. St. Dominic's provides chaplains for several hospitals and convalescent homes and participates in several inner-city social service programs.

The present St. Dominic's was designed by Arnold Constable for Beezer Brothers of Seattle. The handsome gray granite structure was built in cathedral style, but on a reduced scale. The building has numerous areas with carved Gothic designs, notably interlaced, pointed arches, and many niches, empty of statuary. The most striking aspect of the exterior aside from the play of light on its great multiple-molded arches and impressive overall size is a lofty tower crowned with multiple spires and innumerable finials and crockets. This unique structure looks like a skillfully wrought tall crown; in general appearance it is similar to the Harkness Tower at Yale University.

The exceedingly high interior is of cast stone made at the construction site. The stations of the cross were brought from the old building. A rood screen stretching across one of the arches in the apse depicts the Crucifixion. Edmund Schmid of the woodcarving studios of Oberammergau, Bavaria, carved several of the shrines, altars, and confessionals. Alphonse Pieters et Fils of Belgium carved the statues of Mary, the angels, and the saints. The woodwork of the altars, [illegible], pews, confessionals, and other church fittings is very fine. Most of the stained glass windows are by Charles J. Connick of the famed Connick Studios in Boston. The Assumption Window was done by the Cummings Studios of San Francisco. The main altar, designed by Arnold Constable, was carved of botticino marble at Pietrasanta, Italy in the [illegible]. While being shipped to San Francisco, the altar was somewhat damaged, and Albe[illegible]asconi, the famous San Francisco sculptor and stonemason, repaired and installed it under Constable's direction. The rich appointments contribute to the old world atmosphere of St. Dominic's.

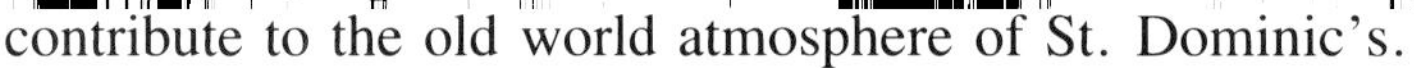

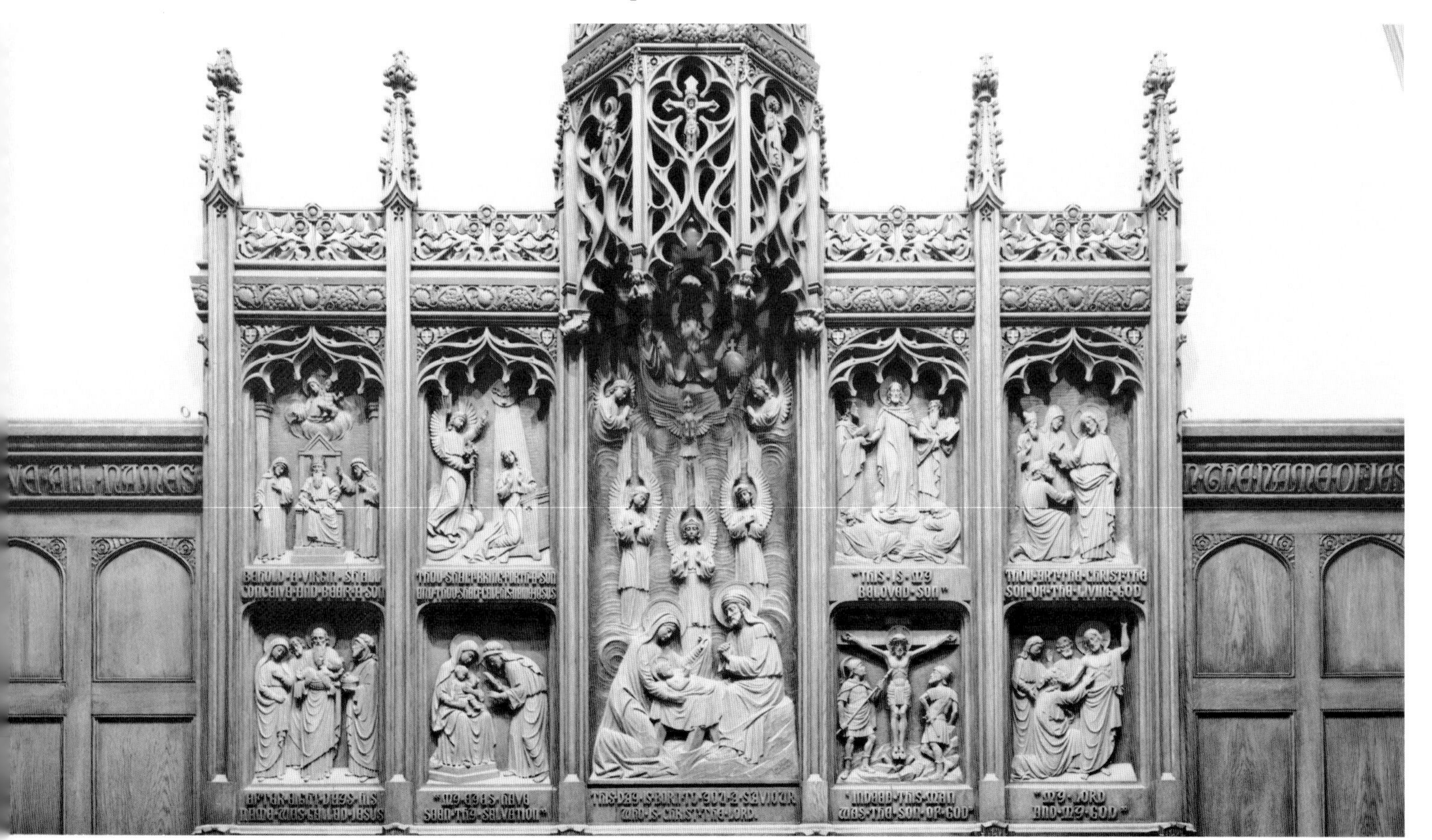

This fine artisan carving at St. Dominic's emphasizes the importance of craftsmanship in all parts of church interiors.

Part of a nationwide movement to the renewed interest in fine Gothic interiors, St. Dominic's altar area is one of the most opulently designed in San Francisco.

Hamilton Square Baptist Church and Theological Seminary

1212 Geary Street, at Franklin Street
Founded February 7, 1881

Swedish Baptists, like the Pilgrims of the American colonial period, fled from their homeland to escape persecution for their religious beliefs. In the mid-nineteenth century a revival of personal religion in Germany influenced some ministers and laymen of the Swedish state church to study and interpret the Bible in a new way, and they came to the conclusion that to be true to those teachings they must be baptized by their own choice, rather than as infants, and in the same manner as the New Testament Christians, by immersion. A lay minister, F. O. Nilsson, after being so baptized by a German minister, returned to baptize five converts and establish the first Baptist church at Vallersvik, Sweden, on September 21, 1848. The state church, until that time inattentive to the revival movement, charged the Baptists with heresy. Nilsson was first imprisoned, then convicted of heresy and banished for life from his homeland; he fled first to Denmark and later to the United States.

Another pioneer of the Swedish Baptist Church was Captain Gustavus W. Schroeder, the founder of Hamilton Square Baptist Church. In November 1880 he placed an appeal in a Boston paper, *The Watchman,* for a Baptist minister "willing to trust God and His people for his support, without waiting for a call from any particular church for any specified salary." The Reverend Joseph S. Bromley answered the call, and Schroeder invited five friends to his San Francisco home on February 7, 1881, to establish the Zion Baptist Church. The group held services first in the Hamilton Hall, later building on property across the square at the corner of Steiner and Post streets, and taking the name Hamilton Square Baptist Church. This sparsely settled area lay beyond the burned main city when disaster struck in 1906. Open space surrounding the church became a haven for homeless victims, to whom the Baptists ministered. In 1912 the congregation erected a new church on the same site.

By the 1940s Hamilton Square was looking for a more central location, and after selling their church to a Methodist group in July of 1944, they bought new property at the corner of Geary and Franklin streets. Ground was broken for the present church on January 7, 1945. The congregation worshiped for several years in the lower level while the building was completed. In 1958, when the Conservative Baptist Ministers' Fellowship of the San Francisco Bay Area was planning to establish a seminary, Hamilton Square offered the use of their Franklin Street wing. The location at the crossroads of the city was considered ideal, and on September 16, 1958, the first class sessions were convened with twelve students.

Architect Donald Powers Smith designed the Gothic-inspired modern building of low interrelated forms with a tower that has a piquant, spired side turret. It is constructed around a hedged garden. Within the sanctuary, the communion table, which antedates the pulpit, is the center of worship. The choir is seated behind the chancel railing, with the baptistry above and behind the choir. Seating capacity of the sanctuary can be expanded to accommodate one thousand worshipers.

SS. Peter and Paul Church

666 Filbert Street, between Stockton and Powell Streets
Founded June 29, 1884

A new ethnic enclave—Little Italy—began to develop in the 1880s, as Italians started to arrive in significant numbers. They settled in the North Beach area, so named because a finger of the bay came inland between Telegraph and Russian hills and a stretch of sandy beach abutted the neighborhood. SS. Peter and Paul Church was established in response to direct orders from Rome for an Italian National Church in San Francisco. It has a citywide parish for all Catholics of Italian birth or ancestry. On June 29, 1884, the Feast Day of Saints Peter and Paul, Archbishop Alemany offered the first mass in the newly built church at the corner of Filbert Street and Grant Avenue.

Little Italy was a lively neighborhood, and in 1897 the Salesian Order was invited to administer the parish. This order, founded in Italy by Saint John Bosco, is noted for its work with youth. Father Bernard Redahan, the first Irish Salesian priest to come to San Francisco, taught English to the immigrants and organized the Telegraph Hill–Montgomery Street Club, which won the city baseball championship in 1912. The Salesian Boys' Club, famous for redirecting excess youthful energy into productive channels, was started in 1921 by Father Oreste Trinchieri.

From 1900 on, Italian-Americans participated actively in every phase of San Francisco's existence. Their festive "Continental Sundays"—devoted not only to religion but also to socializing—quickly became the norm for much of the city. In the 1930s the most influential banker, the mayor, and the national head of the American Legion were all San Franciscans of Italian ancestry. Italian Americans are prominent in musical and artistic circles as well as in fishing, agriculture, the building trades, and the wine and wholesale produce industries.

Archbishop Edward Joseph Hanna laid the cornerstone for the present church in 1922, and it was dedicated March 20, 1924. At the time SS. Peter and Paul was finished, there was a wave of bombings in San Francisco. The mysterious bomber made five attempts to destroy the church. During his last attempt, the person planting the dynamite was killed by detectives hiding in the church. His partner was captured alive, but the "mad bomber" himself was never identified.

The traditional Easter Week parade, a popular religious event for Catholics from the 1920s to the 1950s, started from SS. Peter and Paul. The Annual Blessing of the Fishing Fleet, the first Sunday of each October, still proceeds from there to Fisherman's Wharf; the Madonna del Lume (Our Lady of Light) is asked to protect those who harvest food from the sea. Columbus Day is a major local holiday with a parade up Columbus Avenue and an outdoor mass held in Washington Square Park.

SS. Peter and Paul faces Washington Square in North Beach, today still the heart of the Italian community, although the neighborhood has grown more cosmopolitan. In the square, children of many ethnic groups frolic at the foot of a statue—not of Columbus, but of the Quaker Ben Franklin. The church has offered some masses in Chinese since 1978.

Architect Charles Fantoni designed the concrete building to house a parochial school a hundred feet above the street along each side of the building behind the spires. Artificial illumination behind the stained glass windows gives the effect of natural sunlight streaming into the sanctuary. Although the church history describes the location as being advantageously quiet and affording a good view, the sequestered classrooms were built at a time when tax laws exempted only church properties used in worship. The plan was thus both practical and aesthetically satisfying.

The stone-faced exterior of SS. Peter and Paul has a Gothic sharpness of silhouette, with Romanesque touches in its multiple rounded arches, twisted colonnettes, and tympana of the main portal, modest arcade above, and plain rose window. Four symbols of the Evangelists sit at the base of four paneled wall sections that divide the facade. Roundels of wheat ornaments frame the center. The tall, squared towers have an aspirant verticality, with multiple spires, finials, crockets, and variant forms of corbel tables to add variety. A quotation from Dante's *Paradiso* is worked in mosaic across the front of the church. Translated, it says, "The Glory of the All-Mover penetrates through the Universe."

The inscription is a fitting introduction to the interior of this church, which is executed with distinctive lavishness and contains a diversity of marbles, statuary, and other manifestations of old world craftsmanship. There is botticino rosato marble and Carrara marble, with onyx from Morocco and Brazil. The sanctuary floor is calacata marble with inlaid crosses of breccia violetta from Seravezza. The white marble altar from Italy has a sculptured reproduction of Leonardo da Vinci's *Last Supper* on it. Several other shrines have marble altars, and the rich interior is redolent of beeswax and incense. A treasured sixteenth-century carving of Christ graces the church. The painting of the beckoning Christ above the altar was begun by the Los Angeles artist Ettore Sebaroli and (after he became ill) completed by his daughter Giuditta. The marble copy of Michelangelo's *Pietà* that flanks the altar was a gift from Rome, originally intended for the new St. Mary's Cathedral but considered more appropriate for the style of SS. Peter and Paul.

A Gothic wedding cake, SS. Peter and Paul has a lusciously decorated silhouette that forms a rich backdrop to Washington Square and North Beach.

The vivacious outline of SS. Peter and Paul's exterior is echoed in the pinnacled reredos of the interior.

The Salvation Army

101 Valencia Street, at McCoppin Avenue
Founded July 22, 1883

"Denizens in and around the Barbary Coast" received public notice in the *San Francisco Chronicle* of July 27, 1883, that the building at 815 Montgomery Street was going to serve as headquarters from which a certain "24 year old Irish Major" planned to "sally forth daily and do battle with sin and the devil." The Irishman in question was Major Alfred Wells, handpicked by General William Booth to establish the pioneer corps of the Salvation Army in western America. Wells and Captain Henry Stillwell came in response to a plea from a local Holiness Band who felt they could accomplish more by joining forces with the already well-known Salvation Army. A plaque on the building commemorates the July 22, 1883, meeting at which the nucleus of seventy resolute people established the army that now serves San Francisco from eleven churches and service centers.

As in England, where the movement started, the Salvationists tried to take the Gospel to those who would never enter a church. Their methods were designed to attract attention—parades, street-corner band concerts, visits to gambling halls and saloons—and they were often pelted with rotten eggs, decayed vegetables, or rocks and broken bottles. In those early days there was no fixed income, and Wells depended on his prayers. The first answer came when a young man, recently converted by the Salvation Army, came in saying he had received some money and wanted to share. When he learned that this was an answer to prayer, he raised his five-dollar donation to ten. Soon more and more came from unexpected sources and by 1891 the Army had their own headquarters. Sales of their publication, *War Cry,* brought in extra revenue.

Soon they rented a small steam launch, *Little Nell,* in which they chugged about the bay from San Francisco to Carquinez, visiting with sailors aboard the schooners, clippers, and steamers at anchor, as well as with the people living on the banks, all the while selling their *War Cry*. Next they formed an "Evangelistic Cavalcade," buying—and breaking—six wild horses to pull their wagon load of intrepid evangelists on an eight-hundred-mile trek through the Mother Lode.

Fong Foo Soo, a young Cantonese working in Sacramento, embraced Christianity after reading a copy of *War Cry #87*. He became a Salvation Army officer and after serving for some years in the San Francisco Corps he was able to enter Pomona College in southern California. In later life, after many years as an influential Christian civic leader in China, he was awarded the third honorary doctorate ever given at his alma mater.

San Francisco is the home of the Salvation Army's famous Christmas soup kettle campaign. In 1891 Captain Joseph McFee was determined that the Army would provide free Christmas dinners for a hundred needy persons. But where to get the money? He recalled seeing people toss coins into a pot for charitable causes in Liverpool, England. The heaviest foot traffic, he reasoned, was at the ferry landing at the foot of Market Street. He quickly secured city permission to put a large cauldron at the passenger entrance to the ferry boats and another in the waiting room. Signs were added saying "Keep the kettle boiling," and the tradition took off from there. The familiar bell, a dimestore handbell, was added by Amelia Davis, who joined the Army in 1901.

San Francisco has one of the four schools in the country for officer training, where volunteers pursue a two-year course. The purpose of the Army is the "spiritual, moral, and physical reformation of all who need it." Physical regeneration is regarded as an important aid to spiritual regeneration, and the Army has many social service programs. There are emergency shelters, soup kitchens, help and shelter for alcoholics, the family welfare bureau, a senior residence and activity center, the Red Shield Youth Center, the League of Mercy (which sponsors hospital visits), and of course the well-known thrift stores, which provide work, therapy, and income. There are also maternity homes and hospitals, emergency disaster services, correctional counseling centers, services to prison inmates and their families, and a highly successful agency for locating missing persons. Flamboyant methods are no longer necessary, as public encouragement has replaced hostility. Salvationists still play tambourines and other traditional instruments on street corners and in parades, but they also play guitars on beaches where young people congregate.

The Army has no particular architectural focus. Their San Francisco offices are housed in a four-story brick building of twentieth-century Mannerist Georgian style, but that is a happenstance.

Pine United Methodist Church

426 Thirty-third Avenue
Founded in September, 1886

Early in 1876 a young man named Kanichi Miyama knocked on the door of the Chinese Methodist Mission with a note to its superintendent, the Reverend Otis Gibson. Despondent over his failure to be accepted at a military academy in Japan, he had determined to build a new life in America. What he asked was an opportunity to learn English. The following year the young man became the first Japanese convert to Christianity in America, and shortly thereafter he began to study for the ministry. In the fall of 1877, Miyama and some other Japanese students established the Japanese Gospel Society, the first Japanese organization in the United States. Among the members were several students who attended the First Congregational Church, and in the mid-1880s that group withdrew to form the Tyler (Street) Gospel Society. When Miyama completed his studies, the society requested permission to establish a church, and the Methodist Board of Missions authorized the necessary financial aid. The Japanese Methodist Episcopal Mission was formally founded in September 1886, with the Reverend Kanichi Miyama as the minister and Bishop Merriam C. Harris as the superintendent.

For a time they worshiped in a borrowed Sunday school room at the Central Methodist Church on Jessie Street. One of the most significant services rendered by the church in its early years was the English School under the supervision of Dr. Milton S. Vail, who had previously established a similar school in Tokyo. More than 6,000 Japanese immigrants were taught the English language in a twenty-year period. After a religious revival in 1889, laymen moved to other West Coast communities, bearing the Gospel and establishing new churches.

During the ministry of the Reverend Suenoshin Kawashima (1897–1902), the congregation moved to their own new building on Pine Street, adopting the present name. The church erected there was destroyed in 1906. The *Official Journal of the Pacific Japanese Mission* records a devoted member's rescue of the pulpit Bible along with photographs of Gibson and Harris "in the midst of the horror and excitement when thousands were fleeing for their lives." Today they are treasured mementoes of those early beginnings.

Like other churches with largely Japanese congregations, Pine Methodist closed its doors during World War II. The church was reopened the first Sunday in 1946 with the Reverend Shigeo Shimada as pastor; services were in English until April of that year when Japanese services were resumed. Beginning in 1948 the church had two pastors, and in 1953 they became financially independent. Ground was broken for the present building in January 1965, with Bishop Donald H. Tippett officiating at the consecration services the following December. In 1973 the church was able to burn the mortgage.

The long, low building on Thirty-third Avenue was designed by architect Roy Watanabe, widely known for his modular designs for schools. Modern and Gothic elements are crisply blended in a neatly organized form. To the left of the entrance is a tiny Japanese-style atrium; bonsai trees augment the Oriental feeling. The interior is functional but stately, under a many-dormered roof. Light pours through clerestory windows at the ridgepole, and a large wooden cross against a colored glass window adorns the end gable above the pulpit.

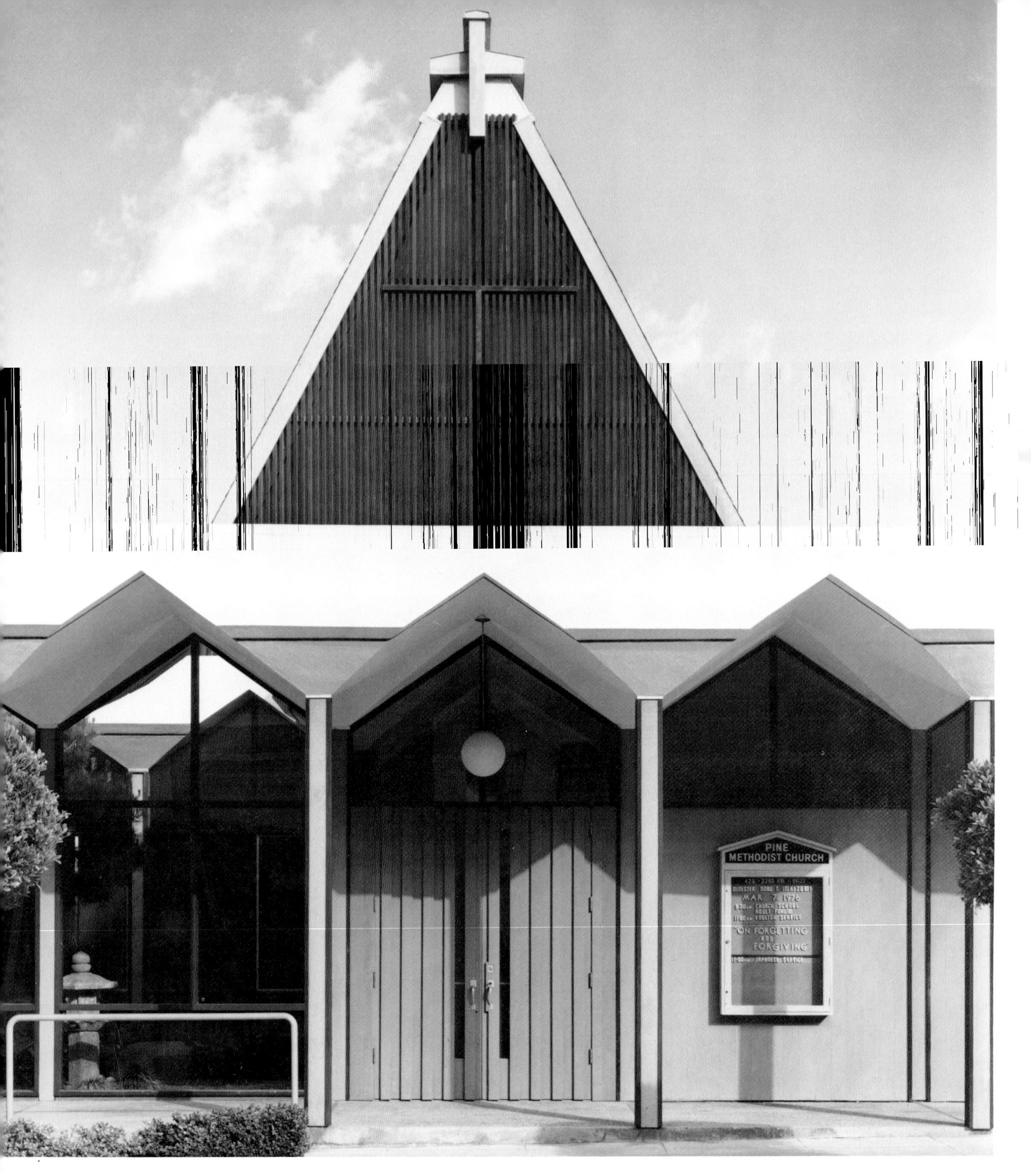

The raking eave lines of Pine United Methodist bespeak the sharp profiles of northern churches, as does its wood construction.

St. Mary the Virgin Episcopal Church

2301 Union Street, at Steiner Street
Founded March 3, 1889

In the late 1880s dairy farms began to give way to residences in the area then known as Cow Hollow. Among their owners were enough Episcopalians to aspire to a church of their own. In 1888 St. Luke's Church started a Sunday school in Cow Hollow, calling it the Mission of St. Mary the Virgin. The following year saw the arrival of an English minister, the Reverend William W. Bolton, whose whimsical memoirs have been preserved. He presented his credentials to the local bishop, who at first tried to discourage him because he was not an American, but later changed his mind and appointed the young priest to the mission.

At first the small group met in a vacant grocery store, then in the Republican Wigwam, "used on weekdays, but free on Sunday." There were protestors, but the owner of the hall ignored them and gave the rector full use. Soon the time came for a real church, and Bolton set out to find a location. "At the foot of one of the hills," he later wrote, "was an oasis in the desert of sand and poor class buildings. One whole block of land had been turned into a bower of trees and in their midst was a lovely bungalow—a city editor's home—and all around, other blocks of land were his. He was the uncrowned King of Cow Hollow, his name Frank Pixley, his sheet *The Argonaut* known from west to east the continent over."

The rector then began what he termed "The taming of the editor," whom he described as "an agnostic with a touch of atheism." Unperturbed by Pixley's reputation, Bolton approached him with British courage and frankness. Pixley so admired the young man's spirit that he donated a lot on which to build the church. When the church was dedicated, Pixley took down a fine copy of Murillo's "Virgin and Child" from his own wall and presented it to the church; the painting still hangs there. Pixley also deeded a small house and lot to William Bolton personally. Later, Bolton turned this into a diocesan gift. The two men remained friends throughout Pixley's life.

Several stories indicate that Bolton must have been an unusual man. He is reported to have tracked down a parishioner's wife who had disappeared—run away without a trace. Using methods that would be no insult to Agatha Christie's Hercule Poirot, Bolton uncovered a trail that led through several cities; he finally located the missing woman in New York. He traveled across the country and appeared one day, unannounced, in her drawing room. She had left, she said, under the impression that her husband no longer cared for her as he kept so busy with his work. Bolton convinced her otherwise and brought about a joyous reconciliation—a step or so beyond the usual in marriage counseling.

St. Mary the Virgin Church is a frame structure built of redwood and pine and covered with handsomely weathered shingles. The building is simple Victorian Gothic mingled with Shingle Style; dark wood shingles, indeed, suggest a country church, a feeling that is enhanced by the lovely English-style garden alongside the church surrounded by a picket fence and eugenia hedge. The church, with its sturdy buttresses, strong walls, and soundly planned interior trussing, survived the earthquake of 1906, as did many frame structures that did not burn in the fire afterwards. It was remodeled and enlarged in 1953; a small belfry with cross rises over the east end and the building nestles in its urban setting with disarming serenity. Architects Warren Perry and Ellsworth Johnson did the sensitive remodeling; Johnson, the altar end with its decorative painted ceiling. At that time, the entrance was changed from Steiner Street to Union, with a small but effective courtyard upon which church, parish house, and nursery open. Dirk Van Erp, the well-known San Francisco metal craftsman, designed the sanctuary lamp and the spout for the tiled Reading memorial fountain in the court. The waters of the fountain, from an artesian spring that runs under the church, are said to be from an old Indian watering place with curative powers. The spring's murmur can sometimes be heard if one stands quietly near the church altar. On a nearby court wall is a large fresco mural of the life of Christ done in 1966 by Lucienne Bloch with Stephen Dimitroff as technician. An overhanging wood canopy protects the long narrative mural.

This church contains many fine furnishings and works of art, including a richly carved Renaissance-style pulpit, a curiously Baroque pastor's bench nearby, and a striking eagle-form lectern—all in richly polished dark woods. The general effect of the interior is equally dark but soothingly calm. After one passes through the doors and under the entrance loft with its Tudor arch support and quatrefoil, Gothic-inspired decorative enrichments, the repose of cool, dark wood paneling, a lower side ceiling and lofty gabled main roof serve to highlight the more brilliantly lighted altar. Rose-colored, frosted glass windows with deeper rose inserts further soften the light that enters the church. Inside the building, one feels that such an intimate and personally meaningful church has been and continues to be an important part of the lives of its congregation.

The attractive humility of St. Mary the Virgin gives a quiet elegiac suggestion of the country on Union Street.

First Church of Christ, Scientist

1700 Franklin Street, at California Street
Founded July 1, 1889

Ten members of the relatively new Church of Christ, Scientist, met in a vacant lot to organize the first San Francisco congregation on July 1, 1889. Services were later held in the Steinway Hall, 223 Sutter Street, and several other locations, but it was twenty-two years before the present church rose near the intersection of the city's main east-west and north-south thoroughfares.

The Church of Christ, Scientist, was founded in 1879 when fifteen students of Mrs. Mary Baker Eddy voted to "organize a church designed to commemorate the word and works of our Master, which should reinstate primitive Christianity and its lost element of healing." The church comprises the Mother Church in Boston together with branch churches and societies all over the world. This optimistic faith holds that sickness, sin, and death, as aspects of falsehood, can be overcome by understanding spiritual truth. Members are expected to study the Scriptures and the writings of the founder, *Science and Health, with Key to the Scriptures,* and to live by these teachings. There are no ministers as such in the church; each congregation elects a first and a second reader for a specified term of office; the weekly lesson-sermon is the same in Christian Science churches everywhere.

The present church, designed by architect Edgar A. Matthews, was completed in 1911 and dedicated in 1913, when the debt was retired. Like Old First Presbyterian, First Church is built in a form of North Italian Romanesque, also out of varied tones of tan tapestry brick. Large flattened arches, a heavy roof overhang, and plain Lombard corbel tables with Renaissance-style cornices along the rooflines and on the squared belfry suggest a simple form of country Romanesque. With its simple silhouette and thick walls, the church gives a feeling of substantiality. Heavy doors and the metalwork in the fence are of fine-cast bronze, patined by time and climate to a soft blue-green that is echoed in the detail work below the roofline. With this and the varicolored bricks, the building has a rich texture. Terra cotta detailing in early Florentine Renaissance style surrounds the windows and is especially rich around the facade doors and their lunettes. The traceried windows and colored glass add a harmonious note to this muted ensemble. Like all Christian Science churches, the First Church building is meticulously maintained and attractively landscaped.

The First Church of Christ, Scientist uses a form of Romanesque rather than the Neoclassicist designs often chosen by this faith.

St. James' Episcopal Church

4620 California Street, between Eighth and Ninth Avenues
Founded August 10, 1890

St. James' Church began as the first Episcopal mission authorized by Bishop William F. Nichols. Before seeking official sanction, a group of thirty people led by the Reverend Floyd Mynard and Miss Florence Gay had established a Sunday school and the guild and fund-raising committees necessary to demonstrate their eagerness for a neighborhood church. They met first in a private home and then in a storeroom.

Within two years the congregation was able to build a guild hall on Clement Street between Fifth and Sixth avenues. Altar linens and other gifts came from St. James' Episcopal Church in Philadelphia, where Bishop Nichols had once been rector. For the next ten years the guild hall served a growing congregation; then in 1904 it was enlarged and remodeled, with a schoolroom added, and St. James' was declared a parish church. By that time Clement Street had become quite commercial, so the congregation bought two lots on California Street between Eighth and Ninth avenues. Mayor James Rolph's brother William laid the cornerstone of the present building on December 2, 1920.

One of the congregation's early community interests was the Ministering Children's League, a religious education service to orphans. Currently, the church operates the St. James' Early Childhood Education Center, founded in 1963, an all-day kindergarten with an average attendance of about sixty children. The Inner Richmond district has become a microcosm of the city of San Francisco, and communicants of St. James' Church represent the wide variety of separate cultural, ethnic, and racial traditions within the Episcopal church. The membership of the church is less than one hundred families, but—as a church publication points out—the key word is *family*, the best word to describe the parish which "views itself as a happy and useful part of the family of God."

The building, designed by architect Harvey E. Harris, was completed in 1923. Like other Episcopal neighborhood churches, notably St. Mary the Virgin, St. James suggests a simple country church set in a garden courtyard. A massive street entrance in wood, with traceried and trussed gables over the balustraded gates, leads to the unassuming wood and stucco church with its squared, buttressed tower and colored glass windows crowned with a high gable roof. The church contains many interesting and beautiful memorials in wood, metal, stained glass, and needlepoint. St. James' Church is a favorite for small weddings.

The massive size and rough strength of St. James Episcopal's entrance elements give an attractively modest and countrified look to its design.

Congregation Chevra Thilim

751 Twenty-fifth Avenue, between Balboa and Cabrillo Streets
Founded in 1892

Congregation Chevra Thilim is significant for its strict observance of all the 613 laws revealed to Moses on Mount Sinai. Orthodox Jews believe the laws to be inseparable from Judaism, and that the only proper observance of their religion requires total observance at all times, in all places, and in all manners.

In 1892 a small group of faithful Jews established a house of worship on Russ Street between Folsom and Howard streets. They always recited psalms before beginning services, so they named themselves Congregation Chevra Thilim, which means "a society for the recitation of psalms." In 1906 the synagogue was destroyed by the fire that swept the city after the great earthquake, but the congregation reorganized and relocated a few doors away at the corner of Russ and Howard streets.

In 1932 the congregation moved to the Richmond district, erecting a synagogue on two lots purchased at 745 Twenty-fifth Avenue. Additional adjoining land has been acquired from time to time, and the present synagogue, built in 1946 and enlarged in 1960, is the focus of an extensive religious and educational plant. The congregation's Hebrew Day School became affiliated with the Bureau of Jewish Education in 1949, and in 1961 they opened a daily Hebrew nursery school—the first in Northern California—where children ages three to five receive, in addition to a general nursery school program, instruction in Hebrew language, prayers, blessings, songs, dances, Bible stories, and celebrations of the Sabbath and Jewish holidays.

Architecture has little significance to Judaism; the Book or Torah is sacred rather than the temple as such. According to Jewish law, a synagogue consists of the Torah and ten men, wherever they can meet. Consequently, the exterior of a synagogue often assumes the architectural form of its time and place. The street facade of the quietly dignified, rose-painted synagogue of Congregation Chevra Thilim—dedicated to strict observance of ancient laws—is adorned in tall Moderne paneled pilasters and a pair of arched openings holding the tablets of the Law. The altar displays the Torah, as is traditional, and the sanctuary is divided to separate the sexes, according to Orthodox Jewish law. An unusual feature of the temple is the seating—comfortable theatre-style seats rather than benches or pews. The interior is unadorned; following tradition, it has no statues or images. The building was designed by Rabbi Morris Fishel, the first official rabbi of Congregation Chevra Thilim.

Chevre Thilim is one of the few San Francisco synagogues where male and female worshippers are physically separated.

Sparely and quietly geometric, Chevre Thilim's exterior has an Art Deco quality.

Amazzasti-no Hotoke

Japanese Tea Garden, Golden Gate Park
Opened January 1, 1894

Appropriately named "The Buddha that sits throughout the sunny and rainy weather without shelter," this serene figure continues to inspire contemplation in young and old visitors to the Japanese Tea Garden, as did the vandalized wooden Buddha that it replaced in 1947. From the opening of the Midwinter Fair on New Year's Day, 1894, to the present time, this enchanting garden has been a popular attraction. Constructed by a dealer in Oriental art, George Turner Marsh, lovingly tended and developed by the family of Makota Hagiwara from 1894 to 1942, it provided the American public with an early example of Japanese temple art and reverence for nature four years before the first missionaries arrived from Kyoto to establish their faith in North America.

Originally cast in 1790 in Tajima, Nasa Prefecture, Japan, for the Taioriji Temple, the Buddha was imported in 1928 by the Gump family and later given to the city as a memorial to the firm's founder. The handsome bronze statue stands ten feet eight inches high and weighs one and a half tons. The Buddha has his hand raised in the traditional "have no fear" gesture. He is seated on a lotus blossom, a Buddhist tradition. Today more than 254 million people worldwide follow the Buddha's teachings of wisdom, nonaggression, and compassion.

Almost overgrown by vegetation in Golden Gate Park, the Buddha's stylized curls and elongated ear lobes recall his youth as Prince Gautama Siddhartha.

St. Matthew's Evangelical Lutheran Church

3281 Sixteenth Street, between Dolores and Guerrero Streets
Founded February 10, 1895

The 1890s brought new waves of German-speaking immigrants, many of whom settled in the Mission district. The Synodical Home Missions Committee authorized the Reverend Hermann Gehrke, at that time assistant minister of St. Mark's, to establish a church for them. Gehrke rented and renovated an unoccupied church building on Eleventh Street between Howard and Mission, and the new Lutheran Church was dedicated with twenty-eight charter members.

The building was demolished in the 1906 disaster. Although St. Matthews had already bought the site of their present church, construction was not yet begun. A nearby Swedish congregation, Ebenezer Lutheran, offered use of their facilities during the interim. Despite the loss of members who moved away after losing their homes, St. Matthew's proudly dedicated its new building on March 29, 1908.

Gehrke died in 1936, having served his church for forty-one years. His successor, the Reverend Herman Lucas, served for the next twenty-five years, until 1961. During World War II, Lucas was asked to provide religious services and counseling to the five thousand German prisoners of war interned at the Presidio and Treasure Island. After the war, St. Matthews, like St. Boniface Catholic Church, sent substantial contributions to the various relief funds in war-ravaged German-speaking countries. St. Matthew's Church still offers services in German as well as in English; they have never interrupted their bilingual tradition. Music remains an important part of their services; members sing the old Bach chorales lovingly and well.

The church is said to have been designed after a church in Gehrke's hometown of Hildesheim, Germany. It is picturesquely and sharply Gothic, with forms that have clearly been translated from masonry into wood. The exterior is of painted shingles. The complex elements in the portal cohere into a symphony of pointed arches rising to a traceried rose window and high corner tower.

Stained glass windows honor several early San Franciscans. Among them is the Resurrection window over thc altar givcn by Mrs. Helena Strybing in memory of her husband, a silk merchant and owner of a diamond mine in South Africa. Mrs. Strybing is probably even better remembered by her gift of the arboretum in Golden Gate Park. Another window honors Judith and Albrecht Kuner. Kuner, a steel engraver who came to San Francisco in 1849 and later became a state senator, designed the first gold coins minted in San Francisco and also the state seal of California. A third window is dedicated to the daughter of what has been called a typical family of the early congregation. They were German immigrants who went into the grocery business, prospered, and gave the window in gratitude for their good fortune.

The church interior is both simple and elegant. There are arches over the sanctuary and an unusual ceiling of curved beams. The pews are oak, and a high, gilded pulpit with a canopy embellishes this graceful church.

As in all Protestant churches, a pulpit for preaching assumes a major role in the interior of St. Matthew's Lutheran.

Buddhist Church of San Francisco

1881 Pine Street, at Octavia Street
Founded July 30, 1898

Between 1890 and 1900, the Japanese population of San Francisco increased from 590 to 1,781. Most of the immigrants were young bachelors, not particularly interested in religion. A youth named Nisaburo Hurano, however, went back to Japan in 1896 and requested that Buddhist missionaries be sent to the Japanese community in San Francisco. Out of that request grew the San Francisco Young Men's Buddhist Association (the first Jodo Shinshu—True Pure Land Teaching—organization in the mainland United States) and later the Buddhist Mission to North America.

There was a warm welcome for the two priests from Kyoto, the Reverends Eryu Honda and Ejun Miyamoto, on their arrival in San Francisco on July 6, 1898. These two came on a goodwill tour with the hope of establishing a mission in the United States. Dr. Katsugoro Haida invited about thirty acquaintances to his Sutter Street office for the purpose of establishing a Young Men's Buddhist association on July 14. By the end of the month an official ceremony was held at the Pythian Castle auditorium on Market Street to formalize this association. They held services at 7 Mason Street until the increasing membership required a larger hall. April 15, 1899, found them gathering at 532 Stevenson, still without regular religious leadership. Finally on September 1 two resident missionaries arrived in response to a petition sent to Japan. Later that month the group moved again, this time to 807 Polk Street, where they were designated a branch office of the mother church, Hompa Hongwanji of Kyoto.

Local newspapers printed stories with photographs of the two new arrivals. They were distinguished religious leaders: Dr. Shuye Sonada, at that time head of the Academy of Literature (which later became Ryuku University), and one of his disciples, the Reverend Kakuryo Nishijima. Lectures and study classes were organized and opened to the American public. On May 16, 1900, Caucasian members organized the "Dharma Sangha of Buddha" club, and beginning in April of 1901, the Buddhist magazine *Light of Dharma* was published bimonthly by a group of twenty-five American and twenty Japanese staff members. The organization was officially named the Buddhist Church of San Francisco in 1905, the year that the Reverend Koyu Uchida assumed ministerial duties.

The church building lay in the path of the earthquake of 1906. Temporary quarters at 1906 Buchanan served as a refugee center for the homeless and injured for a few weeks until a new church was dedicated at 1617 Gough. Church programs were westernized by the addition of a Sunday school in 1913, and on April 15, 1914, The Buddhist Church of San Francisco occupied its first building at the present location, 1881 Pine Street. This was a Baroque temple very similar to those used by Protestant churches of the period, except for the presence of a stupa and an emblem signifying the four "L's" or Loves of Buddhism: love of the teachings, of one's parents, of one's community, and of one's country.

In July 1914 the San Francisco church was host to the first conference of ministers and lay representatives from all the Jodo-Shinshu churches in the United States. At that time the group formed a national association, the Buddhist Mission of North America, with headquarters in San Francisco. The following year, in conjunction with the Panama-

Pacific Exposition, that group was host to the International Conference of Buddhists. Religious leaders came from Hawaii, India, Ceylon, Burma, Mexico, Japan, and the United States. In 1918 a new title was bestowed upon the San Francisco minister; he became Socho (Bishop) Uchida of the Buddhist Mission of North America.

During the Golden Gate International Exposition on Treasure Island the church presented colorful "Buddhist Day" pageants in 1939 and again in 1940; these spectacles were warmly received by the general public. But after the events of December 7, 1941, all persons of Japanese ancestry were viewed with suspicion by many Americans; Buddhist leaders were unable to convince the authorities of the loyalty of their followers. Ultimately most San Franciscans of Japanese ancestry were interned at the Topaz Relocation Center in Utah. For the duration of the war, the headquarters of the Buddhist Mission of North America was established at the Topaz Buddhist Church. There, under the leadership of Bishop Kenju Misuyama, a conference of delegates from Topaz and other centers formed a new corporation, Buddhist Churches of North America, which was registered with the State of California on May 2, 1944. During the war years, Caucasian members looked after the San Francisco church building and the goods stored by Japanese members who were interned. After the war the church served as a hostel for returning members and friends during a critical housing shortage.

Thousands of Jodo Shinshu members from Japan, Brazil, Canada, Mexico, and the United States converged on San Francisco during the week of August 24 through September 1, 1974, for the largest celebration of the denomination's history. A panorama of cultural, social, educational, and religious events commemorated the 75th anniversary of the founding of the oldest Buddhist group in the United States, the 750th anniversary of the founding of the Jodo Shinshu sect, and the 800th anniversary of the birth of the founder, Shinran Shonin. From a group of thirty young Japanese immigrants, the Buddhist Church of North America had expanded to a total of one hundred temples with a hundred thousand followers in the continental United States. Buddhism had become a widespread religion in America, encompassing a broad spectrum of racial, social, and linguistic groups.

The present Buddhist Church of San Francisco, like its predecessor on the same site, is an essentially Western building. It is built in a modified Roman Baroque style with broken pedimented entrances at either side. Except for the stupa above, there is no exterior indication that this is a Buddhist church. But inquiry into its background reveals an exciting story beginning in the year 1935. While accompanying a group of pilgrims to Japan, Bishop Misuyama was invited to the Royal Court of Siam to receive a significant gift for the Buddhist Mission of North America—a portion of the Holy Relics of the Buddha—along with a two-inch Golden Buddha and a two-foot sculptured figure of Sakyamuni Buddha. Ceremonies honoring the gift were held in Kyoto and Tokyo before the group left Japan. When they arrived in San Francisco harbor on August 13, they were met by a procession of six hundred jubilant Buddhists and given a police escort from the pier to church headquarters.

After much discussion it was agreed that the San Francisco church and the national organization would jointly construct a temple suitable to house the treasures. Land was purchased adjacent to the Pine Street church, which was demolished to make way for the new temple. On February 19, 1937, ground was broken for the "Busshari Hoto," or "Sacred Tower of the Holy Relics." Fund raising was difficult; the nation was making a slow recovery from the Great Depression. Kikutaro Nakashima, a member of the building committee, left his nursery business and devoted his entire time to raising the needed capital.

Together with Bishop Masuyama he traveled through every district, visiting members in their homes. About sixty thousand dollars was raised through pledges from the various districts, and twenty-five thousand dollars from members of the Buddhist Church of San Francisco. The San Francisco Japanese Carpenters' Association assumed responsibility for constructing the Shrine.

Gentoko Shimamato, a young nisei architect who had earlier designed the Oakland Buddhist Church, drew the plans for the Buddhist Church of San Francisco. The Muneage Ceremony (fixing of the ridge pole) was held on July 25, 1937, and the enshrinement of the Holy Relics along with dedication of the new building took place on February 10, 1938. Each member who had donated fifteen cents or more to the building fund had his name written on a paper lotus petal. Approximately twenty thousand petals were subsequently boxed and placed in the building cornerstone.

On the roof is the stupa, a domed receptacle with elaborate upper parts—the whole intensely symbolic. Enshrined in the stupa are the Holy Relics of the Buddha—the first (and believed by the church to be the only) such relics in America. Ancient writings describe the death and cremation of the Buddha, the division of his mortal remains into eight portions (each to be enshrined in a stupa in one of the Indian kingdoms) and their subsequent subdivision into many small portions to be enshrined in Buddhist stupas throughout the world.

The ornate interior of the church expresses the Asian background of the Buddhist faith. The Hondo (worship hall) located on the second floor, bears a strong resemblance to that of the mother church in Kyoto, though on a smaller scale. It has a grid ceiling pattern and large columns in front of the altar that are typical of Japanese timber construction. The gilded carvings above the shrine recess are from Kyoto. Folding screens can be closed in front of the elaborate shrine, and Oriental-style painted screens flank the shrine recess. The carved and painted wooden figures above the shrine are Chinese-inspired dragons. A large urn for incense rests on a lacquerware table in front of the shrine, and the pews are ornamented with the eight-spoked Wheel of the Dharma (or Law), representing Buddha's teachings of the eightfold path.

The fine materials and workmanship of traditional Japan are combined in a stage-like altar for the Buddhist Church of San Francisco.

This stupa holds the only relics of the Buddha in the Western hemisphere, a gift of the Imperial Crown of Siam in 1935. The top of the (Japanese) Buddhist Church recalls the early Buddhist stupas of India, with its domed area for relics of the Buddha.

Vedanta Society of Northern California (Old Temple)

2963 Webster Street, at Filbert Street
Founded in 1900

Although comparatively few emigrants from India have settled in the United States, American interest in the richly textured religious traditions of that ancient land has mounted steadily since the days of Transcendentalism. For most Americans, the first exposure to the religions of India came through the World Parliament of Religions held in connection with the Columbian Exposition in Chicago in 1893. After the exposition, Swami Vivekananda, a disciple of the great mystic theologian Sri Ramakrishna (1836–86), stayed on to found the Vedanta Society of North America in 1897, with centers in a number of major cities. The Vedanta Society of Northern California was established in San Francisco in 1900. The society's publications and lectures have given Americans a larger appreciation of Indian religion generally.

The Vedanta Society is affiliated with the Ramakrishna Order, one of the most important religious institutions in India. Considered one of the world's oldest religions, Vedanta is based on ancient Indo-Aryan scriptures called the Vedas. Vedanta followers study the Upanishads, which form the last part of the Vedas. It is their belief that all religions teach the same basic truths, which are adapted to the needs of different times and peoples. Followers of Vedanta revere all the great teachers and prophets.

In San Francisco the society conducts services in the New Temple at 2323 Vallejo Street. Designed by the architect Henry Gutterson with Swami Ashokananda and dedicated in 1959, the building is not beholden to any specific type of architecture. One doorway contains a design that blends the cross, Star of David, thunderbolt, lotus, and crescent, showing the harmonizing potential of all religions. There is a flame motif in the front door grill that is repeated in the inner stairway and symbolizes the inner light within all beings. Within the temple, the Sanskrit word OM on the altar represents the many aspects of God revealed in varied forms. Beneath are shrines devoted to Sri Ramakrishna, Jesus Christ, and Buddha.

The Vedanta Old Temple (now a monastery) at 1963 Webster Street was consciously designed to incorporate many traditions and styles of architecture. The architect was Joseph A. Leonard with Swami Trigunitananda. The first two floors were built in 1905, and the third floor and various towers were added in 1908, after the earthquake. It has been called one of the most unusual buildings in San Francisco, yet its first two floors are also typical of the indigenous San Francisco use of bay window forms—here, slanted bays on the long north facade and rounded Queen Anne bays on the shorter east one. The departure from this convention on the lower floors is the treatment of the ground floor windows, with their "lobated" arches, which are echoed once on the second floor and again in the open arcade of Moorish inspiration on the third level, surrounding that floor. This is a rare feature in San Francisco building, but even more rare is the collection of towers on the building's roof.

The southeast corner has a medieval European-style crenellated tower. Next to it is a bulbous dome on a round tower, styled after temples in the Bengal region of India. Next along the northern side is an octagonal tower with a two-stage dome and Saracenic crescent with a trident or pinaka above, the latter modeled after Hindu Shivite temples. The cluster of pointed domes farther along the side represents a miniature of a temple in Benares, India. This cluster also suggests the multiple domes of Russian Orthodox churches, often called onion domes. The last dome, separated from the others and on a squared base, is a higher and smaller variant of that on the Taj Majal. The various pointed arches and domes symbolize the heavenly aspiration of the spiritual seeker, and different domes represent the harmony of all religions. A "skin" of scalelike shingles provides yet a final touch of both exoticism and unity to the upper levels, contrasting with the solid horizontal sheathing below as if these dramatic accents rise to the skies from a calm lake.

Intended to symbolize the eclectic nature of Vedanta's teachings, its former headquarters (now a monastery) combines forms from all parts of the world.

St. Vincent de Paul Church

2320 Green Street, at Steiner Street
Founded in 1901

Originally a mission of St. Brigid Church, St. Vincent de Paul first held services in a storefront on Fillmore Street under the ministry of Father Martin P. Ryan. In 1903 the young congregation bought an old Presbyterian church and arranged to have it placed on rollers and moved directly from its original location at the top of the Green Street hill to their present address. Within a few years, the group bought additional lots and moved the original church to the side in order to begin construction of their present building. St. Vincent de Paul became very popular with people visiting the 1915 Panama-Pacific Exposition, and was frequently referred to as the Exposition church. There is an underground stream flowing beneath both St. Vincent de Paul and the nearby St. Mary the Virgin Episcopal Church. By 1941 the water had damaged the church foundation, necessitating extensive repairs. The church interior was remodeled at the same time. Today the church has a school and a gymnasium, and offers some masses in Italian. A gold-leafed statue of Saint Vincent de Paul stands at the entrance to the church, beckoning. The motto of the church is "And the greatest of these is charity."

The most unusual feature of the present church, built in 1914, is the massive, projecting, bracketed gambrel roof. Architect Frank Shea of the firm Shea and Lofquist incorporated this feature (rarely used in church building) at the request of Father Ryan, who had been impressed by Swiss architecture on a visit to Europe. Brick is used for the lower floors, emphasizing the horizontal; wood above stresses the vertical. The detailing of the wood facade is sharply prismatic, and the movement is continued in the lofty, squared tower. Framed window arches under the gambrel roof are repeated in a triple-arched portal below. Exteriorly, the church has an assertive power that contrasts with the blue and white interior, which is more open and receptive. The stained glass windows are dominated by a brilliant blue. Sunlight streaming through these windows upon the blue and white interior walls gives a visitor the impression of standing in the center of a cut jewel. The ceiling of bracketed and trussed dark wood suggests the timbered churches of England.

A massive gambrel roof and lofty tower with vertical reinforcements give a sturdy northern air to St. Vincent de Paul.

St. Francis Lutheran Church

152 Church Street, between Duboce Avenue and Fourteenth Street
Founded May 15, 1903

By the turn of the century the population had increased sufficiently for several of the multinational denominations to establish missions for the various ethnic groups within their constituencies. In 1899 the city had Lutheran congregations offering services in the German, Swedish, English, and Norwegian languages. Most of the Danes who had come with the gold-seekers had joined the Norwegian Synod, but in 1902 the United Evangelical Lutheran Church of America agreed to sponsor a Danish church in San Francisco. For a year these people met in homes and a hall loaned for the purpose. In May of 1903 when their missionary, the Reverend P. L. C. Hansen, arrived from Oregon, the St. Ansgar Danish Lutheran Church was officially organized, the present property purchased, and a drive for building funds begun. A generous gift from Queen Louise of Denmark spurred this effort and soon money began to pour in from California congregations and even from the East. The groundbreaking ceremony on September 17, 1905, found ministers of Swedish and Norwegian churches participating, with offers of assistance during the organization period.

By February of 1906 the ground floor and the parsonage were complete. Fires sweeping the city after the earthquake reached Dolores Street a block away, but the church was not damaged. Breadlines formed along Church Street for emergency rations being distributed from a nearby building. Folding chairs from the Sunday school were given to the old people waiting in line because it moved so slowly. Both the United States Army and the Red Cross used St. Ansgar as their downtown headquarters. A temporary hospital was set up in the Sunday school room. Hansens's daughter, who had just completed her nurse's training, assisted a volunteer doctor in setting broken limbs, treating wounds and infections, and delivering several babies. The church was finally finished and dedicated on December 2, 1906.

The Reverend J. H. Vammen became pastor in 1934 and served until 1951. It was during his pastorate that the Crown Prince and Princess of Denmark attended a service at the church. The name of the church was changed in 1964 when St. Ansgar united with a neighboring Finnish congregation, Gethsemane, taking the name St. Francis Lutheran in honor of the patron saint of the city. They kept both buildings; the former Gethsemane Church at 50 Belcher is now St. Francis Child Care Center. Today the congregation includes both old-time Scandinavian families and other ethnic groups.

St. Francis Church still worships in its original building, designed by its first pastor. The red brick structure is a fine example of a plain Gothic architectural type with Romanesque details. A tall, squared tower is topped by a well-proportioned shingled, faceted spire, very northern in its aspiring elevation. Along the eaves, corbel tables give medieval authority to both the portal and the glass-filled pointed windows topped with hood molds. The interior, painted white and simply furnished, is highlighted by a handsome gold and white altar.

San Francisco Registered Landmark #39

The corbel tables and lancet windows of St. Francis Lutheran combine the Romanesque and Gothic background of this northern faith.

St. Mary's Chinese Mission

902 Stockton Street, at Clay Street
Founded in 1903

In 1894 the Paulist fathers were asked to administer the parish of Old St. Mary's Church. Father Henry H. Wyman, observing what he termed the "appalling environment" of the thousands of people crowded into the Chinatown area at the threshhold of his parish, urged the General Chapter of the Paulist Fathers to establish a Chinese Apostolate in San Francisco. In the Year of the Hare (4601 on the Chinese calendar and 1903 on the Gregorian calendar), Paulist Father Henry I. Stark returned to the city of his birth to begin the new mission.

At that time the Chinese Exclusion Act was still in effect; the Chinese people were barred from becoming citizens, owning property, and attending the same schools as Caucasians. They were also mindful of the antagonism of the labor unions and much of the public. For about a year, Stark conducted a Sunday school in the basement of Old St. Mary's, which the Chinese people called Dai Chung Lou, or The Church of the Big Bell. Gradually the attendance increased. Mrs. Bertha Welch, one of several lay volunteers, enlisted the help of Archbishop Patrick Riordan to secure the assistance of the Helpers of the Holy Souls, a European community dedicated to service among the poor. She also arranged for their expenses and found a house for them at 2030 Howard Street. The first sisters arrived in 1904, and the following year a China-born Eurasian nun, Mother Saint Ida, came to assist in the work. The Chinese women were fond of Mother Saint Ida, who spoke their language and visited Chinatown nearly every day. They brought their children to the kindergarten at the mission and stayed to learn English from the friendly nun.

Mission activities were curtailed during the three years following the earthquake. In 1909, when Old St. Mary's had been rehabilitated, Stark opened the first Catholic night school for Chinese people. In 1910 Father Charles Bradley started his work with the mission; he remained for seventeen years, becoming known as the Apostle to the Chinese. With the help of Mother Saint Ida, Mother Saint Rosa (a second China-born Eurasian nun), and a group of dedicated Caucasian volunteers, Bradley was able to establish the mission in larger quarters, first on Washington Street and later at the corner of Jackson and Stockton streets. In 1920 a native Chinese catechist came to teach and hear confessions in Cantonese.

The Oriental public school (now Commodore Stockton School) was always overcrowded. In 1920 Mrs. Welch offered to finance the building of a permanent school and social center. The cornerstone was laid on December 8, 1920, at the corner of Clay and Stockton streets, and the school opened six months later with 217 students from kindergarten through the eighth grade. Evening classes in Americanization and the English language were taught by Caucasian volunteers, and afternoon classes in the Chinese language were taught by Chinese lay people. Dr. Chu Chew Shong, a young herbalist who had been converted at the mission, served as principal of the Chinese language school for thirty-five years. Chinese children came daily, after regular school hours, for instruction in their native tongue.

The mission was named the Holy Family Catholic Chinese School and Social Center, but it soon came to be known as Sing Ma-Li, or St. Mary's. Mission programs have been adapted to changing needs over the years, but the Chinese Day School and Chinese Language School have functioned continuously. St. Mary's is probably best known for its Chinese Girls' Drum Corps, formed in 1940. In their colorful Chinese costumes, they frequently appear in parades and other community events. In January of 1961 they traveled to Washington, D. C., to represent the city of San Francisco in the inaugural parade honoring John F. Kennedy as President of the United States.

The building exterior is a plain, basically three-storied structure with tall arched windows on the main floor, doubled windows above, and a deep-bracketed roof at the top which gives a kind of Oriental aspect to the whole. The chapel is a separate building connected to the school. It has triple Romanesque-style windows at the lower sides and an ornamented portal to give additional medieval grace. The organ was given by the students of the Chinese Language School as a memorial to Dr. Shong, their former principal. The chapel interior was refurbished by the parishioners in the summer of 1969. The handcarved rosewood altar, sanctuary chair, and tables came originally from a Buddhist temple in Taipei, Taiwan. A miniature statue of the Madonna and Christ Child and one of Joseph flank the altar. The Madonna has Chinese features, and the child has a forelock that denotes royalty in China. The statues were imported from China in 1938. On the annual feast day honoring Mary the Blessed Mother (the first or second Sunday of May), children from the school carry the statues in a colorful procession through the streets of Chinatown from the school to Old St. Mary's Church.

St. Mary's Chinese Mission combines elements of West and East with particular sensitivity.

The mother and child theme, here seen in a more specifically Chinese form, is recurrent in almost all religions.

Holy Trinity Greek Orthodox Church

999 Brotherhood Way
Founded December 25, 1903

Holy Trinity is the oldest Greek Orthodox Church in the western United States, and the second Orthodox congregation to be established in San Francisco. Greek immigration to California began to increase in the 1890s, and by 1903 there were at least a hundred new arrivals from Greece living in the city. A group of about twelve devout Orthodox Christians formed a parish council and wrote home for a priest to lead them. Church records do not disclose their earliest meeting place, but other sources suggest use of St. Alexander's Church (otherwise unidentified) somewhere in the vicinity of Rincon Point, the present location of the San Francisco–Oakland Bay Bridge terminal. Father Tsapralis came from Greece and conducted the first services on December 25, 1903, and the new parish was officially registered on March 23, 1904. In this early period, the parish included Greeks living in both California and Nevada. By 1906 the congregation was ready to build its first permanent church. Fortunately, they did not begin the project until October of that fateful year. The attractive edifice designed by architect J. P. Morgan was the first entirely new religious structure to be built after the earthquake and fire. First occupied in 1907 and enlarged the following year, the building served the congregation well for nearly sixty years.

The rate of immigration reached massive proportions between 1900 and 1914. By the 1920s there were at least ten thousand Greeks living in the area south of Market Street. Twenty-four coffee houses clustered around the intersection of Third and Folsom streets (now the location of Moscone Center); in the evenings, the men gathered to drink strong Turkish coffee and play intricate card games. Each year on Good Friday evening the congregation paraded through the streets around the church carrying lighted candles and following the "epiphania" (a coffin) which commemorated the crucifixion of Jesus Christ. By 1912 the church had established a school where new arrivals studied the English language and their American-born offspring mastered the language of their church and their ancestors. Like other immigrant churches, Holy Trinity was quick to westernize in some ways, such as installing pews and replacing the cantor with a choir. Beginning in the 1960s Holy Trinity offered English language services in addition to the traditional Greek liturgy.

In 1920 a portion of Holy Trinity's membership formed a second church, Saint Sophia, on Hayes Street, later moving to a remodeled theater at 245 Valencia Street. This later became the Greek Orthodox Cathedral of the Annunciation, seat of the Bishop of the West, whose diocese includes California, Oregon, Washington, and Nevada. Holy Trinity Church and the Cathedral of the Annunciation fall under the jurisdiction of the Archbishop in New York and the Patriarch of Constantinople.

After World War II San Franciscans of all ethnic groups and all faiths tended to move to outlying districts of the city or to suburban communities, and many churches followed. Holy Trinity was among the congregations to relocate on Brotherhood Way, a park-like boulevard stretching along the southwest corner of the city and restricted by the Board of Supervisors to religious and educational uses. They sold their venerable church on Seventh Street to the newly established Ukrainian Orthodox Church of St. Michael.

The present building, dedicated on January 26, 1964, was designed by the architectural and engineering firm of Reid, Rockwell, Banwell, and Tarics. Robert Olwell of that office worked with Father Anthony Kosturos to make use of traditional forms in a modern, newly functional manner. The style suggests traditional Byzantine architecture like that of Hagia Sophia in Istanbul. Twelve massive pier buttresses, seventy feet high, support a dome that spans the sixty-foot center. A twenty-foot gold cross surmounts the copper-clad dome. The pier buttresses are hollow at the base, large enough (ten by twelve feet) to contain confessionals, stairs, and washrooms. A footbridge leads from the parking area to the nave; ground level entrances provide access to the office, service, and Sunday school facilities below. A separate building at the perimeter of the property accommodates a day school offering instruction for grades kindergarten through nine.

Structurally, the building commemorates the several groupings of twelve in the Christian tradition—twelve apostles, twelve tribes of Israel, twelve sons of Jacob. Twelve soaring stained glass windows in colors of rose, purple, blue, and green join the twelve pier buttresses. The circular form of the church is said to express the concept of unity or oneness; worshippers circle the periphery and file into the pews from the sides. The church is softly lighted by large chandeliers resembling clusters of iridescent bubbles supporting tall sconces topped by candle-flame bulbs. The striking mosaics on the iconostasis were designed by Robert J. Andrews of Hingham, Massachusetts. Richly ornamented with gold mosaic tiles, they were made in Italy and show scenes from the earthly life of Christ. The large vertical panel above and behind the altar represents Death, the Descent into Hell, and the Transfiguration. The interior walls are lined with mosaic icons of colored and chipped glass, also by Andrews. The church represents a reverent and successful union of the traditional and the modern to express the infinite.

The chaste and dignified interior of the Greek Orthodox Church of the Holy Trinity.

Massively buttressed and with a triple portal that echoes the Trinity, this church is a modern adaptation of other Byzantine ideas.

St. Anne of the Sunset Church

850 Judah Street, at Funston Street
Founded in 1904

The plain gray Catholic church founded at Irving and Funston in 1904 was named for the mother of Mary and for its location in the Sunset district of San Francisco. Father Joseph McCue was charged with the responsibility of building a new parish in the largely vacant area south of Golden Gate Park. The earthquake of 1906 affected this Irish-German congregation in two ways: first, the building was damaged, but could be repaired. Second, so many new families began moving into the western part of the city after losing their homes in the older residential neighborhoods that the building soon became inadequate. St. Anne's began planning for a larger church.

In prosperous 1929, the goal seemed near. A new lot was purchased at 850 Judah. Then troubles multiplied. Architect Will D. Shea dropped dead before the building was completed. The contractor was among those who went bankrupt when the Great Depression throttled business everywhere. World War II caused another delay. Almost twenty-five years went by before the church was plastered on the outside, and eighteen more before the interior was finished. Despite these inconveniences, St. Anne's parish continued to flourish. Today more than two thousand families belong to this church, and over six hundred children attend the church school. In 1984, fifty-two percent of the school children were of Asian descent. One of the highlights of the church year is the Novena of St. Anne, held from July 18 to July 26, with a procession on the Saturday falling within those dates.

The true beauty of St. Anne's became apparent after its rehabilitation in the 1970s by Denis Shanagher. The painted stucco (pink, rose, and white) design of the church is French Romanesque with chevron-bound, rounded arches above colonnettes, faceted corbel tables, and lofty towers that do not match. A large rose window dominates the upper facade. The lower part is reminiscent of the pilgrimage church of Saint Trôphime at Arles, France, although it has been classicized and modernized. A Corinthian colonnade supports a frieze with a plethora of figures created by Sister Justina Niemierska, a Dominican nun from Mission San Jose. From the rear, the church silhouette is powerfully architectonic, with its many clearly articulated parts.

After passing a narthex, one comes to a replendent interior in tones of pink, rose, and white, like the exterior. Its oversized Corinthian columns support massive arches and a barrel-vaulted ceiling; they repeat those of the facade. Frosted glass clerestory windows brighten the interior. The lower windows in stained glass, brought from the original church, are colorful yet with enough light glass to further illuminate the church. The mosaics along the nave were done by Edith and Isabel Piczek, two sisters who fled from the Communist regime in their native Hungary. These mosaics are the only examples of their work in San Francisco, but they have done mosaics, frescoes, and stained glass windows in southern California, where they now live. The massive crossing, overscaled like all parts of this theatrically designed church, is domed, and there is a deep apse behind the high altar.

Based on southern French Romanesque facades, St. Anne of the Sunset recalls the portal of St. Trophîme at Arles, with Classical overtones.

St. Anne of the Sunset has an almost theatrical presence, set against rolling hills and the Golden Gate Bridge.

All Saints' Episcopal Church

1350 Waller Street, between Masonic Avenue and Ashbury Street
Founded in 1904

All Saints' was the third mission established by St. Luke's Church. Although small in size, the church has played an important role in San Francisco history. During the 1960s the Haight-Ashbury district became famous as the focal point of the hippie movement. As thousands of young people—often more idealistic than practical in their expectations—converged on the city, numerous churches instituted social service programs to meet their needs. Parishioners often held conflicting views about the hippies and the church's responsibilities to those who questioned so many conventional values. By virtue of its location, All Saints' became the community church of the "flower children." On one occasion the Reverend Leon P. Harris, rector, sent out a letter reminding his flock that the church is not a private club existing for the comfort of the members, but rather a regiment of Christian soldiers dedicated to supplying food, clothing, and comfort to those in need, "and hippies often need these things." Today the church serves the University of California Medical Center and three other hospitals, as well as a heterogeneous parish. The Haight-Ashbury, located close to the geographic center of the city, is undergoing a dramatic period of restoration and rehabilitation. All Saints' continues to serve that neighborhood. The church follows the Anglo Catholic (high church) liturgy.

All Saints' is one of several small, out-of-the-way churches that are among the pleasant surprises San Francisco neighborhoods offer exploring pedestrians. Half-timbered, with leaded and colored glass windows, the high-gabled church is a miniature of the late medieval English style more frequently found in large, early twentieth-century suburban homes. The inside is paneled in redwood and has an elaborately trussed and beamed ceiling of high-pointed form. The ceilings and the three-aisled arrangement of the pews were part of the original central portion of the building moved from Masonic Street to the present location.

Lilliputian, but well tuned to its residential setting, All Saints' Episcopal is a humble cottage variant of urban late medieval design in England.

St. Francis Xavier Mission for Japanese

1801 Octavia Street, at Pine Street
Founded December 1912

The Catholic Order of the Divine Word, founded in Germany, is a European version of the Maryknoll missionaries. They established missions in Japan, with a high school and university at Nagoya. San Francisco, with its growing Japanese population, was the next logical field, and in the year 1912 a French bishop established St. Francis Xavier Mission (named for the Jesuit who introduced Christianity to Japan in 1549) in a small building on Buchanan Street. A school was added for children from kindergarten through sixth grade when the mission moved to its present location in 1929. The church serves Japanese and Korean Catholics from all over the San Francisco Bay Area. Mass is offered in Japanese and Korean twice monthly.

Architect H. A. Minton successfully combined qualities of East and West in this wood and stucco building, which was completed in 1939. The structure has a slight Mission Revival quality, but it is basically eclectic, with its upturned roof forms, squared tower with Moorish arched openings, and orientalizing multiple-arched entrance. There is a statue of the Madonna in a small, hedge-enclosed alcove-shrine to the right of the church entrance, but the other side of the garden shows its Japanese heritage in trimmed pine and plum trees.

St. Francis Xavier's orientalizing roof form recalls that saint's ministrations in the Far East.

Fourth Church of Christ, Scientist

300 Funston Avenue, at Clement Street
Founded in 1912

The Fourth Church of Christ, Scientist, reflects the movement to the suburbs that took place during the early twentieth century. A group of Christian Scientists living in the Richmond district founded this congregation in 1912, holding services in a hall on Arguello Boulevard for the first year.

The present church was first used on December 30, 1913. The building, designed by the architect Carl Werner, is a good example of the period styles (here Classical and Baroque) that were popular at the time. The facade has a set of three fine bronze doors and grills set in high, arched reveals with rusticated walls around them. Tall, simplified Corinthian pillars are set back in the center of the facade and then project forward at the side. These capitals show the architect's reworking of older forms; like the tobacco leaf capitals designed by Benjamin Latrobe for the United States Capitol, they use leaves only and not the traditional corner spirals and other details of the ancient Corinthian. As at First Congregational, the side "wings," topped with large urns above the well-detailed entablature that runs across the whole front, provide a framing of the center in the Baroque manner. These are echoed by paired tripods at either side of the entrance steps. The white exterior provides a note of sober dignity in its urban and residential setting.

The auditorium of the church is topped by a large central dome with a small circular stained glass skylight. A deeply coffered ceiling surrounding the main dome is painted in subtle tones of three or four different "colors," although the combined effect is of a modulated monochrome. The church contains a three-manual Kimball organ, recently rebuilt by Swain and Kates. Some of the original pipes were kept when it was rebuilt to enhance the beauty of the organ and maintain its mellow tone. It is considered to be one of the better of such instruments in the city. The basement below the church has an open-area Sunday school; this was built long before the open classroom approach to education became popular in the public schools. The reading room that opens onto the garden was added to the church at a later date.

A classical shrine with flowing side wings represents the usual mode of Christian Science (here Fourth) churches.

4

A New Century, A New City

1915–1985

Rebuilt, refurbished, and with a nationally acclaimed Civic Center, San Francisco had become a major American city in every respect. Then, in August of 1914, World War I broke out in Europe. A city made up of people from all the areas involved in hostilities was soon torn by divided loyalties. Bowing to public opinion, some German-speaking congregations introduced worship services in the English language. In an effort to "offer the discipline of free speech under a definite moderatorship," First Unitarian Church sponsored a series of open forums on Sunday evenings; the forums were well attended, though "perhaps better supported by outsiders than by the congregation," according to the church history.

Though far from the Atlantic seaboard, the Bay Area shipbuilding industry played an important role in the war effort. There were bond drives and housing shortages as workers moved to new jobs in San Francisco. Labor-management troubles flared up again, but these were contained during the war years. In October of 1918 the whole nation was hit hard by a flu epidemic that took many lives, particularly among the young, the old, and the caring. Among those who sacrificed their own lives by attending the sick and the dying was the Reverend Arthur Burton, especially beloved by the children of his Church of the Advent parish. Churches continued to function; at Grace Cathedral both clergy and choir wore surgical masks to prevent the spread of contagion. Despite the epidemic, the local population continued to grow, fueled by both the normal east-to-west movement of Americans and the influx of thousands fleeing homelands disrupted by the toppling of three major empires between 1914 and 1920—the Austro-Hungarian, Czarist Russian, and Ottoman Turkish. By 1921 San Francisco was a city of well over half a million people with more than two hundred sixty churches and chapels encompassing a wide variety of faiths.

New arrivals tended to settle in enclaves, often in older residential areas. During this same period established San Franciscans were following their automobiles and the expanding system of streetcars, streets, and tunnels to newly built homes in outlying districts. Districts formerly residential became commercial, and downtown San Francisco took on the character of a metropolitan area, with high-density housing, many-storied office buildings, and few if any single-family dwellings. Church affiliations were affected too. Congregations had to decide whether to sell their property and follow their flocks to the suburbs, or remain in the central city, augmenting their rolls with new members often of an ethnic origin different from that of the founding members. Three pioneer churches—First Congregational, Old St. Mary's, and St. Patrick's—found new congregations amongst the business community. Congregation Emanu-El, having worshiped in their rebuilt synagogue for twenty years after the earthquake, sold the 450 Sutter Street property and, in 1926, dedicated their masterful new temple complex at Arguello and Lake Streets. The Union Square area, formerly surrounded by imposing ecclesiastical structures, now had a medical building in place of a synagogue, a restaurant and upstairs shops at 133 Geary in place of First Unitarian, a home furnishings store where St. Mark's Lutheran once stood, and the St. Francis Hotel in Calvary Presbyterian's former location.

As churches and temples were demolished to make way for commercial structures, religious leaders sought ways to preserve the presence of sacred places in the central city. Someone proposed multiple use of valuable downtown real estate—enclosing a church within a high-rise. Such churches were actually built in New York, Chicago, and San Francisco. Under the sponsorship of the Methodist Board of Home Missions, four pioneer congregations agreed to participate in such an effort. Howard (1851–1927), Central (1864–1927), Wesley Simpson Memorial (1882–1927), and California Street (1893–1927) Methodist congregations sold their properties and pooled resources to construct the ultimate twentieth-century church, a place of worship combined with "a fine hotel where Christian travelers could feel at home." The profits from the hotel were expected to implement the Methodist missionary activities. The twenty-eight story William Taylor Hotel, at the corner of McAllister and Leavenworth streets, opened on January 15, 1930, and the magnificent ground-level sanctuary, Temple Methodist Church, was dedicated the following Easter Sunday.

Additional water for the growing city was assured by the start of the new water system in 1919, the Hetch Hetchy aqueduct, which was expected to provide plentiful water as well as electrical power starting in 1925. The water did not actually flow into the city until the mid-thirties, but the knowledge that it was coming gave confidence to those charged with planning the city's expansion. City ownership of the basic utilities—public transportation, water, power-generating systems, and later, a municipal airport—had been provided for in the 1898 city charter.

The prosperous and expansive mood of San Francisco was reflected in its religious structures. As new residential areas developed, new congregations were formed. During the twenties numerous churches were built in the new and mostly middle-class Richmond, Sunset, and West Portal districts, with their rows of shoulder-to-shoulder houses. Many churches started locally and informally. People might meet in one another's homes. A Mrs. Hansen described the formation of Portalhurst Presbyterian, recalling that they always took their babies with them to church meetings. "They played contentedly on the kitchen floors with the lids of cooking utensils, dried onions (which rolled around beautifully), and potatoes (whose movements were more erratic)." From such simple beginnings, new neighborhood congregations established themselves.

Most denominations expanded their social services during this period. The Episcopalian Good Samaritan Mission, moving to new quarters at Eighth and Natoma streets, took the name Canon Kip Neighborhood House in honor of its founder. The Reverend W. J. Byers, pastor of First A.M.E. Zion, was instrumental in establishing the Booker T. Washington Center for the black community. The Presbyterian Board of Missions engaged the noted architect Julia Morgan to design the Potrero Hill Neighborhood House for the predominantly Molokan Russian community being served by Olivet Presbyterian church. St. Mary's Chinese School and Social Center occupied its first permanent home and opened a day school for children who could not gain admittance to the overcrowded Chinese school (now Commodore Stockton). Protestant groups in Chinatown, long accustomed to teaching English as a second language to newcomers, now joined forces to operate the Hip Wo School, which offered late-day instruction in Chinese language and culture to both children and adults. A few churches that had been destroyed in 1906 were completed in this time, long after the initial flurry of rebuilding had ended. SS. Peter and Paul and St. Dominic's are examples, both impressive structures requiring substantial outlays of time, effort, and money.

The Bolshevik Revolution in Russia inspired a flood of immigrants from Eastern Europe, the Balkans, and the Middle East, while at the same time making it impossible for the Patriarchate of Moscow to support an overseas mission. Serbians, White Russians, and Syrians established their own national Orthodox congregations in San Francisco between 1919 and 1938. Another branch of Eastern Christianity, the Armenian Apostolic church, began holding regular services in various Episcopal and Orthodox church buildings as their countrymen migrated to the city from the Fresno area after the collapse of the raisin industry there.

Large public religious events started to become popular in the 1920s. Among Roman Catholics, the annual Easter week celebration was a major holiday, and people worked hard to create a memorable time. SS. Peter and Paul was the first stop on a pilgrimage that covered a twelve-mile route and seven churches—SS. Peter and Paul, St. Francis of Assisi, Our Lady of Guadalupe, Old St. Mary's, Nôtre Dame des Victoires, St. Brigid's, and St. Patrick's or St. Boniface. The parade started after ten o'clock mass on Holy Thursday. Italians, Tuscans, Genovese, Lucchesi, Sicilians, French, Spanish, German, and Irish San Franciscans joined the throng. Everyone was well dressed, of course; the women especially showed off their new hats. Some people walked or traveled by streetcar; some covered the route in their automobiles, giving rides to relatives and friends, waving to more friends as they slowly passed.

A second city-wide religious tradition started in 1923 with the first Easter sunrise service on top of Mount Davidson. This was and continues to be a nondenominational event that begins before dawn on Easter morning. Pilgrims climb the tallest mountain in San Francisco just as pilgrims of all faiths have climbed mountains all over the world to move closer to heaven for their prayers.

Prosperity came to an abrupt end with the Wall Street crash of 1929 and the Great Depression it signaled. Churches under construction were often put to use at the current state of completion. Grace Cathedral and St. Anne of the Sunset were not finished until after the end of World War II. Like several of its counterparts in other American cities, the Methodists' skyscraper church-hotel was financially unsuccessful. Stained glass windows and pipe organ were removed and the building sold to satisfy creditors (the fine organ now graces the chapel of the University of the Pacific in Stockton). Temple Methodist Church then merged with First Congregational, a union which lasted five years, and then moved to the Scottish Rite auditorium. The structure itself, next known as the Empire Hotel, was converted to United States government offices during World War II and to apartments for students attending Hastings College of the Law in the 1980s. Few people remember the original function of the yellow brick and terra cotta structure, which is clearly visible in the photograph of St. Boniface Church.

Almost no new religious buildings were started in the early years of the Depression with three exceptions—the ecumenical Post Chapel at the Presidio (built by the United States Army), the Buddhist Church of San Francisco–Buddhist Mission to North America complex, and Glide Memorial Methodist Church. Glide, exceptional in many respects, was financed by an oil well discovered in 1931. The Japanese-Caucasian Buddhist headquarters at 1881 Pine Street was demolished and rebuilt in order to enshrine the only Holy Relics of Sakyamuni Buddha in the Western world. Attendance in most churches increased during this time, and some congregations reported their largest membership during the troubled thirties and forties. People sought comfort and a sense of hope in religion.

Eventually various public building projects were begun, funded by the New Deal under the administration and guiding hand of President Franklin D. Roosevelt. Various federal agencies employed artists to do public work for the city. Murals at the Presidio Post Chapel, the Beach Chalet, Coit Tower, and Rincon Annex Post Office were executed by groups of painters working together under the leadership of a head artist, somewhat in the manner of the European studio system. These brilliantly colored murals, highly revealing social documents of the thirties, are still generally available for people to see. Another federal agency, the Public Works Administration, funded construction of Pulgas Water Temple at the confluence of Hetch Hetchy and San Francisco's Crystal Springs reservoir waters. This graceful structure may be the last manifestation of the Greek Revival movement that impelled nineteenth-century Americans to erect temples in secluded areas symbolizing the bringing of civilization to the wilderness.

Until the late 1930s the only way to cross the bay was by boat. The Ferry Building at the foot of Market Street had been operating since the beginning of the century, but ferry traffic reached its height in the 1930s. This changed dramatically when the great bridges were completed. Historical photographs illustrate how much these immense human creations have come to seem a natural part of the environment. A photograph showing the entrance to the bay without the Golden Gate Bridge is somehow shocking. This evocative bridge spans the entrance to one of the world's finest harbors. Over the years nature's provision was supplemented by human endeavor, and San Francisco developed a fine port with a prosperous shipping industry that contributed greatly to the financial base of the city.

San Francisco's third world fair, the Golden Gate International Exposition, held in 1939 and 1940 on man-made Treasure Island, was planned to celebrate the completion of the two Bay Area bridges. The theme of the exposition emphasized San Francisco's affinity with other cultures of the Pacific Basin. Seventeen million people visited the island, which was soon to serve a very different function. When war was declared by the United States, Treasure Island became a naval base. Many of the original fair buildings were quickly converted to military purposes.

The outbreak of the war in Europe had a profound effect on San Francisco and brought about radical changes in American society. There was a widespread feeling of enthusiasm and of working together wholeheartedly for a good cause. The local population grew dramatically as people came from all over the country to work in war-related industries, especially shipbuilding. The already crowded city felt the pressure of even more people, and—as during the Gold Rush—struggled to meet greatly increased demands for housing, transportation, social services, and recreational facilities. Families were encouraged to rent unused rooms to war workers. Low-cost "temporary" housing was built near the Hunters' Point shipyard.

Sunday, December 7, 1941, had a dual significance for two new congregations. On that day St. John Armenian Apostolic Church dedicated the altar of its first church building at 7 Elgin Park, and College City–Lakeside Presbyterian Church was formally established as the Reverend Harry Clayton Rogers, recently retired after serving thirty years as the pastor of a Kansas church, stood at an open window of his St. Francis Wood home and delivered a sermon to the more than one hundred neighbors assembled in his garden. The group, which had grown steadily since the first informal service the preceding June, had already made plans to build a church, but the attack on Pearl Harbor caused a moratorium on civilian construction, so they rented a vacant store on Ocean Avenue near Nineteenth Avenue.

Then, with America's entry into the war, young men and women left their homes as earlier generations had done before them to defend the values of Western civilization. The

Reverend David H. Youngdahl resigned as pastor of the First Swedish Baptist Church to become a chaplain in the United States Army. Along with many others, he was lost at sea when his troopship was torpedoed in the North Atlantic on February 7, 1943. Soldiers and sailors came through San Francisco on their way to the Pacific. The local churches welcomed military personnel, and most congregations organized social events for them, or participated in the war effort in other ways.

Although the congregations of many churches increased during these troubled times, some churches closed when their Japanese-American members were required to leave their homes, businesses, and places of worship to spend the war years in internment camps. Pine Methodist closed entirely. Caucasian members of the Buddhist Church of San Francisco cared for the temple and the personal belongings of absent members; the Soto Shu Mission employed Caucasian caretakers to oversee their facilities during the war years.

The needs of the defense industries stimulated a flood tide of immigration far greater than that of the Gold Rush, the 1880s, or the 1920s. Census figures show an increase from 634,536 in 1940 to 775,357 in 1950. The most noticeable ethnic change was a tenfold increase in the city's black population. In the early forties a group of young adults calling themselves the Sakai group (they were living in the former home of the Japanese Sakai family) approached the Reverend Albert Fisk, a professor of philosophy at San Francisco State College, with the idea of establishing an interfaith, interracial church. As a result of their efforts the highly successful Church for the Fellowship of All Peoples began its life in the building vacated by the Japanese Federated Church of Christ. Financial support came from Unitarian, Jewish, and Protestant sources.

As World War II drew to a close, President Roosevelt, Premier Stalin, and Prime Minister Churchill, meeting at Yalta, had called for a conference of the heads of the allied nations to draw up a charter for an international organization to maintain world peace. The site selected for this United Nations conference, scheduled to begin on April 25, 1945, was San Francisco, perhaps because its location across the country from Washington, D.C., might symbolize nationwide support for the international peace effort. Practically speaking, San Francisco was also more readily accessible to the representatives of the forty-five participating countries than other American cities.

The city assumed a festive air as delegates, many of them in colorful native dress, gathered from around the world. Fashionable stores recruited personnel from alterations and warehouse departments to serve as interpreters. Temple Sherith Israel was selected to serve as host for one of the founding sessions. The first meeting of the representatives took place at the War Memorial Opera House. President Harry S. Truman welcomed the nations of the world via a radio connection from the White House. With characteristic straightforwardness, he said, "If we do not want to die together in war, we must learn to live together in peace." An alternative to war became a necessity for world survival when we entered the atomic age two months after the United Nations charter was signed.

By the end of World War II America had become a strong industrial nation, a world superpower, and the home of an international organization seeking world security and peace. Industry, geared up for war, adapted to a peacetime economy that included a baby boom, a housing boom, and the development of several new industries made possible by wartime technology. The postwar period was a time of national confidence and financial expansion, felt in San Francisco as well. At the same time, fifty million human beings had been killed in the most destructive war the world had ever known. Both the war and its aftermath had a tremendous effect on people, their religious beliefs, and their needs. The war's end, the highly visible United Nations conference, and the use of nuclear weapons across the Pacific were gateposts into the modern age. Eventually old values would be questioned and new explanations sought. But for the present—at the war's end and for the next decade—people only wanted to return to a blessed ordinariness. They wanted to go to work or to college, to buy homes, to have children, and to raise them in peace. They wanted to settle down and in, and that is what they did.

The end of the war, however, had left a host of urban problems in its wake. Thousands who had lived in, or merely passed through, San Francisco during the hostilities wanted to live in "everybody's favorite city." Others were coming home to the city of their birth. Five thousand or more Japanese-Americans returned only to find their previous homes unavailable to them. New housing was needed. Demands grew for more public services—transportation, education, recreation facilities, health care—and private goods and services—stores, theaters, baby sitters, restaurants, churches.

The city took stock. A study commissioned by the board of supervisors found that wartime growth coupled with restrictions and labor shortages had left a legacy of traffic and parking problems, of city services in need of overhauling, and of older residential neighborhoods degenerating into slums. Bond issues approved by the voters provided new playgrounds, swimming pools, branch libraries, and public schools in record time. A redevelopment agency was established to take some action on the upgrading of older districts. First efforts were focused on the Western Addition, but legal difficulties delayed actual construction for more than a decade.

The only sizeable tracts of vacant land lay in the southwest corner of the city. Private developers, quick to assess the market, were soon advertising split-level homes and garden apartments in the area. Within a short time the new residents had a choice of churches within walking distance. St. Stephen's Catholic parish took the overflow from St. Cecilia's. College City–Lakeside Presbyterian built two churches on Nineteenth Avenue, first a small chapel at Ocean Avenue and then the present edifice at the corner of Eucalyptus Drive. First Swedish (now Temple) Baptist, a pioneer congregation, moved from the Mission district. And Temple Methodist, after unsuccessful attempts to repurchase their hotel-church from the federal government in 1948–49, relinquished the idea of a downtown location and put up the present impressive church complex at the intersection of Nineteenth Avenue and Junipero Serra Boulevard. Nestled among the churches was the city's first regional shopping center, Stonestown.

The period had begun on an optimistic note. People looked forward to a happy new world of peace and prosperity. Young couples, Depression-bred, set about acquiring all the things they had dreamed of during wartime service and separation—a secure, middle-class way of life and in many cases families larger than those in which they had grown up. Apart from home ties, families looked to the churches for both religious and social needs. Church programs were expanded to provide for toddlers, singles, couples of various ages, professional people. Camps and weekend retreats were organized. This extended-family environment was as much appreciated by transplanted Americans as by the foreign-born. America's wartime efforts seemed to have produced a better life for all.

Religious thought took a new turn within a year or two, however. It began to appear that another conflict was in the offing. Winston Churchill described the Russian presence as an "iron curtain" that had descended across the continent of Europe; Joseph Stalin announced that communism and capitalism were inevitably fated to clash; and Congress had appropriated funds for the protection of Greece and Turkey. Disillusioned by the turn of events and shocked to find that much of the world, while eagerly accepting American aid, mistrusted American motives, many people sought answers in religious studies. Protestant, Catholic, and Jewish seminaries were crowded. Theologian Reinhold Niebuhr, who had been insisting since the thirties that human beings are irretrievably selfish and sinful, became a kind of national sage. Though the existentialist philosophy of Jean-Paul Sartre and Albert Camus influenced some to become atheists, many more followed the Danish theologian Sören Kierkegaard's religious version of existentialism, accepting the leap of faith to a belief in Christ. By the mid-fifties San Francisco church membership, like that of the nation as a whole, was rising twice as fast as the general population. There was a huge increase in church building and contributions to churches. The historian Robert Kelley equates this national revival of religion to the "Great Awakenings" of the past.

Several churches bought land adjoining Stanley Drive, a wide, curving boulevard along the southwestern perimeter of the city. Sensing an opportunity for tangible expression of the city's traditional tolerance, they successfully petitioned the board of supervisors to rezone the undeveloped, parklike area exclusively for religious, educational, and fraternal organizations, and in January of 1958 the boulevard was officially renamed Brotherhood Way. The various property owners have jointly developed such amenities as sidewalks, streetlights, and access roads.

Brotherhood Way is both a street and a concept. Along its winding contours are located a number of faiths, a return to the happy admixture of diverse beliefs and believers characteristic of San Francisco's early history—a cheek-by-jowl sharing of traditions that enrich and enliven the city's character. Both pioneer and postwar congregations and their service organizations are represented. St. Thomas More Catholic Church (with its school and convent) was founded in 1950. Temple Beth Israel–Judea (which combines a Conservative congregation founded in 1860 with a Reform group established nearly a century later) adjoins the Brotherhood Way Jewish Community Center and Nursery School and the Brandeis-Hillel Day School. Both the city's earliest Armenian church, Calvary Congregational (founded in 1926) and its next door neighbor, Lake Merced Christian Church (dating from 1895) attract members from the entire community. A new day school and community center are already in operation on the future site of St. Gregory Armenian Apostolic Church. Brotherhood Masonic Lodge (a fusion of two pioneer San Francisco lodges) occupies a handsome temple here. At the westernmost end of the wooded ravine stand the temple and day school of the city's earliest Greek and second oldest Orthodox congregation, Holy Trinity, established in 1903. Brotherhood Way attracts visitors from all over the world.

Elsewhere in the city, new Eastern Orthodox church buildings included Our Lady of Kazan (Russian Church in Exile) and St. John the Baptist Serbian Orthodox. The city's three oldest black churches—Third Baptist, Bethel A.M.E., and First A.M.E. Zion—all built new churches in contemporary styles during this period. And by the time the Church for the Fellowship of All Peoples had moved into its permanent home, the practice of interfaith, interracial worship had become a matter of individual choice.

Non-Western religions, too, found new adherents in the 1950s. The Vedanta Society of Northern California, outgrowing its original quarters, dedicated a New Temple. Ch'an Buddhists, relatively inactive in California since the Chinese Revolution of 1911, put up the four-story Buddha's Universal Church—the sect's largest temple in the United States—using only hand tools and all volunteer labor. A high-ranking priest came from Hong

Kong to establish the Jeng-Sen Buddhist-Taoist Temple for the benefit of newly arriving immigrants.

Possibly the most significant spiritual event of the decade, however, came about because of a singular dream—or was it a vision? Mrs. Dorothy Lister Rogers, president of the San Francisco Council of Churches, awoke during the night with the idea of an enormous prayer meeting—all faiths, all races—praying together for peace on the tenth anniversary of the founding of the United Nations. In the morning she contacted President Eisenhower to ask if he would attend such a service. He accepted, saying that if necessary, John Foster Dulles would represent him. When approached, officials of most religious groups indicated their support for the idea. Only the local hierarchy of the Roman Catholic Church seemed disinterested. Undaunted, Mrs. Rogers telephoned friends in Rome who were able to present the idea to the Vatican. Papal permission was granted for San Francisco Catholics to hold a similar, simultaneous service in another location. This Festival of Faith, held on June 19, 1955, in the great arena of the Cow Palace, attracted sixteen thousand people who read together from the sacred books of the faiths represented—Protestant and Orthodox Christian, Unitarian, Jewish, Moslem, Buddhist, Hindu, Baha'i. Forty-two radio stations and three of the fairly new television networks covered the event, which received front page publicity as far away as Guam and Bombay. Expenses were covered by private sponsors, and after the ceremony a freewill offering of five thousand dollars was sent to UNICEF. The Festival of Faith was repeated in 1965; by that time the Roman Catholic Church had liberalized its policies, and Archbishop Joseph T. McGucken not only approved but officiated.

As the fifties drew to a close, there were more than one hundred churches, temples, or halls in which some services were offered in one or another of at least twenty-three languages including Estonian, Greek, Old Slavonic, Japanese, Syrian, and Tagalog. The religious concepts represented in this theological panorama included the Jewish, Buddhist, Muslim, Taoist, Hindu, and Shinto faiths, the liberal Unitarian and Swedenborgian teachings, and the Armenian Apostolic, Roman Catholic, Eastern Orthodox, Protestant, and Mormon branches of Christianity. The Watchtower Bible and Tract Society, popularly called Jehovah's Witnesses, held a series of conferences, moving from the Masonic Temple to the Civic Auditorium to Candlestick Park as attendance grew to a peak of fifty thousand people in 1961. Temple Emanu-El and First Unitarian continued to hold joint services on Thanksgiving. San Franciscans celebrated St. Patrick's Day with the Irish, Columbus Day with the Italians, and New Year's with the Chinese, while respecting the right of the Jewish population to be excused from work or school on their High Holy Days. The Buddhist *Obon* or Festival of Souls was celebrated by the young dancing the *Odori* in Buchanan Street while the older generations honored their dead in the temples with offerings of incense and flowers.

The turbulent sixties began quietly enough. The cosmopolitan nature of the city's religious heritage became newly apparent as impressive new temples rose to punctuate the San Francisco skyline. Eastern Orthodoxy had become well established in America, and by 1961 most national Orthodox churches were members of the World Council of Churches (heretofore almost exclusively Protestant). In San Francisco the Greek and Syrian congregations dedicated new churches; the Ukrainians established their first congregation in the former Greek church; and ground was broken for an elaborate new cathedral of the Russian Church in Exile. The distinctive foliated cross of the Armenian Apostolic Church rose above new edifices in the Jordan Park and Midtown Terrace districts. As the legal obstacles to redeveloping the Diamond Heights district were finally resolved, the residents of the new homes, apartments, and condominiums there could choose from a variety of churches—St. Nicholas Antiochan Orthodox, St. Aidan's Episcopal, Shepherd of the Hills Lutheran, or St. Philip's and St. Brendan's Catholic. The various branches of Buddhism, especially Zen, began to interest many Caucasian Americans, and religious leaders from the Asian countries attracted new followers. Chevra Thilim, an Orthodox Jewish congregation, extensively remodeled its Richmond district temple and opened the city's first daily Hebrew nursery school.

The practice of ancient religious laws was in dramatic contrast to much of what was happening in San Francisco and elsewhere during the sixties. Religious fervor broke the confines of buildings and moved into the streets with the hippies. (The term *hippie* was an English import taken from a pair of pants, but the movement was American and particularly focused in San Francisco, where it probably took some cues from the Beatniks of the fifties.) If hippies had no catechism, no liturgy, and no central belief, they had plenty of energy, righteousness, and disdain for the conventional middle-class values—the same ones their parents held most dear. Defining their creed as one of peace, love, and brotherhood or community, they experimented with dress, communal living, sex, and psychedelic drugs. During the summers of the mid-sixties, young people from all over the United States flocked to San Francisco to join the eight thousand or more somewhat permanent residents of "the Haight"; they slept in the Golden Gate Park Panhandle or in Buena Vista Park until evicted; they roamed the streets, often barefoot, and crowded all available living areas. Many were very young and had run away from home to become "flower children" and join the "love generation."

Older residents were upset about the hippie movement, which they considered fraught with danger for the young people as well as for society. Mutual antagonism characterized relations between the generations as each questioned the other's values. Despite the reservations of some parishioners, churches in the area provided coffee houses, medical treatment, and employment, legal, and pastoral counseling. Hamilton Square Baptist and Glide Memorial Methodist churches drew up lists of families who would provide young strangers with bed and breakfast for from one to three nights; First Baptist opened a storefront facility called The Living Room for counseling and referrals. All Saints' Episcopal, located in the heart of the district, became the unofficial parish church of the hippie movement. In the turbulent days to follow, Jewish, Catholic, Protestant, and Orthodox leadership consolidated programs in order more effectively to meet the needs of the disabled, the disaffected, and the incarcerated. The Night Ministry, which provides a pastor in clerical garb on the street of the Tenderloin district nightly from ten o'clock until dawn, was established by seven denominations and later sponsored by the San Francisco Council of Churches.

San Francisco had become the hub of a truly metropolitan area, and by the early 1960s both the Golden Gate and the San Francisco–Oakland Bay bridges reached capacity. The need for public transportation to minimize automobile traffic and resulting parking congestion was a cause for concern. Just as in the days of the volunteer fire departments, people formed associations to meet what they saw as an emergency situation. Cooperative efforts produced, in 1974, the Bay Area Rapid Transit (BART) district's system of speedy rail transportation between San Francisco and the East Bay. Always independent, San Francisco voters were the first in the nation to reject the concept of a continuously expanding freeway system. Following the defeat of several proposals designed to improve traffic flow into and out of the city, a citizens' committee began an initiative that restored commuter ferry service between San Francisco and Marin County by 1976.

Cities across the nation were experiencing problems with inner-city deterioration as the middle classes migrated to the suburbs. Almost alone among American cities, San Francisco maintained the vitality of its downtown retail section, as merchants hastened to upgrade their establishments in response to the appealing new tourist and trade complexes being created out of old factories and warehouses in outlying districts. During this same period the number of tall buildings going up in San Francisco increased dramatically. Skyscraper office buildings towered over the older structures in the financial district, and multi-story hotels, condominiums, and apartment houses blocked views and caused controversies elsewhere. A new zoning ordinance was passed, and the financial and lower Market Street districts began to blossom with outdoor gardens and other public spaces as builders took advantage of the extra height permitted in exchange for specified set-backs and other amenities.

As familiar landmarks tumbled, everyone had opinions on what to build, how much, and where. Progress, and hence building, once worshiped without hesitation or qualification, was seen to have its costs and attendant problems. Among the casualties was Kong Chow Buddhist-Taoist Temple, one of America's two oldest Chinese temples, razed in 1970 to make way for an office building. Concern that the city would become overbuilt and lose its architectural identity became widespread. A list was begun of buildings too important architecturally or historically to be demolished; owners of such property were then required to obtain city approval before making any external alterations. Five of the first six structures to be designated San Francisco Registered Landmarks were churches: Mission Dolores, Old St. Mary's, St. Patrick's, St. Francis of Assisi, and Holy Cross Parish Hall (the second St. Patrick's building).

Urban redevelopment programs kept the city in a turmoil during the sixties and seventies, and even into the eighties. Traditional ethnic and socioeconomic neighborhoods were threatened, and all proposals were hotly contested, delaying the projects interminably. The Western Addition, first to be undertaken, ultimately produced one of the most striking groupings of ecclesiastical architecture to be found in the city. The rerouting of some cross-town thoroughfares produced odd-shaped parcels of land adjacent to several churches, who have utilized them effectively. Approaching Cathedral Hill from the east, one comes upon Hamilton Square Baptist's contemporary church and seminary at the corner of Geary and Franklin, directly across from First Unitarian's traditional Gothic gray stone church and contemporary center. The red brick Victorian Romanesque/Gothic facade of St. Mark's Lutheran rises to the south, with St. Paulus Lutheran's pristine white Gothic church beyond. The ultra-modern St. Mary's Cathedral crowns the hill directly to the west, so skillfully adapted to its site that neither parking nor educational facilities are visible from the street. A Presbyterian-sponsored retirement community lies diagonally across Geary Boulevard from the cathedral, and to the west of that can be seen the Peace Pagoda supplied to the Japanese cultural center as a gesture of friendship by the people of Japan. An informal "Brotherhood Way" has sprung up along Laguna Street, with Buddhist, Konko, Presbyterian, and Jehovah's Witnesses groups located side by side.

As San Francisco celebrated its two hundredth birthday in conjunction with the national bicentennial celebration, a large interfaith parade through the downtown area was combined with the customary Pontifical Mass at Mission Dolores and birthday luncheon at the Presidio Officers' Club. The city of Saint Francis, always cosmopolitan, entered its third century with a population more varied than ever before. In the tempestuous years since World War II, new ethnic, cultural, and idealogical groups of all kinds have demanded attention. In the response the city has shown itself "tolerant of Bohemianism but not radicalism" (as noted by historians Robert W. Cherney and William Issel). And underneath all the confrontations and conciliations, the heart of the city has continued to beat as people are born, married, and buried, for the most part observing these rites of passage within the churches of their choice.

Newly arriving minorities establish their spiritual headquarters in a small way. The American Indian Baptist Church, founded in 1978, offers services in English because the native tongues of the members include Creek, Navajo, Piute, Choctaw, Siouan, and Seminole. Because of the distance from the Islamic Center on Crescent Avenue, St. Ignatius Catholic Church has made space available for the five daily prayer periods of the Moslem students attending the University of San Francisco. Filipino Christians established Iglesia ni Cristo in a former Christian Science church. Innumerable new Buddhist and Taoist centers have opened in the last decade. Homosexuality, a sensitive point with many religious groups, has become a part of the city's diversified political, social, and religious life; Congregation Sha'ar Zahav (Jewish), the Golden Gate Metropolitan Community Church, the Parsonage (Episcopal), Dignity (Catholic), and four Lutheran churches minister to the gay community.

With the passage of time, original congregations have moved away and new parishioners have inherited the elaborate churches designed for large, formal Sunday worship. Some have successfully adapted the stately old buildings to the requirements of inner-city ministry. Others, like the pastor and members of Mission United Presbyterian Church, have petitioned the City Planning Commission for permission to demolish the structure and build something more suitable to current programs and less costly to maintain. Permission is necessary in this case because the building has been assigned Landmark status. As 1984 drew to a close, twenty-two churches and church-related structures held that designation, and the nomination of First Congregational was being delayed because of a protest by the church. Landmark status restricts but does not preclude future remodeling; the interior of the long-closed B'nai David Orthodox Synagogue (San Francisco Registered Landmark #118) has been converted into artists' studios and apartments while the exterior remains unchanged. Historic Trinity Methodist Church at 2299 Market Street near Sixteenth and Noe streets was spared this dilemma by a fire in 1980; the remains of the building have been razed in preparation for a new, multi-purpose church building that will include shops, condominiums, and underground parking.

In contrast, recent years have seen an explosion in lavish ecclesiastical architecture of several major religious groups. The city boasts two newly completed cathedrals—St. Mary's Roman Catholic, and Holy Virgin Russian Church in Exile. The various ethnic congregations of the Eastern Orthodox faith have built new sacred places, as have two Armenian Apostolic churches. Konko Church has graced the Nihonmachi (Japantown) area with a sparkling example of traditional Japanese architecture. New Buddhist churches abound. The interest in organized religion continues to grow. The city's population decreased from 775,357 in 1950 to 678,974 in 1980. During that same period the number of churches increased by thirty percent, from approximately four hundred twenty to five hundred fifty.

Redevelopment in the eighties is focused in two areas, the Performing Arts Center adjacent to the already impressive Civic Center complex, and the area recently christened Yerba Buena Center between Market and Folsom, Third and Fourth streets. The long-awaited Performing Arts Center has become a reality with the opening of the new and architecturally exciting symphony hall and ballet theater; new restaurants and condominiums add to the festive atmosphere. A new convention center named for former Mayor George Moscone has opened in the Yerba Buena Center. Plans recently submitted for the area, which has been slated for redevelopment since the mid-sixties, include provisions for commercial, hotel, theater, restaurant, shopping, and residential facilities.

At the heart of the current Yerba Buena Center design is a plaza that surrounds and highlights two old San Francisco structures. One is an abandoned power station, the other is St. Patrick's Church, built in 1868 and rebuilt after the earthquake and fire. When St. Patrick's was first built, the area was a residential one where the town's successful merchants made their homes. If the plan is carried out, the new will come round to pay homage to the old. The lovely old brick church will serve yet another congregation, just as the many sacred places of San Francisco have served people faithfully since the city's beginnings.

St. Cecilia's Church

2555 Seventeenth Avenue, at Vicente Street
Founded January 6, 1917

In 1916 the southern Sunset district was still a remote and breezy wide-open space where members of glider clubs gathered to fly their craft. It was here that Father John Patrick Tobin met the challenge of the fifty-nine Catholic families who had by that time ventured to build homes in the area. The founder of St. Cecilia's parish had won his spurs in the preceding fourteen years, during which he had revived and rehabilitated the Old Mission Dolores founded by the Franciscan fathers in 1776. His work and that done by the architect Willis Polk in the 1920s are responsible for preserving the mission as the historical landmark it is today. As a reward for those labors, Archbishop Patrick Riordan offered the Irish priest his choice of two new parishes to be added to the archdiocese. Tobin chose the one that spread from Twin Peaks to the ocean and from Pacheco Street to Sloat Boulevard and Los Angeles Street (now Monterey Boulevard). Then he knocked on doors, raised funds, hired a contractor, and picked up his hammer to help build a church on the sand. St. Cecilia's first mass was celebrated in the garage of a remodeled house at 1215 Taraval Street on January 6, 1917.

Mayor "Sunny Jim" Rolph donated the old Parkside schoolhouse to the congregation, and the Parkside Fire Department gave them a bell. The school and the house were moved to a lot at Fifteenth Avenue and Taraval Street, where they were transformed into a church and a rectory in time to be dedicated on Sunday, June 15, the day after the opening of the Twin Peaks Tunnel.

Monsignor Harold E. Collins became St. Cecilia's pastor in 1946, continuing to serve there until his retirement thirty years later. A native San Franciscan, Collins had attended the Old Mission Dolores school during the years that Tobin was serving there, and had taught classes at a number of institutions—St. Ignatius, Sacred Heart, and St. Vincent high schools, St. Mary's and Mary's Help hospitals, and two convents. He started the distinctive observance of All Hallow's Day which is still observed at St. Cecilia's. On that day all the young who have the names of saints—all the Johns, Annes, Cecilias, Peters, Josephs, and others—form in ranks under their personal banners, march around the block, and proceed into the church for a special religious service. Collins was particularly successful with children, and even in retirement he visited the church playground, where he told jokes or tossed jelly beans into the air for the children to catch. During his long career he was accorded many honors, chief among them his appointment on December 1, 1964, by Pope Paul VI as Prothonotary Apostolic, a title reserved for the seven members of the college of that name in Rome or those ecclesiastics on whom the Pope has conferred the title.

At the suggestion of Archbishop John J. Mitty, Collins compiled information from all the official liturgical books on church buildings, the furnishings of churches, and the proper forms for the official parochial registers. His book, *The Church Edifice and Its Appointments,* first published in 1935 and reprinted numerous times, remains the standard reference work in its field today.

Construction of the present St. Cecilia's Church began on June 1, 1954, and the church was dedicated by Archbishop Mitty on Pentecost Sunday, May 20, 1956. The architect,

Martin Rist, worked closely with Collins in planning the church. This building, which dominates the closely spaced houses of the Sunset district (as St. Anne of the Sunset does in its area), is in a simplified Romanesque and Mexican Colonial Revival style, with a large, traceried Gothic rose window—the whole executed in reinforced concrete with cast stone trim. Tall pier buttresses line the flanks between high, arched windows. Exteriorly, the roof is Mission style with a low, gabled reddish-tiled covering. On the facade, twisted Solomonic columns give dignity to the entrance, which is surrounded by a deep and lofty arch. Ornamental details on the squared bell tower are Ultra Baroque, deriving from the work of Lorenzo Rodriguez in Mexico City—notably the prismatic *estipite* pillars. Brilliant tiles in pale and dark blue, with yellow accents, augment the eighteenth-century Mexican feeling.

Interior architectural elements are done in simulated travertine stucco with rose-painted plaster contrasting. Beyond the narthex, with its painted, recessed ceiling, opens a great high space with wooden dado down the nave and into the transepts. Stained glass windows are set between lofty pilasters and arches; a richly carved balcony fronts the organ loft. This church, which can seat 1,250 people, has a striking altar area, with a large image of the crucified Christ under a gilded dome held up by gilded Plateresque columns. The altar has two small trees in pots on it—an unusual touch. With its plain, rectilinear shape, more decorative facade and tower, and Mission-style painted wooden ceiling, St. Cecilia's is a kind of catalogue of all periods of Hispanic-Mexican-Californian-Mission design—from the plain sixteenth century to the elaborate late eighteenth century.

Lofty Plateresque style columns hold up a coffered dome over the crucifixion at St. Cecilia's.

St. John the Baptist Serbian Orthodox Church

910 Baker Street, at Turk Street
First services in 1919

Serbian sailors arriving aboard ships from the Adriatic were among the earliest to forsake the sea for the Motherlode. When the Gold Rush was over, many established families in Amador County, near Jackson. A smaller contingent settled in the city, where they became fruit brokers, importers and exporters, liquor merchants, restaurateurs, and hotelmen, with a sprinkling of sea captains and fishermen.

Since there were no Orthodox priests permanently assigned to California, chaplains from Russian naval vessels came ashore to conduct religious services from time to time, beginning in 1859. San Francisco's first permanent Orthodox parish was formed on Easter, 1864, when Archbishop Cyril came ashore to celebrate the liturgy with a multinational group called together by Admiral Popov. Twelve of the sixteen founding members of this Russian-Greek-Slavonic Orthodox Church and Philanthropic Society were Serbs. For the first three years, services were held in the home of Petar Sekulovich, with Joakim Chuda serving as psalm reader. By 1867, when the society was officially registered at the city hall, the membership included six more Serbs, among them the honorary Greek consul, George Fischer. Fischer, whose real name was Djordje Sagich, was one of the first Serbs to come to the New World, arriving in New Orleans in 1825. After coming to San Francisco, he served as a judge and as the first secretary of the California land commission.

The first Serbian priest to visit America was Father Sava Matanovich, a Montenegrin, who participated in three liturgies in 1875. About this time, crop failures combined with political repression in the homeland stimulated a new wave of Serbian immigration. By 1880 there were enough Serbs in San Francisco to form the Serbian-Montenegrin Literary and Benevolent Society, which still exists at the First Serbian Benevolent Society of San Francisco.

The year 1892 was a proud one for the Serbian community of California. Sebastian Dabovich, one of the infants baptized in 1863, was ordained as the first native-born Orthodox priest in America. Father Sebastian was assigned first as rector of St. Mary's Orthodox Church in Minneapolis; in 1893 he returned to serve as missionary priest to California. He founded St. Sava Serbian Orthodox Church (California's second permanent Orthodox parish) at Jackson in August of 1894. During the next eight years, the energetic priest continued his work in San Francisco while at the same time serving as pastor of the church in Jackson and publishing, in the English language, a book on the Orthodox faith. In 1902 he was assigned to Sitka, Alaska, and on August 17, 1905, he was named Archimandrite Sebastian, head of the Serbian Mission to North America.

The history of St. John the Baptist Serbian Orthodox Church begins with the arrival of a missionary from Serbia, Archimandrite George Kodjik, shortly after the Bolshevik Revolution. Like his predecessor, Archimandrite George served as pastor to the Jackson church. He also held services in a rented house in San Francisco from 1919 to 1937, when, with his own funds, he bought and remodeled a house at 281 Castro Street. Divine liturgy was first celebrated there on Easter, May 2, 1937, and the Brotherhood of Saint

Methodius and the Sisterhood of Saint Sophia were formed at this mission in 1938. The devoted priest bequeathed his home and all his personal goods to the parish, and shortly after his death in 1945 the Serbian Orthodox Church of St. John the Baptist was chartered. Father Dositei Obradovich became the first pastor; the Brotherhood became the membership, and the Sisterhood continued as the parish auxiliary.

Ground was broken on August 1, 1953, and the present church was consecrated on September 5, 1954. The small, white-stuccoed church is a modern, much-modified variant of one at Graĉanica, Serbia—a monastery church built in the early fourteenth century by King Militun. The church has five domed elements, widely spaced, and elaborated crosses. Simple curvilinear moldings on the building suggest the arched parts of its prototype. The somewhat austere exterior combined with the richly ornamented interior reflects the medieval belief that the internal life of the spirit is more important than the world outside. A large painting of Christ Pantocrator looks down on worshipers from the interior central dome. This mural and the church icons are the work of Victor Shapona. The iconostasis was designed by Stojan Stojanovich and donated by the First Serbian Benevolent Society. Unlike some Orthodox churches, St. John's has installed pews so that members may be seated during services. Weddings and funerals are performed according to rituals that have not changed in twelve hundred years.

Censing angels guard the saintly iconostasis of St. John the Baptist Serbian Orthodox.

Mount Davidson Cross

First Service, April 1, 1923
Easter Sunrise Service

It is singularly fitting that San Francisco's largest regularly scheduled religious observance is held at this, the highest elevation in the city, in a park created and preserved by San Franciscans of all faiths. Every Easter for more than sixty years San Franciscans and visitors representing every branch of Christianity have climbed the trails to gather in the predawn light at the foot of the 103-foot cross in celebration of the Resurrection of Jesus.

Originally a barren, windswept hill, Mount Davidson was claimed by one Jose Yves Limantour as part of a grant giving him title to all the land south of California Street and west of Divisadero. His claim was exposed as fraudulent by the testimony of Coast and Geodetic surveyor George Davidson, who had surveyed the area in 1850 and named it Blue Mountain. In gratitude, the city renamed the peak in Davidson's honor. Adolph Sutro, later to become San Francisco's first Jewish mayor, purchased the Rancho San Miguel of which Mount Davidson was a portion, and with characteristic zeal, not only employed a staff of laborers but also enlisted the aid of schoolchildren to plant young cedar, cypress, and eucalyptus trees on the slopes. After Sutro's death large tracts of his property were acquired by developer A. S. Baldwin, who improved the flourishing forest by building footpaths from the main roadways to the summit of the mountain.

In 1926 the parklike area was threatened with subdivision for residential development. State Park Commissioner Mrs. Edmund N. Brown enlisted the support of the Commodore Sloat School Mothers' Club and the Federation of Women's Clubs to secure municipal funding for the purchase of twenty acres; Baldwin's Residential Development Company donated six more. The land was dedicated as a city park on December 20, 1929. Mayor Angelo Rossi sponsored city purchase of seven more acres in 1941, and in 1950 the board of supervisors approved acquisition of five acres, resulting in a 38-acre park.

The first Easter sunrise service, held April 1, 1923, was organized by James G. Decatur, the Reverend Homer K. Pitman, A. S. Baldwin, Clarence F. Pratt, and others. The first of several wooden crosses was erected on the spot at that time. Beginning in 1930 the services were broadcast over national radio networks, and in 1977 live television coverage began, with CBS news carrying the 1979 services nationally. Attendance reached a peak of seventy-five thousand during the war years.

Designed by architect George W. Kelham, the giant cross can be seen from most parts of San Francisco by day and from a distance of seventy-five miles when illuminated at night. President Franklin D. Roosevelt pressed a golden key in Washington, D.C. on March 24, 1934, to first turn on the one-thousand-watt floodlights—twelve of them, three each on poles concealed among surrounding trees. Until 1955 the cross was lighted only during Easter week. Then a soldier bound for Korea wrote that as he looked back toward his homeland, the one last thing he could distinguish was the lighted cross on Mount Davidson. The Reverend Clarke Neale Edwards read the letter to his congregation at Lakeside Presbyterian Church. Thereafter, members assumed responsibility for providing the funds necessary for year-round lighting of the cross, remembering the injunction of Jesus that a candle on a mountaintop cannot be hid. In the mid-1970s, the City and County of San Francisco assumed this responsibility.

The 103-foot concrete shaft, 10 feet square at the base and tapering to 9 feet at the tip, is the highest cross in the Americas. (The cross held by the Christ of the Andes is but 26 feet tall, although the overall elevation above sea level is, of course, higher.) Seven hundred fifty cubic yards of concrete, made of California sand, rock, gravel, and cement, were used in the construction, as were 30 tons of reinforcing steel and 30,000 feet of form lumber. The foundation extends 16 feet down into solid rock. The arms are 9 feet square and measure 39 feet from tip to tip. Within the base are a granite tablet and a crypt containing stones from the Garden of Gethsemane, water from the River Jordan, Bibles published in 1848 and 1934, a transcript of the title to Mount Davidson signed by the first Mexican governor of California, mementos of Easter sunrise services held from 1923 to 1933, and other memorabilia. Since 1956, the nondenominational services have been sponsored by the San Francisco Council of Churches.

The eternal symbol of Western Christianity is the Latin cross.

Joseph H. Glide Memorial United Methodist Church

330 Ellis Street, at Mason Street
Founded in 1930

Glide Memorial, as it is called locally, is situated in the heart of San Francisco's Tenderloin district, as it was meant to be. Glide is an unusual church with an interesting background. Some time before the turn of the century, a woman named Elizabeth Helen Snider married Joseph Glide, a cattle rancher. She bore him five children, and in the year of the 1906 earthquake, he died. Though he left his "Lizzie" comfortably off, there was not enough money to fulfill her dream of a church in the "Sodom of San Francisco." Elizabeth Glide, who has been described as a direct, outspoken woman though also of conservative, fundamentalist beliefs, prayed for twenty years that her vision might be brought into reality. She spurned personal luxuries "in order to bring the word and helping hand of the Almighty to the poor." One of her early projects was the establishment in Sacramento of a program very similar to today's Alcoholics Anonymous. During the late twenties, after the bulk of her husband's estate had been divided among their children, one piece remained that no one wanted, a desolate parcel of land near Bakersfield. Mrs. Glide kept it, and oil was eventually discovered under the property. A shrewd businesswoman, she formed the Glide Foundation to set up and help maintain a church "to minister to the unmet needs of the core city." Glide Memorial was built and dedicated in 1931, fulfilling Elizabeth Glide's dream only ten years before her death in 1941.

When the Reverend Donald H. Tippet came to San Francisco as the new Methodist bishop in 1948, he upgraded the Glide portfolio so that the trust provided more money for the foundation. He appointed the Reverend Lewis A. Durham as executive director at a time when the congregation was dwindling. The Reverend Cecil Williams joined the ministerial staff in 1963. Williams is an outspoken person who calls church services "celebrations," with Scriptural quotations from "Chairman Jesus." To his racially mixed congregation, Williams' message is to "celebrate being alive; make it mean something."

Glide Memorial and its ministers have become controversial. They actively engage in many social causes, some of them unpopular, while at the same time quietly providing a multitude of community services, including a free dining room (financed jointly by city funds and private donations and staffed by both paid and volunteer workers) which serves 30,000 meals a month. Other programs include theater, dance, and musical participation groups, children's activities, family support and counseling, study groups, service groups, and a skills bank. Although Glide has been termed an experimental church, it is a member of the California-Nevada Conference of Methodist Churches and its clergymen are ordained Methodist ministers. Responding to an article critical of Glide Memorial, Bishop Tippet expressed his pride in the diversity of churches within the Methodist framework, stating that Glide meets certain needs not met by any other church of any denomination.

In design, Glide is a curious mixture of North Italian Romanesque, Georgian, and modern. If a church like First Church of Christ, Scientist, at California and Franklin were raised up to tall-building status and its exterior simplified to a plain stucco coat, one would have an approximation of Glide Memorial. Yet this very Procrustean stretching of period styling, with the addition of Georgian banklike pedimented motifs, tall colored glass windows, and elegant side canvas canopies makes the church fit its central city milieu especially well. A six-story service building with related colored stucco exterior is attached at the west of the Ellis Street side.

A fascinating mix of eclectic forms, Glide Memorial has a modern cast that suits its central city location.

Holy Virgin Cathedral of the Russian Church in Exile

6210 Geary Boulevard, between Twenty-sixth and Twenty-seventh Avenues
Founded May 2, 1927

The Bolshevik Revolution of 1917–19 forced into exile more than a million Russians, including the intellectual and cultural elite of the nation. A number of Russian Orthodox bishops left their sees, leading parishioners into areas considered less hostile to the church. Many settled in Europe, especially France. The founders of this parish, among them several former officers of the White Army and of the Imperial Pacific Fleet, fled first to Manchuria and then through Shanghai, arriving in San Francisco, penniless, in 1920. They settled in the vicinity of Sutter and Divisadero streets.

In czarist Russia the Orthodox church, as the official state religious body, was both directed and supported by the central government. On November 20, 1920, Patriarch Tikhon, probably foreseeing that he might be deprived of the free exercise of his office, issued an order authorizing the Russian bishops to set up temporary ecclesiastical administrative organizations outside Russia. Several such groups were formed. In 1927, when the Russian Metropolitan acknowledged the Soviet government, the Synod of Bishops of the Russian Church Abroad established an independent religious body, now known as the Russian Church in Exile, to meet the spiritual needs of the Russians who had emigrated.

Bishop Appolinary arrived in San Francisco on December 14, 1924, to assess the need for additional Orthodox churches in the city. After gathering a congregation of about ten families, he rented a house at 3537 Sacramento, where he celebrated the first liturgy on May 2, 1927. The new parish was dedicated to the icon of the Holy Virgin, Mother of God, Joy of All Sorrows. Father Shapushnikoff, the first permanent rector, came from Harbin, China, celebrating his first liturgy on St. Vladimir's Day, July 27, and in October of that year he was joined by a second priest from China.

In 1930 the Synod of Bishops of the Russian Church Abroad established the official Western American Diocese with the cathedral in San Francisco. The former St. Stephen's Episcopal Church at 864 Fulton Street was purchased and remodeled to serve the Russian liturgy. The new Bishop Tichon arrived on August 30, and on September 28 a procession of three hundred parishioners carried their treasured icons, vessels, and other liturgical appointments from the temporary church to the handsome redwood cathedral, which could accommodate one thousand worshipers. Additional icons were painted by the artist Gleb Ilyn, who also designed the iconostasis. An old brass central candelabrum from Russia was acquired in 1932. In 1941 the diocese bought an important ancient icon of the Mother of God. This treasured work of art had been appropriated by the Bolsheviks, sold, exhibited in both Paris and New York, and finally put on display by a San Francisco antique store.

In 1945 the government of the People's Republic of China ordered all non-Chinese missionaries to leave the country. An especially large group of refugees, led by Archbishop John Maximovich, went first to the Philippines, hoping to settle in the United States. When they were unable to obtain American visas, the archbishop made a personal trip to Washington, D.C., to secure the necessary permission. The group arrived in San

Francisco in 1949. The group included many children of mixed marriages—Russian and Chinese, Mongolian, British, French, or American—and the congregation of today's cathedral reflects this cosmopolitan population. One of the priests, Father Ilya Ven, is of Chinese ancestry. Archbishop John was born in Russia and educated in Serbia. After becoming a bishop he never again slept lying down, but always in an armchair or in a prayerful, kneeling position. For several years he divided his time among three areas: San Francisco, Brussels, and Western Europe. In 1963 he was permanently assigned to the Western American Diocese.

The cathedral's second rector was Father Michael Polsky, who took over in 1952. In addition to discharging his church duties he has published the first two volumes of a trilogy, *New Martyrs of Russia,* based in part on his experiences in a Nazi concentration camp and in part on interviews with other survivors. Holy Virgin established a day school, from kindergarten through grade ten, as well as a language school. All public worship is in the Old Slavonic language. A member of the parish council mentioned another reason to keep the language: "Russians like to eat, drink, dance, and sing. The songs are in Russian, so of course we need to know the words." As membership continued to grow, additional parishes were formed. There are now eight parishes or institutions within San Francisco and thirty in the archdiocese, which includes the western states except for southern California.

Construction of the present cathedral on Geary Boulevard began on June 25, 1961; among the many speakers was San Francisco's Mayor George Christopher, a member of the Orthodox faith. The one million dollar building debt was retired in time for the official consecration in 1977 on the fiftieth anniversary of the congregation's founding. Archbishop John did not live to attend the consecration; he died in 1966 and today his sarcophagus remains under the cathedral, three floors down in a mural-covered room that is perfumed with incense and the smoke of many candles. The church had to obtain permission for this interment, as burial is no longer permitted within the City of San Francisco. Metropolitan Philaret of New York conducted the consecration ceremony with the assistance of five archbishops. The two thousand worshipers stood for the six-hour service, in accordance with their custom.

American-born architect Oleg N. Ivanitsky designed the Byzantine building. Its five gold-tiled onion domes are topped by gold double crosses with the footrests characteristic of Russian churches. Mosaic panels on the outside depict, on the right, Saint Spiridon, Saint Cyril, and Saint Athanasius the Great; on the left, Saint John Chrysostom, Saint Basil the Great, and Saint Gregory. The cathedral has three entries and three altars. The center altar contains relics of Saint Herman, who established the first Russian Orthodox Church in Alaska in the eighteenth century. The interior of the church is sheer Eastern opulence; nothing is unornamented. The entire interior is covered with icons done by the celebrated New York painter Father Cyprian, who spent his summers in San Francisco until the work was completed. There are no pews or chairs; the congregation stands or kneels for services. There is a balcony with seating for the infirm and the elderly.

San Francisco Registered Landmark #28
(Old Cathedral, 864 Fulton Street)

Eminently traditional, the five onion-shaped domes with Eastern Orthodox crosses on their pinnacles at Russian Holy Virgin Cathedral of Church in Exile remind one of the five-domed churches of the religion's homeland.

Mesmeric in its complex adjustment of saint, symbol, and architecture, the altar scene at Russian Holy Virgin Church in Exile is one of the richest in San Francisco.

Bush Street Temple

1881 Bush Street, between Laguna and Octavia Streets
Congregation Ohabai Shalome, 1895
Sokoji Zen Temple, 1934

This unusual building has been called the most ecumenical of San Francisco's sacred places. It has sheltered the orthodox Jewish Ohabai Shalome congregation, the Soto Shu Mission (now Sokoji Zen Temple), a Christian church, the San Francisco Zen Center, and the Go Club, a center for devotees of the Far Eastern board game, Go. Its roots go back to 1863, when Congregation Emanu-El joined the Jewish Reform movement. Fifty members of the congregation, mostly from Eastern Europe, withdrew and formed Congregation Ohabai Shalome, meaning Lovers of Peace, under the leadership of Rabbi A. H. Bettleheim. In 1866 they erected a synagogue at 414 Mason Street, present location of the Native Sons of the Golden West, where they worshiped for thirty years. On September 18, 1895, they dedicated the impressive structure now known as the Bush Street Temple. This building survived the earthquake of 1906, but was sold in 1934 when the membership declined. Ohabai Shalome moved to Clement Street and then disbanded after the death of their rabbi in 1940.

Members of a Japanese Buddhist sect known as Soto Shu established a mission in the former synagogue in 1934. They were followers of the Zen priest Hosen Isobe, and their leader in San Francisco was the priest Teruro Kasuga. They were developing a good following until World War II and internment interfered. During their absence the building was used briefly by a Christian congregation.

Soto Shu Mission became active again after the war, and membership grew to two hundred fifty. In the late 1950s a priest came from Japan intending to lead the Mission for one year. Shunryu Suzuki, often given the honorary title Suzuki-roshi, practised a form of Zen meditation called *zazen*. Several young Americans living in the neighborhood began to study under his guidance. Eventually they formed the San Francisco Zen Center as a focus for his teaching. Suzuki-roshi remained in America for twelve years until his death in 1971. During that time he founded and became abbot of the Zen Mountain Center at Tassajara Springs above the Carmel Valley, the first Zen training center outside of Asia. His talks have been published in a book called *Zen Mind, Beginner's Mind.* Since his death the Zen Center has expanded to include the Green Gulch Zen Center and several businesses—the two Tassajara Bakeries, Greens Restaurant, and Alaya, a shop selling clothing made from natural fibers. In 1973 the San Francisco Redevelopment Agency bought the old synagogue-turned-Buddhist temple. The Soto Shu Mission, by that time reorganized as the Sokoji Zen Temple, continued to share the building with the Go Club until November 1984, when they dedicated their present handsome temple at the southwest corner of Sutter and Laguna streets.

The wooden synagogue was designed by Moses J. Lyon. Stylistically, the building has been called Venetian-Moorish. The portal is actually modified French Romanesque, with an arcade above based on the Doge's Palace in Venice. The tower entrances have arched windows above them, with painted voussoirs; the towers are topped by Moorish cupolas. Spires once capped the cupolas, but these were removed, probably because of earthquake danger. The wood facade is painted and scored in alternating bands to simulate rustication. Certain details recall Victorian Ruskinian Gothic design. Between the towers there is a kind of catwalk. When the building was a synagogue, the superstructure held religious symbols, including tablets in Hebrew of the Ten Commandments. This building is an excellent example of how multiple masonry architectural traditions were combined and translated into wood during the nineteenth century in San Francisco.

The interior of the Bush Street Temple seats a thousand people. Its walls were once covered with Victorian stenciling in a repeated pattern—an equivalent of wallpaper—somewhat like that of Temple Sherith Israel. The San Francisco Zen Center and the American Victorian Museum of Nevada City, California, had plans to restore and remodel the Bush Street Temple into Pacific Hall, a music hall or public auditorium, art gallery, and museum. The Temple is currently too shabby to photograph well. Federal funds that would have trained craftsmen in the restoration techniques are no longer available, so the future restoration of this historic building is uncertain.

San Francisco Registered Landmark #81

St. Nicholas Antiochan Orthodox Church

5200 Diamond Heights Boulevard, at Duncan Street
Founded September 1938

Antioch, one of the four ancient patriarchates and the original see of the apostles Peter and Paul, is the titular head of that branch of the Orthodox Church serving people of Arabic background—those whose homelands are Syria, Lebanon, Palestine, and Egypt. From A.D. 1300 to 1900, during rigid suppression by the Ottoman Turks, the Antiochan church received funds and other assistance from the Patriarchate of Moscow. Those who came to California found the Russian missionaries meeting the spiritual needs of all Orthodox faithful. Records of the first permanent Orthodox parish in California—now known as Holy Trinity Orthodox Cathedral—indicate the presence of one Syrian family in the last days of the Civil War and several more by the 1870s. The first sizeable number of Arabic-speaking peoples arrived in the San Francisco area around 1905. Those of the Christian faith worshiped first with the multinational congregation already established here.

After the Bolshevik Revolution, the Russian church itself was relentlessly persecuted. At that time each of the national Orthodox hierarchies assumed responsibility for sustaining its own ethnic churches in the New World. In 1922 Father Antony Bashir was sent from the Holy Synod of Antioch to establish churches, parishes, and societies in North America. In order to reach children and grandchildren of immigrants, he introduced English liturgy and Sunday School materials; the wisdom of this move is shown by the number of Antiochan clergy today who were converted in America. Bashir was named Archbishop of the North American Antiochan Church in February 1936. He met with groups of representative Syrians in the San Francisco Bay Area in the fall of 1937. The decision to establish a church here was made on December 5 at a banquet at the Palace Hotel.

St. Nicholas Antiochan Orthodox Church was incorporated in September 1938. The St. Nicholas Ladies' Aid organized fund-raising efforts which led to the purchase and subsequent remodeling of a church at the corner of Gough and Green streets. The first ordained pastor of the parish was Father Ibrahim Corey, who served until his retirement in 1944. He was succeeded by Archimandrite Michael Kaloof, under whose leadership the parish continued to grow and prosper.

St. Nicholas' third pastor was the Archpriest Elias G. Karim, then twenty-three years old and recently ordained as the first officially accepted divinity student under the official archdiocesan priest education program. Father Karim with the help of lay members of the parish set up a program of periodic missionary services in the Northern California area. Meetings were held in private homes and in various churches friendly to the Orthodox movement. Christians of all ethnic backgrounds were invited to join St. Nicholas church.

On December 6, 1963, St. Nicholas parish celebrated its twenty-fifth anniversary by laying the cornerstone of the present church on one of the city's dominant hills in the Diamond Heights district, then just evolving as a residential area. The present priest, Father Gregory O'Feish, arrived shortly thereafter. Today the church provides a school for children from pre-kindergarten through sixth grade and a family counseling service with emphasis on helping the large number of immigrants adjust to life in a new country. The services are similar to those of the Roman Catholic Church. The prayers are sung (in the style of Gregorian chants) in either English or Syrian.

The architect William Hempl designed this white stuccoed building so appropriately located among hills which could be those of Palestine. This modern adaptation of old forms—barrel vaults and a central dome—sits upon a raised octagonal platform, the shape symbolizing the seven days of creation and the day of Christ's resurrection, a reminder of eternity. The squared, open latticework bell tower with its lantern, dome, and cross suggests a Middle Eastern minaret done in Western style. The church dominates Diamond Heights and commands a good view of the entire city. A double tier of stained glass windows—resembling those of eastern Europe but made in Pennsylvania—encircle the interior with themes of holy day sermons. The large, golden iconostasis has royal center gates and two side gates; four brilliant mosaic panels designed and executed in Florence, Italy, are set in Italian marble. Icons representing saints are stationed above the iconostasis. A mosaic representation of Christ Pantocrator against a glittering golden background lines the interior of the dome.

The low profiled Byzantine dome of St. Nicholas Antiochian Orthodox contrasts with the soaring twentieth century delicacy of its bell tower.

St. John Armenian Apostolic Church

275 Olympia Way
Founded December 7, 1941

Armenia became the first Christian state when Gregory the Illuminator converted King Tiridates III before A.D. 300. As the name implies, the Armenian Apostolic Church considers its clergy to be in direct succession to the original apostles of Jesus. This is one of the so-called Lesser Oriental churches (Armenian, Coptic, Ethiopian, Malabar Indian, Monophysite Syrian, and Nestorian Assyrian), which do not recognize the authority of either the pope in Rome or the ecumenical patriarch in Istanbul. Each of these churches developed its own distinctive liturgy and traditions. The Armenian Book of Divine Liturgy includes the Prophets, Proverbs, Epistles, Gospels, and the Nicene Creed. Services are conducted in classical or fifth-century Armenian. Confirmation follows baptism, which is by immersion. Every seventh year, special envoys gather at Holy Echmiadzin in Soviet Armenia, residence of the Supreme Patriarch and Catholicos of all Armenians, to prepare the holy oil used in baptism, confirmation, and ordination. Each day for forty days, a different floral essence is added; the oil is then blessed and hand-delivered to churches all over the world. Despite a long history of oppression and persecution, the Armenian church has survived and is flourishing today. Headquarters of the Diocese of the Western States, once in Fresno, is now in Los Angeles.

The first Armenian mass in San Francisco was offered in the chapel of Grace Cathedral by Bishop Papken Gulesarian sometime between 1915 and 1920. Occasional services were held by other visiting dignitaries, but it was not until the slump in the Fresno raisin industry prompted migration to the city that regular services were held. From 1925 to 1941, as the Armenian population increased, services were held at various locations—the Greek Holy Trinity church on Seventh Street, the cathedral of the Russian Church in Exile (newly established in a former Fulton Street Episcopal church), an Episcopal church on Fifteenth and Julian streets, and the Anglo-Catholic Church of the Advent on Fell Street.

St. John Armenian Apostolic Church was officially organized in 1941 under the leadership of Archbishop Karekin Hovsepian. A Lutheran church at 7 Elgin Park was remodeled to serve the Armenian liturgy. The altar was dedicated on December 7, 1941, and the church consecrated a month later, on Armenian Christmas. In 1953, expansion of the Soviet influence in Armenia prompted a portion of the membership to form St. Gregory Armenian Apostolic church with allegiance to the patriarch residing at Antelias, Lebanon.

Postwar development in San Francisco routed a freeway through the church property; after celebrating Easter, 1956, in the old building, St. John Church used rented facilities while constructing the present handsome structure on Olympia Way in the Midtown Terrace district. Stained glass windows and liturgical appurtenances were brought from Elgin Street; the altar-tabernacle, built by a previous pastor, is a replica of the old church. Handcarved Siberian oak doors bear foliated Armenian crosses in the upper panels. One lower panel represents the cathedral at Holy Echmiadzin, while the other commemorates Saint Ghevond Yeretz, the Archpriest, and Saint Vartan Mamikonian, the Prince, leaders in the revolt of A.D. 451 against the Persian King Yezdegird II's decree compelling the Armenian people to renounce Christianity in favor of Mazdaism-Zoroastrianism.

Our Lady of Kazan Russian Orthodox Church

5725 California Street, between Nineteenth and Twentieth Avenues
Founded in 1950

This bit of old Russia proclaims the spiritual vitality of a people forced by religious persecution to change their homeland twice in as many generations. Many of those who left Russia after the Bolshevik Revolution of 1917–19 settled in China and Manchuria. Only a few years later they were uprooted again, this time by the establishment of the People's Republic of China in 1945. All non-Chinese missionaries were ordered to leave the country. Some Russian clergy were repatriated to the U.S.S.R. Others escaped to America, leading their parishioners first to the Philippines and then to California. A large contingent arrived in San Francisco in 1949. The new arrivals often entered the arts or the professions or opened small businesses, mainly in the Richmond district of the city. Additional churches were needed to serve them.

The Church of Our Lady of Kazan is one of several parish churches affiliated with the Holy Virgin Cathedral of the Russian Church in Exile on Geary Boulevard. The name of the church commemorates one of the four theological academies (graduate schools) established in major Russian cities between 1769 and 1842. The Kazan academy specialized in training clergy for missions to Islam. By the year 1903, the liturgy was celebrated in more than twenty languages in the region of Kazan. When Arabic-speaking peoples began to reach the New York area early in the twentieth century, a professor of Arabic languages was sent from Kazan to minister to them.

Our Lady of Kazan is one of San Francisco's house-churches, constructed from a remodeled residence. Although small in size, the church is richly furnished and has a reputation for exceptional music. Like other neighborhood churches, the building has a single entry and a single altar (the cathedral has three of each). Architecturally, the building combines such plain Western Gothic and Romanesque features as an ogival entrance arch and corbel tables with a traditional Russian octagonal tower, spire, and onion dome topped by the double cross and footrest. The diminutive facade furnishes one of the surprises of ecclesiastical architecture to be found when exploring city streets.

The Russian Orthodox Church of Our Lady of Kazan represents the enduring importance of Eastern Orthodox traditions in even a modest neighborhood place of worship.

Fellowship Church

2041 Larkin Street, at Vallejo Street
Founded October 4, 1944

Wartime brought an outstanding religious leader to San Francisco when the Reverend Howard Thurman left his position at Howard University and came with his family to serve as minister for a proposed church unlike any other in America—interfaith and interracial. He came in response to a request from the Reverend Alfred Fisk, a Presbyterian minister serving at that time as a professor of philosophy at San Francisco State College, who had asked him to recommend a black clergyman for the challenging post. The decision to take a leave of absence before his sabbatical year meant a financial sacrifice, but, as he writes in *A Dream Come True,* the call was too urgent to ignore.

The need for shipbuilders in the Bay Area had brought large numbers of blacks from the Deep South (the city's black population increased tenfold between 1940 and 1950). Many of them found housing in the Western Addition, partly vacant because of the relocation of all Japanese. The newcomers, unaccustomed to urban life, made the lower Fillmore such an unruly district that racial tensions resulted. Some young adults living in the former home of the Japanese Sakai family approached Fisk, asking his help in establishing a Fellowship of Reconciliation. They wanted to found a neighborhood church where all races would feel welcome.

The concept—revolutionary for its time—received support from many sources. The Presbyterian Board of National Missions offered the use of the former Japanese-American Presbyterian Church at 1500 Post Street and also underwrote the salaries of both Fisk and Thurman. Their first community-wide service that summer was a day camp financed by the Rosenberg Foundation. The theme, "Adventures in Friendship," was developed through exposure to the music, art, artifacts, and customs of many cultures. The children's interest soon spread to parents, and membership of the Fellowship of Reconciliation grew rapidly. With foresight and courage, they voted to establish a new kind of church, not affiliated with any denomination and not located where it would become an exclusively black congregation.

The Church for the Fellowship of All Peoples was officially inaugurated on October 4, 1944, at the First Unitarian Church. The location was chosen in tribute to their former minister, the Reverend Thomas Starr King, a staunch friend and supporter of the black churches of San Francisco before and during the Civil War. Representatives of the city's leading faiths participated, and a number of religious groups continued to support the new congregation in various ways. Several denominations supplied interns to serve as assistant ministers. Each summer the church conducted a children's workshop based on the study of a different culture—Navajo, Nigerian, Indian, Japanese, Mexican. Participants included black, Caucasian, and Asian children from Protestant, Catholic, and Jewish families. The congregation continued to be integrated theologically, racially, and culturally, and many people living elsewhere sent regular contributions as members-at-large.

Thurman, who had been named by *Time-Life* as one of the nation's greatest preachers, left in 1953 to accept a position as dean of the Marsh Chapel at Boston University. His dream of an integrated church had been realized, and a number of denominational churches had become interracial. Sixty days before the Church for the Fellowship of All Peoples celebrated its tenth anniversary, the United States Supreme Court handed down its historic decision on public education. In the 1970s Thurman and his wife retired to San Francisco to write, lecture, and oversee the Thurman Educational Trust for young people. On March 13, 1977, in connection with the first public presentation of a British Broadcasting Company film about his life, he was given the first Distinguished Citizen's Award of the San Francisco Council of Churches by its president, Mrs. Donneter Lane.

After worshiping in several locations—the Japanese-American Presbyterian Church, the Philippine Methodist Church, and the Little Theater on Washington Street (originally built as a church), Fellowship Church occupied its present home on Larkin Street in 1949. Originally a German Evangelical Lutheran church, it is a simple Art Deco building with a single off-center tower and three triangular-headed arched doorways, flanked with plain buttresses. A muntined window in the upper center of the facade rises above two Latin cross ornaments. The church has one of the oldest handmade organs in the Bay Area. This unusual instrument, which has possibilities for musical expression similar to those of a piano, is well-suited to the playing of Renaissance music.

Buddha's Universal Church

720 Washington Street, at Kearny Street
Founded in 1952

The congregation of Buddha's Universal Church are Ch'an Buddhists, a Chinese sect related to the Zen Buddhists of Japan. Ch'an Buddhism was founded by Hui Neng in the sixth century, though Buddhism was introduced to China earlier by Bodhidharma. The temple is the largest of this sect in the United States, and the only Buddhist temple built voluntarily by interfaith and interracial cooperation. The church refers to itself as a living symbol of America's freedom of religion.

In 1952 Dr. Paul F. Fung, a physician with a Ph.D. in Buddhist studies, together with members of a Buddhist congregation, bought an old nightclub—the Mandalay. They planned to renovate the building for a new church, but found the structure was defective beyond repair and had to be torn down. The group was left with a $20,000 mortgage on a large, muddy pit. Given the discouraging financial situation, Paul Fung and his brother George, also a physician, came up with the idea of a temple built entirely by its members. Money for the building was raised by cookie sales, contributions, and the congregation's annual bazaar. Only one paid professional worked on the temple, architect Worley K. Wong of Campbell and Wong. Wong said he had to study the Buddhist teachings before he felt he could do his work well.

All the money went into materials, none to labor. All of the work was done by hand, without benefit of such power equipment as bulldozers to level the site or grinders, sanders, or polishers to smooth the terrazzo, teak, walnut, oak, prima vera, redwood, and birch used throughout the church. Nearly twelve years later, on February 29, 1963, the four-story "Temple of a Thousand Hands" was dedicated. The celebration included people of all ranks and all faiths—not only the three hundred Chinese Buddhists who started the project, but Catholics, Jews, and Protestants; yellow, white and black. Hundreds of passersby who stopped to observe had stayed to lend their skills—steelworkers, tilesetters, plumbers, stockbrokers-turned-laborers. It has been estimated that the building could not be duplicated for less than a million dollars.

Buddha's Universal Church presents public lectures twice a month and sponsors an ongoing program of scholarly research and translation. Their first publication, *The Sutra of the Sixth Patriarch on the Pristine Orthodox Dharma,* relates the ten sections of the life and thought of the founder, Hui Neng. Translated from the Chinese by Dr. Paul F. Fung and Dr. George D. Fung, the book includes glossaries in Sanskrit, Chinese, and English. The church raises the funds for its youth education program both by the sale of publications and by the yearly Amitabha plays. Members of all ages participate in these bilingual musical dramas with authentic costumes and dances. The plays start during the Chinese New Year's celebration and continue through March each year. They are attended and supported by people from all of the city's religious groups. Members of Buddha's Universal Church contribute their time and skills to the church's maintenance and operation. There is not a single paid person in the employ of the church.

The temple is a modern-style building with crisp metal grillwork on its facade and a kind of theater marquee that recalls the site's original use. There are many circular forms in the church—lights, furnishings, altar canopies. These symbolize the teaching that the path of life should be round and smooth with no hidden angles of selfishness or of self-interest. The main altar is built to symbolize the ship of the Dharma, or holy truth, taught by the Enlightened One. Behind the altar is a six-foot image of Buddha. Panels of gold leaf on either side indicate strength and flexibility. As the church history points out, Buddha is not a god but rather a great teacher and an enlightened human being.

In the assembly area is an image of Buddha done in mosaic, the work of Helen Bruton of Monterey. The church has several chapels. The fountain in the Chapel of the Purifying Water commemorates the great teacher's fondness for talking with his disciples beside such small streams. The Bamboo Chapel on the mezzanine resembles the site where Buddha lectured twenty-five hundred years ago. There are also research and translation rooms, a library, and a small meditation room.

No visitor should leave the temple without enjoying the roof garden. Here are a small grove with a flourishing cutting from the very *bodhi* tree under which Buddha attained enlightenment and a pool with a stylized lotus blossom in it. The lotus, a many-petaled, graceful white blossom that grows in muddy swamps, is a traditional symbol of purity or "living this life of worries and turmoils without being bound or trapped by them." The lotus pool is particularly significant because this temple flowered on the site of the Bella Union, one of the most notorious of the many Gold Rush gambling halls.

The lotus and its pond are a perpetual symbol of harmony and beauty as in Buddha's Universal courtyard.

Universal Buddhist's altar is a striking demonstration of an almost theatrical approach to this once humble faith; yet its restraint approximates the austerities of Buddha's later life.

St. Gregory Armenian Apostolic Church

51 Commonwealth Avenue, between California Street and Euclid Avenue
Founded in 1953

St. Gregory Church was founded by a group from St. John Armenian Apostolic Church who wished to affiliate with the Catholicos of Cilicia residing in Antelias, Lebanon. The church serves some six hundred families and operates a network of benevolent societies. Future plans call for construction of a new church on Brotherhood Way, where the congregation has recently opened a school and community center.

According to tradition, Saint Gregory the Illuminator had a vision in which the Only Begotten (Jesus) descended from heaven at the site of an ancient fire temple at Vagarshapat. As instructed by Jesus, Gregory demolished the pagan temple and built a Christian church on the site. The place has been given the name Holy Echmiadzin, a coined word that means "Place of the Descent of the Only Begotten."

Completed in 1956, St. Gregory Church, with its large entrance courtyard and related buildings grouped about, is considered the most typically Armenian of all the Apostolic churches in America. Armenian ecclesiastical architecture is a forerunner of the Romanesque and Gothic in Europe, as can be seen at Echmiadzin and several other early medieval sites. The cast stone and stucco building, related to its ancestral sources, is low in silhouette, with interpenetrating graduated red tile roofs and a multiple-sided tower, topped with a gold cross. A shallow apse faces the street, as the Armenians insist upon having their high altars at the east and the entrance at or near the west. The overall stylistic effect is of plain early Romanesque; its interlacing decorative motifs relate to those at St. Brigid's on Van Ness Avenue. A lunette mosaic of Madonna and Child crowns the main entrance. The interior is dominated by the windows from the central tower that forms a part of the unusual vaulted ceiling. The tiered altar and tripartite divisions of the tabernacle, standing in a half dome, frame a large painting of the Madonna and Holy Child. There is no iconostasis in the Armenian Apostolic church. Oriental carpets cover the floor in front of the altar. This well-proportioned church was largely designed by Tigran Kiragosian, though the architect Francis A. Constable signed the plans. Kiragosian worked his monogram into the decorative moldings above the large three-part stained glass windows along the side of the church.

Following the formal precedent of early medieval churches in Ani, St. Gregory Armenian Orthodox has an interwoven set of interior spaces crowned with a powerful tower.

Jeng Sen Buddhism-Taoism Association

146 Waverly Place, between Washington and Clay Streets
Founded in 1955

Buddhism, which originated twenty-five hundred years ago in India, and Taoism, which was founded in China two thousand years ago by Lao-tzu, have joint temples in Hong Kong and Taiwan as well as in California. This temple was founded by the Reverend Ng Piu Lam, who studied in China under the teacher Hoi Wan and holds high offices in Buddhist-Taoist associations in both countries. He founded this association to provide a spiritual refuge for Chinese immigrants in San Francisco. The temple name translates roughly as a reaching out from within the self in genuine brotherhood to others. Children accompany their parents to the temple on special occasions but receive religious instruction at home until they are considered to be mature enough to join the temple as young adults. Active membership consists in attending the temple and assisting with maintenance.

On the second floor of its building, the one-room temple features an elaborate altar holding a large portrait of Lao-tzu. To the viewer's right there are three statues of Buddha; to the left are three mentors of Taoism. Lanterns suspended above the altar table are gifts from grateful members, as are numerous bouquets of chrysanthemums. The collection of ribbon banners to the right of the altar bear Chinese inscriptions representing the names of temple members. In contrast to the furnishings of some older temples, Jeng Sen shows contemporary influence in its decor.

A prodigality of offerings characterizes the altar of Jeng Sen Buddhist-Taoist.

Ukrainian Orthodox Church of St. Michael

345 Seventh Street, between Harrison and Folsom Streets
Founded in 1964

Although Greek settlers introduced the Christian faith along the shores of the Black Sea as early as A.D. 100, it was not until A.D. 988 that Saint Vladimir, Prince of Kiev, made it the official religion of the Ukrainian state. The Kiev Theological Academy became an influential seat of learning, providing advisors to Peter the Great (czar of Russia 1682–1725). Under later czars, however, the Ukrainian church lost its national status and some of its clergy were sent into exile in Siberia. Attempts were made to re-establish a separate Ukrainian church after the fall of the czar in 1917, but the Bolsheviks destroyed or confiscated all church properties. Since the 1940s the Ukrainian Orthodox faithful in the homeland have been under the Patriarchate of Moscow. Today Ukrainian Orthodox churches exist around the globe, with the greatest concentration in the United States. The American church is an independent body. Its cathedral is the Church of St. Vladimir in Philadelphia and the administrative center is located in South Bound Brook, New Jersey.

All Orthodox congregations follow the same liturgy, translated from the original Greek into their own languages. The clergy wear elaborate vestments, and the congregation participates extensively with chants and hymns. The liturgy is based on the New Testament and the Sacred Traditions, which include the seven sacraments of baptism, confirmation, the Holy Eucharist, penance (confession), ordination, marriage, and Holy Unction. Saints, relics, and icons (two-dimensional images of Christ, the Virgin Mary, angels, and saints) are honored in the church. The Eastern Orthodox church believes that its clergy represent an uninterrupted succession from the apostles of Jesus Christ.

There were some Ukrainians in America before the Revolution, and a large wave of immigration occurred between 1890 and 1914, but most of them settled in the East or Midwest. However, the first Russian-English newspaper in the United States was published in San Francisco in 1868 by A. Honcharenko, a Ukrainian. After World War II, there were enough Ukrainians among the refugees arriving from the displaced-persons camps of Eastern Europe to form a national church in San Francisco. In 1964 they established St. Michael's Ukrainian Orthodox congregation, purchasing the building about to be vacated by the city's earliest Greek Orthodox church, Holy Trinity.

St. Michael's Ukrainian Orthodox Church occupies the first ecclesiastical structure to be built in San Francisco after the earthquake and fire of 1906. Construction began in October of 1906, and the first services were held in 1907. The following year the church was raised and a hall was added at the ground level. The architect J. P. Morgan designed the building in a stripped classicist style. The interior of St. Michael's is lighted by a series of stained glass windows very close to the ground level, with small round clear glass windows high above. Window and ceiling arches are repeated in the wooden iconostasis or altar screen. The traditional Orthodox cross with its two straight arms and slanted footrest below appears on the table covering, and modifications of the Greek cross occur in the railing and on the iconostasis.

Twin towers (without spires) frame the pedimented center section, with its plain, tubular columns and arched windows. There is an Ionic colonnaded porch before the entrance door. An elaborately balustraded double-ramped stair leads to the landing in front of the main entrances. Trees and shrubbery enhance the walled garden, which provides an oasis of greenery in an area that has become commercial.

The principal feature of the Eastern Orthodox church is an iconostasis, or altar screen, as seen in the Ukrainian Orthodox Church of St. Michael.

St. Mary's Cathedral

1111 Gough Street, at Geary Boulevard
Dedicated May 5, 1971

The history of this modern cathedral begins on Christmas Eve, 1854, with Archbishop Joseph Sadoc Alemany's dedication of the beloved landmark now known as Old St. Mary's Church and located at the corner of California Street and Grant Avenue. When a larger cathedral was needed, a local philanthropist, Horace Hawes, donated land for the purpose at Tenth and Howard, the site of St. Joseph's Church, but ultimately the second St. Mary's was located at the corner of Van Ness Avenue and O'Farrell Street. The cornerstone of the second cathedral was laid in May of 1887, and the red brick German Gothic edifice, officially known as St. Mary's Cathedral of the Assumption, was dedicated January 11, 1891, by Archbishop Patrick William Riordan. For seventy-one years worshipers of all ages, of all races, and from many places climbed the granite steps to bow in reverence before the great arched altar, until flames soared into the dark night of September 7, 1962. The great structure, which had survived the disaster of 1906, lay in ashes. But the spirit of the city on many hills was not dimmed. The very next morning, Catholics were joined by Protestants and Jews making voluntary contributions to create a new St. Mary's, just as they had done for the original cathedral more than a century before.

The timing was, in a way, fortuitous. San Francisco was engaged in massive redevelopment of the Western Addition, adjacent to the location of the burned cathedral. Block after block of old buildings had been leveled and several streets rerouted to make way for a new neighborhood, with amenities of many kinds, along the Geary corridor, an east-west thoroughfare extending from Market Street to the Pacific Ocean. As the archbishop surveyed the locale, he selected one particular knoll as the ideal location for a cathedral, only to learn that redevelopment officials had already authorized construction of a supermarket on the site. After some vigorous campaigning by many segments of the community, the supermarket was relocated. Newly named Cathedral Hill, the knoll was made available to the church.

At about the same time, the Second Vatican Council authorized a new version of the sacred liturgy, emphasizing the concept that the priest and the congregation should be united, with the altar as their focus. Armed with a spacious site and new freedom of liturgical arrangement, the church held an architectural competition. The startlingly modern design of the new St. Mary's Cathedral is the result of the combined talents of a team of world-renowned architects, based on studies made by the San Francisco firm of McSweeney, Ryan, and Lee. Consulting architects Pietro Belluschi of the Massachusetts Institute of Technology and Pier-Luigi Nervi of Rome brought world experience to the project.

It took only eight years until the gold-leafed aluminum cross was hoisted atop the cruciform spire crowning Cathedral Hill. The cathedral, designed to be a "message of a living relationship between man and God," was dedicated on May 5, 1971, by Archbishop Joseph T. McGucken. Use of the hyperbolic paraboloid as the basic structural form produced a strikingly original cathedral that quickly became a landmark in the city. The cupola rises 190 feet from the floor, and the warm-toned concrete reflects the light in ever changing patterns. The exterior of St. Mary's is faced with travertine laid in subtle patterns of horizontal and vertical bands. Elevated plazas, laid in brick and travertine, are level with the entrances and with Geary Boulevard. The level entrances were planned to facilitate the arrangements for funeral services; pallbearers had frequently staggered under their burdens while ascending and descending the one hundred steps at the main entrance of the second cathedral. At the northwest corner of the plaza stands the old bell rescued from the debris of the second cathedral.

Like Coventry in England and Sacre Coeur in Paris, the inspiration of the building must be experienced rather than described. The five bronze doors of the main entrance are surmounted by a bas relief bronze sculpture done by Enrico Manfrini of Milan, Italy. The sculpture is intended as a monument to the spirit of freedom, ecumenicism, and brotherhood. The central figure is the Christ with hands outstretched to two flying angels, visualizing the concept of heaven. To the left, cut-out figures portray primitive man struggling for "freedom to search out a footpath to a lasting kingdom." On the lower right, an Arab embraces a Jew in reconciliation; a black and a Caucasian work side by side; and Mary welcomes the multiracial family of man into the kingdom of her Divine Son. Some of the figures have local significance. There is Saint Francis of Assisi, patron saint of the city, Saint Claire, patroness of the Santa Clara Valley, and finally, kneeling in prayer for all mankind, there is a likeness of Pope Paul VI, a personal friend of the sculptor. Looking out from the inside, with light streaming through stained glass, one sees them all, heroic in their silhouetted stances.

Once inside, eyes are lifted to the scintillating baldacchino. "Like angels dropping stars," is the way one visitor described the mobile, composed of slender silver and gold cylinders suspended above the white marble altar. Richard Lippold of New York designed the sculpture, which measures fifty-five feet from top to bottom and weighs nearly a ton. Monsignor Thomas J. Bowe, pastor of St. Mary's, defined the baldacchino as "a life cord between God and His creatures."

Above and behind the altar is a panel of stained glass harmonizing with the almost overwhelming high, narrow windows that serve as junctures for the four hyperbolic paraboloids. They are six feet wide, start at a height of thirty feet and rise one hundred thirty-nine feet to the top, where they come together in the form of a skylight cross. Designed by Gyorgy Kepes, each represents a vital element. On the north is a blue window for water; to the south, gold for light; green meaning earth to the east; and red fire in the west.

The floor of red brick, durable and warm, pays tribute to the early mission architecture of California. The nave, sanctuary, transepts, baptistry, and narthex—all the elements of a classical cathedral—are here combined into one magnificent space. The pews are so arranged that none of the twenty-four hundred people the cathedral accommodates is more than seventy-five feet from the altar. There is also room for another two thousand people to stand. The organ, one of the finest in the world today, was made by Ruffatti of Padua, Italy. It has eighty-nine ranks and seventy stops. This electro-pneumatic pipe organ contains 4,842 pipes and rests on a "soaring pedestal platform" so that everyone can see it. Entering the cathedral just as the organ is sounding a fanfare gives an instant impression of a corner of heaven on earth. As the brochure states—"How awesome is this place—it shall be called the Court of God."

This is the first cathedral ever built that has more space set aside for social use than for worship. The cathedral itself is 45,000 feet square, and the lower level is 62,000 feet square. The latter contains an auditorium, museum, music library, practice rooms, meeting rooms, education facilities, and offices. Ample parking space is provided on the lower level plazas outside. One of the building's triumphs is its inclusion of the surrounding cityscape. This most modern of cathedrals, with its open vistas of the city from every corner of the great hall, exemplifies the growing concept of the church as a nexus of the community rather than a refuge from the world.

St. Mary's Cathedral is an audacious modern conception of centrality in form, mirroring the faith it houses.

An abstracted crucifixion is appropriately placed above the thorn-like door panels at St Mary's Cathedral.

Richard Lippold's incandescent sculpture cascades like a heavenly vision from the roof of St. Mary's Cathedral.

Konko Church of San Francisco

1909 Bush Street, at Laguna Street
Founded May 27, 1973

Shinto, the ancient, indigenous religion of Japan, includes elements of nature worship, hero worship, tribal cult, and reverence for the emperor. Some Buddhist ideas and practices have also been incorporated. An ordinary Shinto shrine is the domicile of a local guardian deity or tutelar. There are many shrines affiliated with particular emperors. The Ise Jingu or Grand Shrine honoring Amaterasu Omikami, the Sun Goddess–founder of the Imperial House, is believed to guard the Japanese nation. In 1868 the Meiji government reinstated the emperor to power and designated Shrine Shinto as a national institution. There were some advocates of religious Shinto, however, who preferred to remain separate from the national office. The government subsequently classified these groups as Sectarian Shinto and gave them equal footing with other religions. By the end of the nineteenth century they numbered thirteen sects; since the end of World War II the figure has increased dramatically.

Konko Church, although related, is an independent sect. It was founded in 1859 by a man born to the farmer class and called Ikigami Konko Daijin, an honorific name. He is usually referred to as "The Founder." Like many ordinary people, he paid homage in his youth to the local tutelary deities, to Kannon Sama, to the Grand Shrine of Ise, to every god and buddha as a way of preventing misfortune. At the age of forty-two, after a miraculous recovery from a serious illness, he received a divine revelation from Tenchi Kane no Kami, the parent God of the universe, who requires interaction with humanity to effect mankind's salvation. As directed by God, he began to teach others. As his following increased, he quit farming and devoted the last twenty-one years of his life to *toritsugi* or mediation—counseling and praying for others who were experiencing anguish or misfortune, or who lacked understanding of divine virtue. Konko Kyo today has more than seventeen hundred churches, four thousand ministers, and six hundred thousand believers worldwide. There are churches in the United States, in Canada, and in Brazil. In San Francisco services are conducted in English and Japanese.

The present church was constructed in 1973 by the architectural firm of Van Bourg, Nakamura, Katsura, and Karney. The building uses the post-and-lintel form of traditional Shinto architecture and has a small Japanese-style garden flanking the entry stairs. Simple natural materials are used throughout the building, which is executed in the time-honored way using ancient techniques of Japanese carpentry. A deeply projecting roof, patterned after that of the Grand Shrine at Ise, overhangs the building. Light is filtered through translucent windows on the sides. The lightweight sash suggests the shoji screens of Japan. The austere interior is dominated by the expansive roof, ceiling, and altars. Finely made light wood shrines contain offerings of food, flowers, and Japanese rice wine. These offerings are varied and often include simple supermarket foods; they symbolize the varied character of the world's things. Above the shrines is a golden *yatsu-nami,* the Konko Kyo symbol of divine light.

The carefully balanced offerings on the altar of Konko Church are set against an equally planned background of fine wood.

Pulgas Water Temple

Cañada Road, South of Bunker Hill Drive
Dedicated in October 1934

As ablution, offering, for purification or for baptism, water forms part of the ritual of many religions. "We worship the sources of great rivers," wrote the Roman dramatist Seneca in a famous letter. "We erect altars at the place where a sudden rush of water bursts from the bowels of the earth, warm springs we adore, and certain pools we hold sacred on account of their somber darkness or their immense depth."

In California, water has spiritual significance beyond the temple walls. Water has made this desert bloom. Water enables thousands to live where only hundreds could survive without it. The struggle for water on this semi-arid peninsula began in 1776, when Franciscan fathers established their mission beside a small stream. The Gold Rush population depended upon wells or springs, or bought water from peddlers who ferried it across the bay. Lobos Creek in the present Richmond district supplied the city in 1857, but by 1860 it was necessary to tap peninsula sources as well. As early as 1871, the city's engineers, foreseeing the need for a greater supply, began ambitious plans to import water from the mountains to the east.

Some sixty years later, their dreams were realized. The water that serves the people of San Francisco comes from the wilderness of the Sierra Nevada. Impounded by O'Shaughnessy Dam, it flows, entirely by gravity, one hundred fifty miles through the Hetch Hetchy Aqueduct, generating electricity in the process. Completed in 1934, Hetch Hetchy surpasses a previously acclaimed engineering achievement—The Catskill Aqueduct—in every respect. The pure mountain water bursts from its underground pipeline not far from a spring whose Indian name, *uchate,* means "to conceive." Here, too, the travel-weary Spanish soldiers and Franciscan fathers paused as they made their rounds between missions and presidios. They named the area "El Valle de las Pulgas," for the fleas that tormented them.

This symbolic temple is the city's tribute to its source of life. In October 1934, before a crowd of twenty thousand people, Secretary of the Interior Harold Ickes drank the first glass of Hetch Hetchy water and dedicated a full-scale papier-mâché model of the eventual temple (which was not yet built). Michael O'Shaughnessy, engineer on the project for twenty years, was to have been the honored guest at the festivities; unfortunately, he died suddenly at the age of seventy, only twelve days before the water arrived.

By 1938 the completed temple stood in place. Commissioned by the Public Works Administration at a cost of $38,400, it is said to be one of three such American water temples, modeled after the *tholoi,* or round temples sometimes built near their waterways by the ancient Greeks. The surrounding park is a popular place for picnicking and engaging in one's own form of sun worship. While the large city-owned watershed beyond is closed to the public except by arrangement, permission is freely given to schools and nature study groups.

Although often described as a duplicate of the Sunol Water Temple designed by Willis Polk and built in 1910, Pulgas was actually designed in miniature by artist William Merchant. Albert Bernasconi took Merchant's small model, scaled it up to the size he thought best (a difficult task), and built it, using California granite, cast stone, and concrete.

Bernasconi—artist, designer, sculptor, and above all master stonecarver—is one of those artisans who are secretly famous—little known to the public, but highly revered by those in the profession. He worked as a child in his father's stoneworks in Annecy, France, going on to take a degree in architectural ornamentation in Milan and to study at L' École des Beaux-Arts in Paris before coming to San Francisco in 1911. Here he went to work immediately under John Galen Howard, chief architect of the University of California. He worked on so many buildings—in San Francisco the City Hall, the War Memorial Opera House, the Pacific Gas and Electric Company building, Grace Cathedral, St. Dominic's and St. Patrick's churches—that he said he forgot them after a while. But of Pulgas he said, "This is one I don't forget. I built the temple, myself."

Coming upon Pulgas Temple unexpectedly while driving alongside the San Andreas Lakes (also known as Crystal Springs Reservoir) is an awesome experience, like suddenly finding oneself in an ancient land. No other buildings are visible in any direction. The temple, sixty feet high and thirty feet in diameter, stands at the far end of a reflecting pool with a raised circular planting bed in the foreground. It has ten Corinthian columns with characteristic acanthus leaf and corner-scrolled capitals. The eye is drawn to an inscription on the frieze:

I give waters in the wilderness
and rivers in the desert,
to give drink to my people

Isaiah 43:20

Above the frieze is an ornamental band of anthemia and lions' heads. Far below the viewer's feet, water thunders into a circular weir before cascading down the hillside to enter the chain of lakes.

Pulgas Water Temple is a twentieth-century adaptation of a Greco-Roman temple with the words of a Hebrew prophet chiseled on it in English. It was built along the route taken by the Spanish padres who came to California bringing Christianity to the Indians. Its ultimate construction was by an Italian-Swiss stonecarver born in France. The worldly craftsmanship of the man who built Pulgas and the temple itself epitomize the richly international and ecumenical religious tradition of San Francisco.

The Pulgas Water Temple epitomizes the concept of the "temple" as the shrine of all things holy.

Glossary

ACANTHUS LEAF. A conventionalized leaf of the acanthus plant, used in the decoration of Greek, Roman, Renaissance and later Corinthian and composite capitals. The Greek form of the ornament is more sharply pointed and more crisply carved than the Roman and later forms.

ADOBE. Mud brick (earth and straw) dried in the sun.

AISLE. Longitudinal space division of a church interior, generally narrower and at the sides of a central aisle or nave.

ANTHEMION (plural: ANTHEMIA). In Classical architecture, an ornament resembling honeysuckle, based on the flower of the acanthus.

APSE. The polygonal or curved enlargement of the end (traditionally, the eastern end) of a church to provide more space and emphasis for the altar.

ARCADE. A row of arches on columns, piers, or pillars, usually carrying a roof, wall, or some other superstructure.

ARCHITRAVE. Lowest horizontal division of an entablature. Decorated characteristically for each of the orders and their variations.

ART DECO. A style of architecture and ornament popular in the 1920s and 1930s, with streamlined colorful designs of an early modern type. Also called *art moderne*.

BALDACCHINO. Canopy over an altar, throne, or tomb; usually placed on columns or pillars but may be hung from the ceiling.

BALUSTERS AND BALUSTRADE. Balusters are turned, often vase-shaped, vertical support forms which together form the balustrade of a stair or of a balcony, etc.

BAROQUE. Style of architecture and art common to the Western world in the seventeenth and eighteenth centuries; sometimes divided into phases of Early, High, and Late Baroque. Characterized by a controlled organization of minor and major parts, leading to a dramatic focus of design elements, and often showing strong contrasts of light and color as well as movement of parts forward and backward.

BARREL VAULT. A tunnel-like vault; actually of semicircular or half barrel shape.

BEAUX-ARTS. One of the oldest centers for architectural study; the École des Beaux-Arts is in Paris, France. The name now connotes a special kind of elegant classicist Baroque design.

BELVEDERE. A structure erected upon the roof of a building, open to the air and commanding a view.

BOTTICINO MARBLE. *See* MARBLE.

BRACKET. A support or pseudo-support (often used decoratively rather than structurally), based on a ninety-degree angle shape, usually of variable decorative character, and to be distinguished from the more invariable classicist forms that are related to it in shape and function.

BRECCIA VIOLETTA MARBLE. *See* MARBLE.

BUTTRESS. A projecting vertical support for a wall. May be a pier buttress (solid pier attached to wall) or flying buttress (arches brought from upper parts of building to piers at some remove from the wall).

BYZANTINE. Byzantine architecture was adopted in the countries under the influence of the Eastern Orthodox Church, including Constantinople and Greece. Later the style became dominant in Russia and extended its artistic legacy to Venice. Byzantine churches are characterized by the use of domes with a squared Greek Cross plan, whereas the typical medieval church of Western Europe had a Latin Cross plan, with a long nave. Mosaics are used as decoration.

CALACATA MARBLE. *See* MARBLE.

CANOPY. A projecting cover over a niche, window, door, etc.

CAPITAL. The carved top of a column or pilaster; surmounts the shaft.

CARRARA MARBLE. *See* MARBLE.

CLASSICAL. Ancient Greek or Roman architectural forms, or directly imitative of them (as in Classical Revival or Neoclassical).

CLASSICAL REVIVAL (NEOCLASSICAL). The revival of interest in Classical antiquity, dating from the mid-eighteenth century, and especially notable in architecture; divided into two phases—Roman and Greek—in the United States, although they usually overlapped and both often included elements of Baroque planning continuing from the Georgian era.

CLASSICIST. Derived from Classical forms, but variously interpreted in a new context (as Renaissance or Baroque classicism).

CLERESTORY. The top level of a nave wall, with windows.

COFFER. A boxlike recess (often square or octagonal), frequently found in ceilings to extend interior space effects; sometimes simulated in painting.

COLONNADE. A row of columns.

COLONNETTE. A small column, usually very tall and slender in proportion.

COLORED GLASS. In this text, the general distinction is made that stained glass is more medievalizing and made up of smaller transparent pieces of glass, whereas colored glass is in larger parts and may be translucent.

COLUMN. An architectural support of definite proportions, usually cylindrical in shape with a shaft and capital (and sometimes a base). May be free-standing or attached to a wall (engaged) as a half or three-quarter column (that is, a column cut vertically in half or into three-quarters).

COMPOSITE. One of the Roman, Renaissance and later orders—related to the Corinthian, but combining in its capital the leaves of the Corinthian and the volutes of the Ionic.

CONNEMARA MARBLE. *See* MARBLE.

CONSOLE. In architecture a support or pseudo-support (often used decoratively) with a top curving down into a reverse scroll; the scrolls are generally called volutes.

CORBEL. A stone or wooden bracket, usually built into a wall as a support; may be decorative.

CORINTHIAN. One of the main architectural orders—originally taller than the Doric and Ionic; having a fluted shaft, bell-shaped capital with stylized acanthus leaves and corner spirals, and base. Extensively used in Roman and later architecture.

CORNICE. Topmost horizontal division of an entablature. Sometimes isolated and used separately as a strong molding.

CRENELLATION. A form of battlement, created with indentations (crenels) of a low wall; often made by alternating squared blocks or merlons (sometimes with pyramidal tops), with embrasures or empty spaces between. Originally intended for protecting defenders on the upper walls of a fortress; nineteenth-century crenellation was decorative.

CROCKET. Carved ornament in Gothic architecture, resembling a curved leaf; generally projects from a pinnacle or spire.

CROSSING. Area where nave and transept intersect.

CROWN. The uppermost part of an architectural ensemble.

CUPOLA. A curved or domical roof over a circular, square, or polygonal space. The term is usually synonymous with dome.

CURVETTING. Characterized by animated curving and geometric forms on an upper part of a building.

CUSP. In Gothic architecture, the solid stone part of a window shape; cusps divide the area (arched or circular shape) into a series of foils and are usually used as a part of tracery.

DOME. A cupola. A convex roof, usually circular or polygonal at the base and semicircular or paraboloid in elevation.

DORIC. One of the main architectural orders; the Greek Doric had a simple capital with block (abacus) and curved cushion (echinus) over a plain, fluted shaft. The Roman and later Doric was closer to the Tuscan.

DORMER. A gabled window projecting from a sloping roof, having vertical sides.

DRUM. A cylindrical (or polygonal) ring of structure on which a dome is sometimes placed to elevate it.

EASTLAKE. A period term derived from the name of Charles Eastlake, English author of *Hints on Household Taste*. See Stick Style.

ECLECTIC. Borrowing freely from various styles of the past.

ENTABLATURE. The total horizontal section above classical columns or pilasters. In such architecture and its derivatives, the entablature is divided into three horizontal parts from bottom to top: the architrave, the frieze, and the cornice. Each of the orders had a characteristic entablature, with special decorative enrichment of the parts.

ESTIPITE. Special Spanish and Mexican eighteenth-century pillar or pilaster made up of a base, inverted obelisk, various blocks and moldings (sometimes medallions as well), and crowned with a Corinthianesque capital.

FACADE. The front, or frontispiece, of a building.

FINIAL. An ornamental part at the top; architectural element like a pinnacle.

FLEUR-DE-LIS. Flower of a the lily; usually a three-part flower form.

FLORENTINE. From the town of Florence, Italy.

FLUTING. Vertical channeling (usually concave) of a column or pilaster shaft.

FOIL. *See* QUATREFOIL and TREFOIL.

FOLIATE. Leaf formed.

FRESCO (plural: FRESCOES). Paintings done with color and lime water on wet (*buon fresco*) or dry (*fresco à secco*) plaster.

FRIEZE. Middle horizontal division of an entablature. Decorated characteristically for each order and its variations.

GABLE. A high, peaked roof form; the vertical, triangular part at each end of such a peaked roof, or above a dormer window.

GEORGIAN. A period term derived from the names of English sovereigns of the eighteenth century; divided into various phases in American architecture—Early, High, and Late. Classicist Baroque in general character, it utilized features from fifteenth-and sixteenth-century Italian architecture as seen through English eyes of the seventeenth and eighteenth century. Its historic time span was 1700 to 1790, but its forms were revived in the late nineteenth century Colonial Revival.

GOTHIC. A style of architecture and art, essentially of the mid-twelfth to late fifteenth or early sixteenth centuries. Usually characterized by pointed arches of varied shapes—some high and narrow, others low and flat or depressed—but occasionally by arches of double curvature, or ogival shape. Buildings were often rib vaulted and had pier or flying buttresses.

GOTHIC REVIVAL. A revival of Gothic forms in the mid-to-late-nineteenth century.

GRID. An intersecting pattern of lines.

HALF COLUMN. *See* COLUMN.

HALL CHURCH. Church with aisles the same or nearly the same height as the nave.

HELM DOME or HELM ROOF. A form of roof with gables on each of the four faces, and a pyramidal spire rising from the tops of the gables.

HOOD MOLD. A rectilinear molding above a door or window in Gothic Revival architecture, designed to help throw rain water away from the opening below; sometimes called a drip mold.

HYPERBOLIC PARABOLOID. A special form of complex mathematical curve.

ICON AND ICONOSTASIS. Image and image screen; votive paintings of the saints and their positioning on a closed screen that separates the altar from the worshippers in Eastern Greek, or Russian Orthodox churches.

IONIC. One of the main architectural orders; especially characterized by its capital with large opposed spirals or volutes at the corners.

ITALIANATE. A period term which includes forms and ornaments derived particularly from fifteenth-and sixteenth-century Italian architecture, notably from the Mannerist era in Italy (ca. 1530 to 1600); the fashion was especially common between 1850 and 1875 in Northern California.

LAYERING. Characterized by use of several layers of design elements.

LOBATE or LOBATED. Having lobes or rounded parts.

LUNETTE. A semi-circular or crescent-shaped window.

MANNERISM. A style of architecture and art, now especially associated with the mid-and late-sixteenth century. Characterized by tension, ambiguity, lack of balance, crowding of parts, and a proclivity for elongated shapes. Italian Mannerism was both structural and ornamental. It is the inspiration of the nineteenth-century Italianate style.

MARBLE. A form of fine-textured limestone found in many hues and capable of taking a high polish:

botticino: beige marble
breccia violetta: white marble with purple veining
calacata: a family of milky white marbles ranging through many hues of veining
Carrara: white marble
Connemara: green marble
Seravezza (more correctly, breccia di Seravezza): yellowish marble with pink and purple veining
(Note: the modern names of marbles are complex and somewhat inconsistent.)

MARQUEE. A canopy, usually of metal and glass, sheltering the entrance doorway to a building.

MASONRY. Built of stone, brick, or a similar material.

MEXICAN COLONIAL REVIVAL. Style reviving eighteenth-century late Baroque Mexican forms, often called erroneously Churrigueresque.

MISSION REVIVAL. A style reviving the materials and forms of the architecture of California's early missions.

MODILLION. A support or pseudo-support (it was often used decoratively) resembling a console with its flat side uppermost.

MOORISH. The art of Islamic or Moslem North Africa and Spain.

MOSAIC. Form of surface decoration of walls, vaults, domes, and pavements done with small cubes (*tesserae*) of marble, opaque glass, or other hard materials; laid in mortar or plaster.

MULLION. One of the larger dividing bars of a window.

MUNTIN. One of the lesser dividing bars of a window.

MUTULE. A rectangular block under a Doric cornice.

NARTHEX. A porch or vestibule at the entrance to a Christian church.

NAVE. The central longitudinal space or aisle of a church. Traditionally (in medieval Europe) oriented west (the entrance) to east (the altar). The nave is counted as an aisle in, say, a three-aisled church.

NEOCLASSICAL. A phase of architecture and art, essentially of the late eighteenth and early nineteenth century. Characterized by a revival of Classical forms, with special variations for contemporary use; called by some writers Classical Revival.

OBELISK or OBELISKOID. A tall tapering shaft, square in plan, and rising to a pyramidal top; originally used at the entrances to ancient Egyptian temples.

OGIVE or OGIVAL. Arches of ogee or double-curved shape. Formerly, and now erroneously, applied to all of Gothic architecture.

ONION DOME. A dome shaped like an onion and often seen in Eastern European church architecture.

ORDERS. In architecture, the basic columnar or pilaster types of the Classical world: the Doric, Ionic, and Corinthian of the Greeks and the Doric, Tuscan, Ionic, Corinthian, and Composite of the Roman, and later eras.

PALLADIAN WINDOW. A window form with high arched central section and lower flanking rectangular sections—derived from the name of the Italian architect, Andrea Palladio (1518–1580); extensively used in the Late Georgian era, and again in Colonial Revival buildings.

PANEL or PANELLED. Sheets of wood framed together by means of strips of wood to form the lining for internal walls.

PARAPET. Originally a breastwork in fortifications; later, a low wall around a roof or platform, to prevent people falling over the edge.

PEDIMENT. The low triangular space between the raking cornice of a roof gable and the entablature of a Classical temple; by extension, any low triangular shape, with cornice above and below, used to suggest this, as in a pedimented window.

PENDENTIVE. A spherical triangle used as transition from a squared space to a drum or dome; usually in Byzantine architecture.

PERIOD REVIVAL. A term used to define an era roughly from 1895 to 1925, when architects used various older periods as inspiration, but with scholarly correctness of form unlike the more free eclecticism of the nineteenth century.

PIER. A massive architectural support; proportions not fixed.

PIER BUTTRESS. *See* BUTTRESS.

PILASTER. A flattened columnar form, rectilinear in shape, attached to a wall.

PILLAR. A slender architectural support, usually rather tall. Sometimes squared or rounded.

PINNACLE. Sharp spire-like form in Gothic architecture; commonly ornamented with crockets.

PLATERESQUE. Style of architecture and ornament combining especially late Gothic and Renaissance elements, with some Moorish features.

PORTICO. A porch-like columned and roofed projection from a building.

POST AND LINTEL. Architecture based on the principle of upright vertical posts and connecting horizontal bars or lintels. Less dynamic than arch-based architecture.

PYRAMIDAL. In the form of a pyramid.

QUATREFOIL. Four-leaved; in Gothic tracery, an opening having four foils separated by cusps.

QUOINS. Stones, often simulated in wooden blocks, to create an effect of stength or ornamental finish at the corners of a building.

RENAISSANCE. A style of architecture and art of the fifteenth and sixteenth centuries characterized by harmony of parts, (symmetrical) balance, and clarity—strongly influenced by Classical sources. Sometimes subdivided (notably in Italy) into Early and High Renaissance.

REREDOS. An ornamental screen or structure covering the wall behind and above an altar in a church, enhancing the importance of that altar. *See also* RETABLE.

RETABLE. The French and English word for the Spanish *retablo*. Also can refer to a shelf behind the altar in an Anglican church. Some writers use the word reredos in place of retable.

REVEAL. The inside of a doorway or window opening.

RIB VAULTING. Masonry roof constructed either with a network of ribs and curved vault sections or with ribs as ornamental enrichment on the underside of a vault. *See also* VAULT.

RICHARDSON ROMANESQUE or RICHARDSONIAN. An important phase of later nineteenth-century American architecture, derived from the work of Henry Hobson Richardson (1838–1886). Richardson had been inspired by French and Spanish Romanesque building, and by Early Christian architecture of the Near East; from these, and other later medieval sources, he evolved his highly personal Romanesque manner, later popularized in most parts of the United States. *See also* ROMANESQUE.

RIDGE JOINT. The line of intersection produced by the two sides of a sloping or pitched roof.

RIDGE POLE. The piece of timber (strictly known as the ridge-piece) along the line of the ridge, against which rest the upper ends of the sloping rafters.

ROMANESQUE. A style of architecture or art, essentially of the tenth to mid-twelfth centuries, although persisting in variant forms later. Generally characterized by use of semi-circular arches, extremely solid masonry construction, and heavy piers; often with relatively simple masonry vaults.

ROSE WINDOW. A round window, usually with tracery.

ROUNDEL. A disk or circular decorative part; may be applied to a window form also.

RUSKINIAN GOTHIC. A phase of Gothic Revival using Venetian Gothic forms.

RUSTICATION. Masonry construction in which the joints are emphasized, usually in a regular pattern with bevelled edges.

SARCOPHAGUS. A burial chest.

SCAGLIOLA. Plaster or marble dust reconstituted, and painted and stained to represent marble.

SCONCE. A wall bracket for holding candles.

SECOND EMPIRE. The nineteenth-century architectural fashion which derived from the Neo-Baroque work of French architects during the Second Empire of Louis Napoleon, or Napoleon III as he was called.

SERAVEZZA MARBLE. *See* MARBLE.

SHAFT. Section of a column or pilaster between capital and base.

SHINGLE STYLE. The late nineteenth-century architectural fashion which derived from sources in New England of the late seventeenth century, and from certain progressive nineteenth-century eastern architects' variations on them; it often combined features of other late nineteenth-century architectural fashions.

SOLOMONIC. A Solomonic column—that is, one with a twisted shaft, usually with a Corinthianesque capital and base; often grapes and vine leaves (or foliate patterns) cover the twists. So called from the presumed use of such columns in Solomon's temple; columns of various periods now in St. Peter's in Rome are variants of the type.

SPIRE. An elongated pyramid on top of a tower.

STAGED TOWER. *See* TOWER.

STAINED GLASS. Most colored glass used in church windows is stained, in that it derives its color from some metallic oxide added during its manufacture; some stained glass is also painted to give additional detail. Usually stained glass is of intense hue and transparent. *See also* COLORED GLASS.

STICK STYLE. The late nineteenth-century architectural fashion derived from the ideas of Eastlake, often combining various local features; the phrase was especially described in Vincent Scully. It might better be called Strip Style in Northern California. A sub-phase emphasized Moorish details, such as horseshoe arches, etc.

STRIATED. Characterized by horizontal bands of color or form.

STRUT. In any framed structure, a part which is in compression to hold the larger members in shape.

STUPA. A commemorative or sepulchral monument of mound shape to enshrine some relic of the Buddha, on a platform and with other symbolic features and gateways.

THREE±QUARTER COLUMN. *See* COLUMN.

TORCHÈRE. A tall lamp with a holder at its apex directing light onto the ceiling above.

TOWER. A high squared or rounded structure. Sometimes built in levels or stages which diminish in area as they go higher.

TRACERY. Patterns in carved stone in a window or other opening.

TRANSEPT. The interior space of a church at right angles to the nave; where the transept intersects the nave is the crossing, which often has a domical covering higher than the nave or transept. Traditionally oriented north and south.

TRAVERTINE. A soft cream-colored, porous limestone quarried in central Italy.

TREFOIL. Three-leaved; in Gothic tracery, an opening having three lobes or foils separated by cusps.

TRIPARTITE. Of three part divisions.

TRUSS. A beamed form designed to bear a superincumbent weight, as a roof truss.

TUDOR. A term covering the period from about 1500 to 1600 in England, including Elizabethan architecture.

TUSCAN. Roman and later variants of the Doric order with a very simplified capital; uses a base, rare in the Greek Doric.

TYMPANUM (plural: TYMPANA). The space above a main church door and below the framing arch.

VAULT. A masonry arched roof of variant forms.

VESTIBULE. An enclosed entrance to a building.

VOLUTE. A spiral form, especially the spirals used in the Ionic capital.

VOUSSOIR. One of the parts of an arch; the top voussoir is the keystone.

Suggestions for Further Reading

This book is directed to the general reader, rather than to the professional scholar, and has, therefore, no footnotes or detailed bibliography. Nevertheless, it is our hope that the information presented between these covers will stimulate further study of this fascinating subject.

As we began the project, it quickly became apparent that this was an unexplored approach; almost nothing has been written about the collective religious history of any cosmopolitan city. Published works on the churches and temples of other cities or regions tend to focus on the buildings themselves and to be limited to structures of the Judeo-Christian tradition. Religious historians have generally ignored the West, and Western historians have emphasized other aspects of the culture. Few of the excellent histories of San Francisco give the role of the city's diverse religious community more than a passing mention.

Examination of the various congregational histories suggested a new approach to the story of America's first Eurasian city—a text that would encapsulate the many kinds of immigrants who settled here, the beliefs they brought with them, and the relationship of those religious convictions to the richly textured culture of today's San Francisco. Quotations in the text, unless otherwise identified, were taken from the respective congregational histories.

Extensive research was undertaken to place the various groups in historical perspective. Although we found no overall, general reference on this subject, we recommend the titles listed below. Each one has provided authoritative information on some phase of the subject.

Religious Groups in San Francisco

(Arranged alphabetically by congregation.
Self-published in San Francisco unless otherwise indicated)

Bethel African Methodist Episcopal Church, History 1982.

"Black Churches in Urban San Francisco" by Philip Montesano. Typescript, n.d., Special Collections, San Francisco Public Library.

Calvary Presbyterian Church: *Calvary through the Years, 75th Anniversary 1929; Chronicles of Calvary, 90th Anniversary 1944; Many Years, One Message, 125th Anniversary 1979*, all by Carol Green Wilson.

Cameron House: *Chinatown Quest: The Life of Donaldina Cameron* by Carol Green Wilson. Stanford CA: Stanford University Press, 1931, 1950; San Francisco: California Historical Society, 1974.

Chinese United Methodist Church, Centennial, Brief History by David K. Lee, 1969.

Church of the New Jerusalem (Swedenborgian): *The Garden Church of San Francisco* by Othmar Tobisch, 18th printing, 1972.

Congregation Chevra Thilim, 70th Anniversary Journal, 1961.

The Story of Congregation Emanu-El by Reuben R. Rinder, n.d.; *Architects of Reform: Congregational and Community Leadership, Emanu-El of San Francisco 1849–1980* by Fred Rosenbaum. Berkeley: Judah L. Magnus Memorial Museum, 1980.

Ebenezer Lutheran Church, Seventy-fifth Anniversary, a Brief History by J. Orville Martin, 1957.

"Episcopal Church of St. Mary the Virgin, Early Beginnings" by William R. Bolton, Rector 1889–1897, typescript, n.d.

Fellowship for All Peoples Church: *Footprints of a Dream* by Howard Thurman. New York: Harper & Brothers, 1953.

First Baptist Church of San Francisco, One Hundred Years, Lewis J. Julianel, ed., 1949.

First Congregational Church: "The Gold Rush and San Francisco's First Chaplain" by Dr. Harold T. Janes, 1964; "The Story of the First Congregational Church of San Francisco" by Gail Cleland, 1966. Typescripts.

First Presbyterian Church: *A Pioneer Pastorate and Times: Embodying Contemporary Local Transactions and Events* by Albert Williams. San Francisco: Bacon & Co, 1882.

First St. John's United Methodist Church: *Past Images, Events, and Miracle Stories, 127th Anniversary, 1972; Seven Years' Street Preaching in San Francisco*, by William Taylor. New York: Carlton and Parker, 1856.

First Unitarian Church of San Francisco, One Hundred Years, Years 1850–1900 by Horace Davis; Years 1900–1950 by Church History Committee, Clotilde Grunsky Taylor, Chair.

Grace Parish and Cathedral, A Historical Survey by Michael D. Lampen, 1974.

Hamilton Square Baptist Church, History, ca 1950.

Holy Trinity Orthodox Cathedral: *Restoration of Holy Trinity Cathedral 1978; The 100th Anniversary of the First Eastern Orthodox Parish in San Francisco, 1868–1968* by George Afonsky, Robert Hughes, and Olga Hughes, trans.

Kong Chow Temple by William Hoy. Rev. ed., n.d.

Nôtre Dame des Victoires Catholic Church, 100th Anniversary History by Toni Knapton, Jacqueline Carrere, trans., 1957.

Old St. Mary's: Her Story by Marion McClintock, 1965.

"Pagan Temples in San Francisco" by Frederick J. Masters. *The Californian*, vol. II, no. 6, November 1892.

"Pioneer Churches of San Francisco," by Dan Borsuk. *San Francisco Progress*, October–December 1974.

Presbyterian Church in Chinatown, 120th Anniversary, Bradford Woo, ed., 1973.

St. Boniface Parish, 100th Anniversary, 1960.

St. Cecilia's Parish, Golden Jubilee, 1967.

St. Dominic's Church, 100th Anniversary, 1973.

St. Francis Lutheran Church: *Ansgar United Evangelical Lutheran Church, Golden Jubilee, 1953.*

St. John Armenian Apostolic Church, History, 1982.

St. John's Presbyterian Church, The First 100 Years by Roger Deas, 1970.

St. John The Baptist Serbian Orthodox Church, History by Nikola Vucinich, 1974.

St. Joseph's Church, Diamond Jubilee, 1936.

St. Mary's Cathedral, 1972.

St. Mary's Chinese School and Mission, 1971.

St. Matthew's Evangelical Lutheran Church, 75th Anniversary History by H. G. Kurt Adelsberger and Herman Lucas, 1970.

St. Patrick's Church, 125th Anniversary, 1976.

St. Paulus Lutheran Church, A Century Toward Eternity, 1967.

San Francisco Council of Churches: *Heritage and Hope: A History of the Protestant, Anglican, and Orthodox Church Movement in San Francisco.* Helen E. Helton and Norman E. Leach, eds.

Religious Groups in California

Anthony, C. V. *Fifty Years of Methodism: A History of the Methodist Episcopal Church within the Bounds of the California Conference.* San Francisco: Methodist Book Concern, 1901.

Du Brau, Richard T. *The Romance of Lutheranism in California.* Oakland: Lutheran Church–Missouri Synod on the Pacific Coast, 1959.

Kelley, D. O. *History of the Diocese of California 1849–1915* San Francisco: Episcopal Bureau of Information and Supply, n.d.

Kip, William Ingraham. *The Early Days of My Episcopate.* New York: Thomas Whittaker, 1892.

Lattin, Don. "What We Believe," *San Francisco Examiner*, March 27–April 13, 1983.

Le Shane, David C. *Quakers in California.* Newberg, Oregon: Barclay Press, 1969.

Mathes, W. Michael. *Missions.* San Francisco: California Historical Society, 1980.

McGloin, John B., S.J. "The California Catholic Church in Transition, 1846–1850," *California Historical Society Quarterly* vol. XLII #1, March 1963.

———. *California's First Archbishop: The Life of Joseph Sadoc Alemany, O.P.* New York: Herder and Herder, 1966.

———. *Jesuits by the Golden Gate*. San Francisco: University of San Francisco Press, 1972.

Palou, Francisco O.F.M. *Life and Apostolic Labors of the Venerable Father Junipero Serra*. Pasadena: George Wharton James, 1913.

Parsons, Edward Lamb. *The Diocese of California: A Quarter Century, 1915–1940*. Austin, Texas: Episcopal Church Historical Society, 1958.

Stensrud, E. M. *The Lutheran Church and California*. San Francisco: Trinity English Evangelical Lutheran Church, 1916.

Walsh, Henry L. *Hallowed Were the Gold Dust Trails: The Story of the Pioneer Priests of Northern California*. Santa Clara, CA: University of Santa Clara Press, 1946.

Zobell, Albert L., Jr. "The [Mormon] Church in Early California," *The Improvement Era* (Oakland Temple Issue) 1964.

Ethnic Groups in California

Arab History and Culture. San Francisco: St. Nicholas Orthodox Church, 1973.

Austin, Leonard. *Around the World in San Francisco*. San Francisco: Abbey Press, 1958.

Barth, Gunther. *Bitter Strength: A History of the Chinese in the United States*. Cambridge Mass.: Harvard University Press, 1964.

Caire, Helene. "On the Trail of the Slavonic Pioneers," *Slavs of California*. Oakland CA: Slavonic Alliance of California, 1937.

Chinn, Thomas W. "Chinese Temples in North America," *A History of the Chinese in California*. San Francisco: Chinese Historical Society of North America, 1969. (Based on an interview with Chingwah Lee)

———. "Argonauts Become Americans: The Chinese," *Historic Preservation*, April–June, 1979.

Crouchett, Lorraine Jacobs. *Filipinos in California, from the Days of the Galleons to the Present*. El Cerrito, CA: Downey Place Publishing House, Inc., 1982.

Daniels, Douglas Henry. *Pioneer Urbanites: A Social and Cultural History of Black San Francisco*. Philadelphia: Temple Unversity Press, 1980.

Daskarolis, George P. "San Francisco's Greek Colony," *California History*, Summer 1981, vol. 60, 2.

Dicker, Laverne Mau. *The Chinese in San Francisco*. New York: Dover Publications, Inc., 1979.

Gibson, Otis. *The Chinese in America*. Cincinnati: Hitchcock and Walker, 1877.

Glanz, Dr. Rudol. *The Jews of California from the Discovery of Gold until 1880*. New York: The Southern California Jewish Historical Soiety, 1960.

Kiefer, Christie W. *Changing Cultures, Changing Lives: An Ethnographic Study of Three Generations of Japanese Americans*. San Francisco: Jossey-Bass Publishers, 1974.

Lai, Him Mark, Joe Huang and Don Wong. *The Chinese of America 1785–1980*. San Francisco: Chinese Culture Foundation, 1980.

Lai, Him Mark, and Philip P. Choy. *Outlines: History of the Chinese in America*. San Francisco: by the authors, 1971.

Lortie, Francis N. "San Francisco's Black Community 1870–1890: Dilemmas in the struggle for Equality." Thesis, San Francisco State University, 1970.

Montesano, Philip. "Some Aspects of the Free Negro Question in San Francisco, 1849–1870." Thesis, University of San Francisco, 1967.

Radin, Paul. *The Italians of San Francisco: Their Adjustment and Acculturation*. Abstract from the SERA Project 2-F2-98 (3-F2-145): Cultural Anthropology. July 1935.

Saroyan, William, text, Pauline Vinson, water colors. *Hilltop Russians in San Francisco*. Stanford CA: James Ladd Delkin, 1941. By permission of the Works Project Administration.

Speer, William. *The Oldest and Newest Empires: China and America*. Hanford CT: Scranton & Co., and Philadelphia: Parmelee & Co., 1870.

Tadich, John V. "Reminiscences," and "The Jugoslav Colony of San Francisco on My Arrival in 1871," *Slavonic Pioneers of California*. San Francisco: The Slavonic Mutual Benefit Society, 1932.

Thernstrom, Stephan, ed. *The Harvard Encyclopedia of American Ethnic Groups*. Cambridge, Mass.: Belknap Press of the Harvard University Press, 1980.

Zarchin, Michael M. *Glimpses of Jewish Life in San Francisco*. Oakland CA.: The Judah L. Magnus Memorial Museum, 1964.

Californiana

Bolton, Herbert Eugene. *Anza's California Expeditions.* Berkeley: University of California Press, 1930.
Brown, John Henry. *Reminiscences and Incidents of the "Early Days" of San Francisco.* San Francisco: Mission Journal Publishing Company, 1886.
Caughey, John W. *California: A Remarkable State's Life History.* Englewood Cliffs, N.J.: Prentice-Hall, Inc., 1970.
Chandler, Arthur. *Old Tales of San Francisco.* Dubuque, Iowa: Kendall/Hunt Publishing Company, 1977.
Cherny, Robert W. and William Issel. *San Francisco: Presidio, Port, and Pacific Metropolis.* San Francisco: Boyd & Fraser, 1981.
Coy, Owen Cochran. *Gold Days.* Los Angeles, San Francisco: Powell Publishing Company, 1929.
Dana, Richard Henry, Jr. *Twenty-Four Years After "Two Years Before the Mast."* New York: Dutton, 1969.
Downey, Joseph. "Filings from an Old Saw," *The Golden Era.* San Francisco: Jan.–April 1853.
Eldredge, Zoeth Skinner. *The Beginnings of San Francisco.* San Francisco: by the author, 1912.
Hansen, Gladys. *San Francisco Almanac.* San Rafael, CA: Presidio Press, 1980.
McGloin, John Bernard, S.J. *San Francisco: The Story of a City.* San Rafael, CA: Presidio Press, 1978.
Rosales, Vincente Perez. *California Adventure.* transl. by E. Morby and Arturo Torres-Rioseco. San Francisco: The Book Club of California, 1947.
Soule, Frank, John H. Gihon, M.D., and James Nisbet, with the Continuation through 1855 by Dorothy H. Huggins. *The Annals of San Francisco.* New York: D. Appleton & Co., 1855; rept. ed. Palo Alto: Lewis Osborne, 1966.
Starr, Kevin. *Americans and the California Dream, 1850–1915.* New York: Oxford University Press, 1973.
Wilson, George Osborne (1828–1879). "Travel Diary 1849–1851." California Historical Society.

Religious Groups in the United States

Ahlstrom, Sydney E. *A Religious History of America.* New Haven: Yale University Press, 1972.
Albanese, Catherine L. *America: Religions and Religion.* Belmont CA: Wadsworth Publishing Co., 1981.
Antiochan Archdiocese. *A Tribute to the Old Church in the New World.* San Francisco: St. Nicholas Orthodox Church, 1976.
Backman, Milton V., Jr. *Christian Churches in America: Origins and Beliefs.* New York: Charles Scribner's Sons, 1983.
Buddhist Churches of America, 1899–1974. 2 vols. Chicago: Norbart, Inc., 1974.
Chesham, Sallie. *Born to Battle: The Salvation Army in America.* Chicago: Rand, McNally, 1965.
Ellis, John Tracy. *American Catholicism.* Chicago: The University of Chicago Press, 2nd ed., 1969.
———. *Documents of American Catholic History.* Milwaukee: The Bruce Publishing Company, 1962.
Gaustad, Edwin Scott. *A Religious History of America.* New York: Harper & Row, 1966.
Hennessy, James, S.J. *American Catholics: A History of the Roman Catholic Community in the United States.* New York: Oxford University Press, 1981.
Loetscher, Lefferts A. *A Brief History of the Presbyterians* Philadelphia: The Westminster Press, 1958.
Mann, James P., Lawrence Maloney and Alvin P. Sanoff. "Religion's New Turn, a Search for the Sacred," *U.S. News and World Report,* April 4, 1983.
Tarasar, Constance J., ed. *Orthodox America 1794–1976.* Syosset N.Y.: Orthodox Church in America, 1975.
U.S. Department of Commerce, Bureau of the Census. "Religious Bodies," *Statistical Abstract of the United States, 1982–83.*

World Religions

Browne, Lewis. *The World's Great Scriptures.* New York: The Macmillan Company, 1946.
deBay, Theodore, comp. *Sources of Chinese Tradition.* New York: Columbia University Press, 1960.
Ellwood, Robert S., Jr. *Many Peoples, Many Faiths. An Introduction to the Religious Life of Humankind.* Englewood Cliffs, N.J.: Prentice-Hall, Inc., 2nd ed. 1982.
Fedorovich, Father Nicholas. *My Church and My Faith.* South Bound Brook, N.J.: Ukrainian Church of U.S.A., 1969.
McKinley, Edward H. *Marching to Glory.* New York: Harper & Row, 1968.

Offuchi, Chihiro. *How Konko-Kyo Believer Lives*. Nagasaki, Japan: Konko-Kyo Headquarters, 1954.
Ormanian, Malachin. *The Church of Armenia*. London: A. R. Mowbray & Co., Ltd. rev. ed. 1955.
Smith, Huston. *The Religions of Man*. New York: Harper & Row, 1958.
Ware, Timothy. *The Orthodox Church*. New York: Penguin Books, 1982.

Architecture

American Churches . . . A Series of Authoritative Articles on Designing, Planning, Heating, Ventilating, Lighting & General Equipment of Churches as Demonstrated by the Best Practice in the United States, with an Introduction by Ralph Adams Cram. New York: The American Architect, 1945.
American Society for Church Architecture Journal. Chicago.
Anderson, Judith. "A Synagogue's New Life as a Home to Four Artists." *San Francisco Chronicle*, 7 April, 1982, 40.
Baird, Joseph Armstrong, Jr. *Time's Wondrous Changes: San Francisco Architecture, 1776–1915*. San Francisco: California Historical Society, 1962.
Betts, Darby W. *Architecture and the Church*. Greenwich, CT: Seabury, 1952.
Broderick, Robert C. *Historic Churches of the United States*. New York: Funk, 1958.
Bruggink, Donald J. *Christ and Architecture: Building Presbyterian/Reformed Churches*. Grand Rapids, Mich.: Eerdmans, 1965.
Casey, Jay. "Bernasconi the Stone Carver." *The Christian Science Monitor*, 4 December 1969, n.p.
Cone, Lawrence. *Armenian Church Architecture*. New York: Heath Cote, 1979.
Collins, Monsignor Harold Edward. *The Church Edifice and Its Appointments*. Philadelphia: Dolphin Press, rev. ed.; 1940.
Cram, Ralph Adams. *American Church Building of Today*. New York: Architectural Book Publishing Company, 1929.
Faensen, Hubert. *Early Russian Architecture*. New York: Putnam, 1975.
Faulkner, Charles D. *Christian Science Church Edifices*. Chicago: Faulkner, 1946.
Gebhard, David, Roger Montgomery, Robert Winter, John Woodbridge, and Sally Woodbridge. *A Guide to Architecture in San Francisco and Northern California*. Santa Barbara and Salt Lake City: Peregrine Smith, 1976.
Gowans, Alan. *Images of American Living: Four Centuries of Architecture and Furniture as Cultural Expression*. Philadelphia and New York: J. B. Lippincott Company, 1964.
Haskin, Frederic J. *Historic Churches in the United States*. Washington: 1938.
Johnson, Paul C. and Richard Reinhardt. *San Francisco As It Is, As It Was*. Garden City, N.Y.: Doubleday, 1979.
Junior League of San Francisco. *Here Today: San Francisco's Architectural Heritage*. San Francisco: Chronicle Books, 1968.
Kennedy, Roger. *American Churches*. New York: Stewart, Tabori, and Chang, 1982.
Kidder Smith, G. E. *A Pictorial History of Architecture in America*. (Chapter introductions by Marshall Davidson.) New York: American Heritage, 1976, 2 vols.
Kirker, Harold. *California's Architectural Frontier*. Santa Barbara and Salt Lake City: Peregrine Smith, 1973.
McClinton, Katharine Morrison. *The Changing Church: Its Architecture, Art, & Decoration*. New York: Morehouse-Gorham, 1957.
Newcomb, Rexford. *The Old Mission Churches and Historic Houses of California*. Philadelphia and London: J. B. Lippincott, 1925.
Pichard, Joseph. *Modern Church Architecture*. New York: Orion Press, 1960.
Religious Buildings. By the editors of *Architectural Record*. New York: McGraw-Hill, 1979.
Rines, Edward F. *Old Historic Churches of America: Their Romantic History and Their Traditions*. New York: Macmillan, 1936.
Short, Ernest H. *The House of God: A History of Religious Architecture*. London: Eyre and Spottiswoode, 1955.
Stanton, Phoebe. *The Gothic Revival and American Church Architecture, 1840–1856*. Baltimore: Johns Hopkins Press, 1968.
"Six New Churches; Completing a Cathedral." *Theology and Architecture; Architectural Forum*, 103 (December, 1955), 130–151.

Tillich, Paul. "Contemporary Protestant Architecture." *Journal of the Liberal Ministry*, 3 (Winter, 1963), 16–21.

Turak, Theodore. "A Celt among Slavs: Louis Sullivan's Holy Trinity Cathedral." *The Prairie School Review*, 9 (Fourth Quarter, 1972), 5–23.

Watkin, William W. *Planning and Building the Modern Church*. New York: Dodge, 1951.

Woodbridge, Sally B. and John M. Woodbridge FAIA. *Architecture, San Francisco: The Guide*. San Francisco: American Institute of Architects, San Francisco Chapter, 1982.

Works Progress Administration, Northern California Writers' Project. *San Francisco: The Bay and Its Cities*. New York, Hastings House, 1940.

Acknowledgments

So many people have contributed to this publication that it is impossible to acknowledge them all. Much of the information in *Sacred Places* was derived from interviews with clergymen, well over a hundred in all. Many of those first interviewed were no longer in the city when the manuscript was written; therefore, details were re-checked with persons knowledgeable for each faith or denomination. Among the most helpful were Michael Lampen, historian, Grace Cathedral; Col. Carroll E. B. Peake, historiographer for the Episcopal diocese of California; Rabbi Martin W. Weiner, Congregation Sherith Israel; Rabbi David Thaler, Congregation Chevra Thilim; and Dr. Frederick Hong, Buddha's Universal Church. The various Chinese denominations were interpreted by the Reverends Ng Piu Lam, Jeng Sen Buddhist-Taoist Temple; Timothy Taam, Chinese Methodist Church; and Richard Wickman, Presbyterian Church in Chinatown. Japanese Buddhism was explained by the Reverends Ken Yamaguchi, Buddhist Church of San Francisco; and Kyoin Fujikawa, Soto Shu Mission; the Reverend Fumio Matsui explained the Konko-Kyo history and doctrine. Swami Prahuddananda gave insights into the teachings and programs of the Vedanta Society of Northern California.

Questions regarding the Eastern Orthodox faith in San Francisco were patiently answered by Father Seraphim Gisetti, Holy Trinity Orthodox Cathedral; Father Peter Perekrestov, Holy Virgin Cathedral of the Russian Church in Exile; Father Gregory O'Feish, St. Nicholas Antiochan Orthodox Church; Father Dusan Bunjavik, St. John the Baptist Serbian Orthodox Church, and Father Anthony Kostouros, Holy Trinity Greek Orthodox Church. Bishop Aris Shirvanian, St. John Armenian Apostolic Church, and the Reverend Datev Kaloustian, St. Gregory Armenian Apostolic Church, interpreted that ancient branch of Christianity.

Donneter Lane, Norman E. Leach, Mary Woodward, and others at the San Francisco Council of Churches graciously supplied information about various ecumenical programs of the Protestant and Orthodox community.

The Roman Catholic clergymen who were generous with their time included Monsignors Robert Hayburn, St. Francis of Assisi; James McKay, St. Cecilia's; John T. Foudy, St. Anne of the Sunset and the late Thomas Bowie, St. Mary's Cathedral; and Fathers Charles Donovan, St. Mary's Chinese Mission; John Daly, St. Patrick's; Alfred Boeddecker, St. Boniface; Joseph Constanzo, SS. Peter and Paul; James McGee, St. Joseph's, and Charles R. Hess, St. Dominic's. Dr. Richard S. Waters solved the mystery of St. Vincent de Paul's gambrel roof.

Undoubtedly, many librarians assisted the various researchers in their efforts. Outstanding help was given by Judy Sheldon, California Historical Society; Judith Wainwright, the Richard E. Gleeson Library of the University of San Francisco; Gladys Hansen, San Francisco Archives; Michael Peterson, San Francisco Theological Seminary; and Seizo Oka, the Japanese-American Library of the California First Bank.

Architecture, per se, is relatively unimportant to individual congregations except while a new church is being constructed, and information about many of the older buildings and their architects was hard to come by. Among the community consultants contributing their professional knowledge were the architects Warren Wachs, William Diffenbach, Edward Merrill, and Charles St. George Pope. The Reverend Kirby C. Hansen, chancellor of the

Archdiocese of San Francisco, did extensive research to provide the names of architects of a number of Roman Catholic churches. Philip Choy and the late Chingwah Lee provided insight and information about the city's Chinese temples. Dr. Albert Shumate, an authority on San Francisco history and a past president of the California Historical Society, kindly read the entire preliminary manuscript with a sharpened blue pencil, contributing knowledge from his own research.

Any local history is brought to life by the inclusion of first person accounts. Among those lending unpublished papers of pioneer pastors and congregations were Mr. and Mrs. Guilford Congdon, *The Letters of Mr. Bannister and Elizabeth* (his great grandfather and the second minister of First St. John's United Methodist Church); Edna Crandall, the script from the 50th anniversary celebration of Portalhurst Presbyterian; Mrs. Clarke Neale Edwards, letter from a homesick serviceman which resulted in the Lakeside Presbyterian congregation's underwriting the cost of lighting the Mt. Davidson cross nightly for some twelve years; Dr. "Lefty" Rogers, correspondence regarding the Festival of Faith organized by his late wife Dorothy during her tenure as president of the San Francisco Council of Churches. Dr. and Mrs. George McGinnis lent a memorial book honoring a great uncle, the Reverend George Adams, minister of First Congregational Church at the time of its destruction in 1906 and subsequent rebuilding; Bertha Weiss supplied congregational histories by George Bufford and the Reverend Gail Cleland. Mrs. Carroll E. B. Peake, great granddaughter of Canon William Ingraham Kip, lent materials on the Kip family, their journey to California, and his long service as California's first Episcopal bishop.

Personal recollections were contributed by Mrs. May Coombes, Religious Society of Friends; Mrs. Othmar Tobisch, Swedenborgian Church of the New Jerusalem; Sergei Lauper, historian, Church of Jesus Christ of Latter Day Saints; Mrs. Peter Ilyn, Holy Virgin Cathedral of the Russian Church in Exile; Mrs. Cora May Jackson, historian, Third Baptist Church; Constantine von Frederick, historian, Church of the Advent of Christ the King; and Sally B. Famarin, St. Joseph's Church. Among the members of Congregation Emanu-El providing personal insights were Mr. and Mrs. Oscar Geballe, Mrs. and Mrs. Edgar Goldstein, and Mrs. Reuben Rinder. Margaret Hong, Keeper of T'ien Hou Temple, explained the role of popular religion in the Chinese community, and Lana Vukovich gave valuable information about the Serbian Orthodox church.

Many, many more people have contributed time, information, and advice. The preparation of this book has been an ecumenical undertaking typical of the heart of the city of St. Francis.

Index

This is a selective index. It includes the following: present and previous names of the various sacred places; names of the architects and artists involved in their construction and furnishing; and names of clergymen associated with specific sacred places. References to ethnic groups are included when the information pertains to their first arrival in California or to places founded by or for a specific ethnic group. When appropriate, cross references are provided under the various denominations to sacred places for which there is a specific essay.

Abbreviations: Archbishop, *Abp.*; Bishop, *Bp.*; Archimandrite, *Archim.*; Brother, *Br.*; Monsignor, *Msgr.*; Reverend, *Rev.*; Sister, *Sr.*

Bold face numbers indicate essays on specific sacred places.